FITZGERALD AND HEMINGWAY

Also by Matthew J. Bruccoli

The Composition of Tender Is the Night
As Ever, Scott Fitz— (editor, with Jennifer Atkinson)
Profile of F. Scott Fitzgerald (editor)
F. Scott Fitzgerald in His Own Time (editor, with Jackson Bryer)
F. Scott Fitzgerald: A Descriptive Bibliography; Supplement to F. Scott Fitzgerald: A Descriptive Bibliography; F. Scott Fitzgerald: A Descriptive Bibliography, Revised Edition
F. Scott Fitzgerald's Ledger (editor)
The Great Gatsby: *A Facsimile of the Manuscript* (editor)
Bits of Paradise: 21 Uncollected Stories by F. Scott and Zelda Fitzgerald (editor, with Scottie Fitzgerald Smith)
The Romantic Egoists (editor, with Scottie Fitzgerald Smith and Joan P. Kerr)
"The Last of the Novelists": F. Scott Fitzgerald and The Last Tycoon
Ernest Hemingway, Cub Reporter (editor)
Ernest Hemingway's Apprenticeship (editor)
Hemingway at Auction (editor, with C. E. Frazer Clark, Jr.)
The Notebooks of F. Scott Fitzgerald (editor)
F. Scott Fitzgerald's Screenplay for "Three Comrades" by Erich Maria Remarque (editor)
The Price Was High: 50 Uncollected Stories by F. Scott Fitzgerald (editor)
Correspondence of F. Scott Fitzgerald (editor, with Margaret Duggan)
F. Scott Fitzgerald: Poems 1911–1940 (editor)
Some Sort of Epic Grandeur: The Life of F. Scott Fitzgerald; Revised Edition
New Essays on The Great Gatsby (editor)
Conversations with Ernest Hemingway (editor)
The Short Stories of F. Scott Fitzgerald: A New Collection (editor)
The Sun Also Rises: *A Facsimile of the Manuscript*, 2 vols. (editor)
F. Scott Fitzgerald Manuscripts, 18 vols. (editor)

The Cambridge Edition of the Works of F. Scott Fitzgerald, (editor): *The Great Gatsby* and *The Love of the Last Tycoon*

Zelda Fitzgerald: The Collected Writings (editor)

F. Scott Fitzgerald: A Life in Letters (editor, with Judith S. Baughman)

FITZGERALD AND HEMINGWAY

A Dangerous Friendship

Matthew J. Bruccoli

Carroll & Graf Publishers, Inc.
New York

First Carroll & Graf edition 1994

Carroll & Graf Publishers, Inc.
260 Fifth Avenue
New York, NY 10001

Library of Congress Cataloging-in-Publication Data

Bruccoli, Matthew Joseph, 1931–
Fitzgerald and Hemingway / Matthew J. Bruccoli.—1st Carroll & Graf ed.
p. cm.
ISBN 0-7867-0077-7 : $21.95 ($29.95 Can.)
1. Fitzgerald, F. Scott (Francis Scott), 1896–1940—Friends and associates. 2. Hemingway, Ernest, 1899–1961—Friends and associates. 3. Friendship—United States—History—20th century. 4. Authors, American—20th century—Biography.
PS3511.I9Z5593 1994
813'.52—dc20 94-4669
CIP

Manufactured in the United States of America

For Arlyn at thirty-seven

Acknowledgments

A shorter version of this book was published as *Scott and Ernest: The Authority of Failure and the Authority of Success* in 1978. Ernest Hemingway's letters had not yet been published and, under the terms of his will, could not be quoted. Accordingly, I and the readers had to make do with paraphrases of his letters. At that time I conceived the bad idea of writing the book without footnotes. This experiment in "reader-friendly" scholarship did not result in a best seller, but it did result in a book with limited usefulness. Biography without documentation is a species of fiction.

The ability to print Hemingway's letters as well as the discovery of new evidence about Fitzgerald and Hemingway during the seventeen years since *Scott and Ernest* justified an enlarged and rewritten study. I was able to convince Kent Carroll and Herman Graf to back my plan.

Scott and Ernest was written with the help of Scottie Fitzgerald Smith and Mary Hemingway. It was edited by Albert Erskine, the great Random House editor. The original research was aided by Alexander Clark at the Princeton University Library and by Jo August, William Johnson, and Robert Stocking at the John F. Kennedy Library. The present book was aided by Don Skemer, John Delaney, and Alice V. Clark at Princeton and by Megan Desnoyers at the Kennedy. Beth Alvarez of the University of Maryland Library provided prompt, friendly help. My friend Charles Scribner III assisted me in using the Charles Scribner's Sons Archives at Princeton. Patrick Hemingway advised me about the intricacies of Hemingway rights. Lydia Zelaya, Charles Scribner's Sons, provided necessary assistance in clearing permissions.

When I was writing *Scott and Ernest,* James Charters sent me long letters about Paris in the old days. I am also obligated to Merrill

Cody and Duncan Chaplin for searching their memories. Carlos Baker answered question after question.

For this augmented edition Michael Reynolds shared his research with me. Marcia and Maurice Neville granted me access to their superb Hemingway collection, and Nick Beck did some of my work for me.

Judith S. Baughman improved my work in progress with her belligerent advice. Robert W. Trogdon was head checker; Cy League was head fetcher and indexer. My Arlyn removed infelicities of style.

I am gratified to be at the University of South Carolina, where I can get my work done.

M.J.B.
March 19, 1994

Editorial Note

The letters between Fitzgerald and Hemingway are printed as written, within the restrictions of typography; but the spacing of Hemingway's punctuation has been normalized. The other letters in this volume are printed in accurate reading texts. Fitzgerald's and Hemingway's letters have a density of references to people, books, and events. Only references that are crucial to the meaning of a letter have been footnoted. Thus Fitzgerald's vetting report on *A Farewell to Arms* is carefully explained.

The Fitzgerald-to-Perkins letters are printed here from the texts in *F. Scott Fitzgerald: A Life in Letters* (New York: Scribners, 1994) or from *Dear Scott/Dear Max,* edited by John Kuehl and Jackson R. Bryer (New York: Scribners, 1971). The Perkins-to-Fitzgerald letters are printed here from *Dear Scott/Dear Max.* The Hemingway-to-Perkins letters are printed here from *Ernest Hemingway: Selected Letters,* edited by Carlos Baker (New York: Scribners, 1981) or transcribed from the original documents when not in Baker. Perkins-to-Hemingway letters are transcribed from the carbon copies in the Scribner Archives, Princeton University.

Three unpublished sections of *A Moveable Feast*—the alternate account of Hemingway's first meeting with Fitzgerald, the report of Bumby's setting an example of proper drinking for Fitzgerald, and the account of Hemingway's visit to Ellerslie—have been paraphrased here because of copyright restrictions.

Chronology

Fitzgerald		Hemingway
October 1924: Fitzgerald recommends Hemingway to Maxwell Perkins of Charles Scribner's Sons.		
April 10, 1925: Publication of *The Great Gatsby.*		
	Late April 1925 First meeting of Fitzgerald and Hemingway in the Dingo bar, rue Delambre, Paris.	
		October 5, 1925: Publication of *In Our Time.*
February 26, 1926: Publication of *All the Sad Young Men.*		*February 1926:* Hemingway goes to New York to meet Maxwell Perkins at Scribners.
		May 28, 1926: Publication of *The Torrents of Spring.*
	Summer 1926 Hemingways join the Fitzgeralds and Murphys at Juan-les-Pins. The Fitzgeralds turn the Villa Paquita over to the Hemingways and move to the Villa St. Louis. Fitzgerald reads typescript of *The Sun Also Rises.*	
		Fall 1926: Hadley and Ernest separate.
		October 22, 1926: Publication of *The Sun Also Rises.*
December 1926: Fitzgeralds return to America.		

January 1927: Fitzgerald goes to Hollywood to write *Lipstick* (unproduced) for United Artists.

March 1927–March 1929: Fitzgeralds rent Ellerslie, near Wilmington, Delaware.

May 1927: Hemingway marries Pauline Pfeiffer.

October 14, 1927: Publication of *Men Without Women.*

April-August 1928: Fitzgeralds spend spring and summer in Paris.

April 1928: Hemingways make first visit to Key West, Florida

November 19–20, 1928
Fitzgeralds and Hemingways attend Yale-Princeton football game at Princeton; the Hemingways spend the night at Ellerslie.

December 6, 1928
Fitzgerald delivers cash to Hemingway at North Philadelphia Station following the suicide of Dr. Hemingway.

March 1929: Fitzgeralds return to Europe.

May-October 1929: Serialization of *A Farewell to Arms* in *Scribner's Magazine.*

June 1929
Fitzgerald and Hemingway in Paris. Fitzgerald reads typescript of *A Farewell to Arms.*

June 1929
Hemingway and Callaghan box in Paris; Fitzgerald is timekeeper.

September 27, 1929: Publication of *A Farewell to Arms.*

November 24, 1929: Account of Hemingway-Callaghan bout appears in *New York Herald Tribune.*

April 1930: Zelda Fitzgerald has breakdown in Paris. In June she is placed at Prangins Clinic near Geneva.

September 1931: Zelda Fitzgerald is

released from Prangins. Fitzgeralds return to America permanently.

September 1931-May 1932: Fitzgeralds rent a house in Montgomery, Alabama.

October 1931
Fitzgerald and Hemingway meet—probably in New York.

December 1931: Fitzgerald goes to Hollywood to work on *Red-Headed Woman* at MGM.

February 1932: Zelda Fitzgerald has second breakdown; is placed at Phipps Clinic of Johns Hopkins Hospital in Baltimore.

May 1932-November 1933: Fitzgerald rents La Paix near Baltimore.

September 23, 1932: Publication of *Death in the Afternoon.*

October 7, 1932: Publication of Zelda Fitzgerald's novel, *Save Me the Waltz.*

January 1933
Fitzgerald and Hemingway meet in New York.

October 27, 1933: Publication of *Winner Take Nothing.*

December 1933-February 1934: Hemingways on safari in Africa.

January-April 1934: Serialization of *Tender Is the Night* in *Scribner's Magazine.*

April 12, 1934: Publication of *Tender Is the Night.*

May 1934: Zelda Fitzgerald's third breakdown.

October 1934: Publication of "In the Darkest Hour," the first Philippe story.

March 20, 1935: Publication of *Taps at Reveille.*

October 25, 1935: Publication of *Green Hills of Africa.*

1935-1937: Fitzgerald in North Carolina, mostly staying at the Grove

Park Inn, Asheville. The "crack-up" period.

April 6, 1936: Zelda Fitzgerald is placed in Highland Hospital, Asheville, N.C.

February 1936: Publication of "The Crack-Up" in *Esquire.*

August 1936
Publication of "The Snows of Kilimanjaro" in *Esquire.*

March 1937: Hemingway goes to Spain as war correspondent for NANA.

June 4, 1937
Fitzgerald and Hemingway meet in New York when Hemingway addresses American Writers' Congress.

July 1937: Fitzgerald moves to Hollywood, under contract to MGM. Meets Sheilah Graham.

July 1937
Final meeting of Fitzgerald and Hemingway in Hollywood at showing of *The Spanish Earth.*

October 15, 1937: Publication of *To Have and Have Not.*

October 14, 1938: Publication of *The Fifth Column and The First Forty-Nine Stories.*

January 1939: Termination of Fitzgerald's MGM contract.

Late summer 1939: Fitzgerald begins writing *The Love of the Last Tycoon.*

October 21, 1940: Publication of *For Whom the Bell Tolls.*

November 21, 1940: Hemingway marries Martha Gellhorn.

December 1940: Hemingway buys the Finca Vigia, outside of Havana.

December 21, 1940: Fitzgerald dies of a heart attack at Sheilah Graham's apartment, 1443 N. Hayworth, Hollywood.

October 27, 1941: Publication of *The Last Tycoon.*

May 1944-March 1945: Hemingway in London and France as *Collier's* correspondent.

August 12, 1945: Publication of *The Crack-Up.*

March 14, 1946: Hemingway marries Mary Welsh.

June 1947
Death of Maxwell Perkins.

March 10, 1948: Death of Zelda Fitzgerald in a fire at Highland Hospital.

September 7, 1950: Publication of *Across the River and into the Trees.*

September 8, 1952: Publication of *The Old Man and the Sea.*

October 1954: Hemingway is awarded the Nobel Prize.

July 2, 1961: Hemingway commits suicide in his home at Ketchum, Idaho.

May 5, 1964: Publication of *A Moveable Feast.*

OLD LADY: You know I like you less and less the more I know you.
Madame, it is always a mistake to know an author.

—*Death in the Afternoon*

FITZGERALD AND HEMINGWAY

Introduction

> The first time I ever met Scott Fitzgerald a very strange thing happened. Many strange things happened with Scott but this one I was never able to forget. He had come into the Dingo bar in the rue Delambre where I was sitting with some completely worthless characters, had introduced himself and introduced a tall, pleasant man who was with him as Dunc Chaplin, the famous pitcher. I had not followed Princeton baseball and had never heard of Dunc Chaplin but he was extraordinarily nice, unworried, relaxed and friendly and I much preferred him to Scott.
>
> —*A Moveable Feast*

Thus begins Ernest Hemingway's posthumously published account of his friendship with F. Scott Fitzgerald, which portrays him as a drunk, a weakling, a hypochondriac, a fool, an irresponsible writer, a nuisance, sexually insecure and wife-dominated—and ridicules his tie. It is a highly persuasive recollection, utilizing Hemingway's "rat-trap memory" for details. Moreover, there was a witness to this first encounter: Hemingway specifies that Fitzgerald's Princeton friend Duncan Chaplin was there. But Chaplin has stated that he was not there at the Dingo bar in the rue Delambre that spring day in 1925. Chaplin was not in Paris in 1925; Chaplin was not in Europe in 1925; Chaplin never met Hemingway.*

Perhaps it was someone else—another Princetonian. But Chaplin is carefully identified as part of the sense of exact factual recall Hemingway develops in *A Moveable Feast.* As the scene is set up, the witness has to be Chaplin. One wrong detail undermines the truth of the whole thing: all of it has to be right. Hemingway's Chaplin error raises larger questions about the Fitzgerald/Hemingway relationship, for Hemingway is the only source for some of the most widely circulated anecdotes about Fitzgerald that have become enshrined as literary history.

*After fifty years Duncan Chaplin has no recollection of ever having met Hemingway: "I left Genoa for home about Dec. 15- to Jan. 15-1920 & did not return to Paris after my short stay in 1919—" (to MJB, 26 November 1976). Chaplin served with the U. S. Naval aviation in Italy from August 1918 to the end of 1919. Since Hemingway was with the Red Cross in Italy from June 1918 to January 1919, it is possible that they met in Italy and that Hemingway's memory later moved Chaplin to the Dingo.

Chaplin's photo in the Princeton '17 classbook.

The story about Fitzgerald that has become the defining anecdote about the two writers appears in Hemingway's 1936 short story, "The Snows of Kilimanjaro": "He remembered poor Scott Fitzgerald and his romantic awe of them [the rich] and how he started a story once about them that began 'The very rich are different from you and me.' And how someone had said to Scott, 'Yes they have more money.' But that was not humorous to Scott. He thought they were a special glamorous race and when he found they weren't it wrecked him just as much as any other thing wrecked him."[1] This exchange is intended to demonstrate Fitzgerald's fatuity and Hemingway's tough-mindedness. Hemingway quotes Fitzgerald's sentence from "The Rich Boy" accurately, although it does not begin the story. The rest of the anecdote is untrue (see pp. 190–192).

An examination of all the evidence in the Fitzgerald/Hemingway case is required because the anecdotes about these two great writers have become commonplaces of literary history or literary gossip. There are admirable biographies of both Fitzgerald and Hemingway,

Fitzgerald and Hemingway first met at the Dingo.

but these volumes perforce focus on one or the other of them. A documentary reconstruction of their friendship and estrangement enlarges reader understanding of these geniuses—especially of Hemingway, who became his own most enduring character.

There is no need to aggrandize either Fitzgerald or Hemingway at the other's expense. That his works will be read for as long as books are read is what really mattered to each of them. Partisans or groupies have been moved to enhance the stature of one by diminishing the other, often adducing biographical evidence; but the personal relationships and cross-influences between Fitzgerald and Hemingway have become mythologized. Things that did not happen have been treated as truth. What did happen has been distorted. It is therefore necessary to repeat the fabrications and distortions here in order to correct the record.

The mortality rate of literary friendships is high. Writers tend to be bad risks as friends—probably for much the same reasons that they are bad matrimonial risks. They expend the best parts of themselves in their work. Moreover, literary ambition has a way of turning into literary competition; if fame is the spur, envy may be a concomitant.

Fitzgerald and Hemingway had strong friendship needs. Both

sought admiration and companionship. Hemingway needed a claque. Fitzgerald needed heroes. The roll call of Hemingway's literary ex-friends is impressive; his feuds were conducted in print or in public—as he broke with Sherwood Anderson, Gertrude Stein, John Dos Passos, Archibald MacLeish, Donald Ogden Stewart, Robert McAlmon, Ford Madox Ford, Morley Callaghan, Harold Loeb, and Ernest Walsh. The pattern of Hemingway's friendships—especially during his apprentice period—makes it difficult to avoid the conclusion that the young Hemingway had a compulsion to declare his independence from, or non-indebtedness to, writers who could be said to have helped or influenced him. Fitzgerald commented in his *Notebooks* that ''Ernest would always give a helping hand to a man on a ledge a little higher up'' (see Appendix, 1819). A few of his writer friends managed to stay the distance: Ezra Pound, James Joyce, Evan Shipman, and—in a special way—F. Scott Fitzgerald. Hemingway never saw Pound after 1924. Hemingway and Joyce were not close friends, although Hemingway indicated that they were. Evan Shipman, a minor poet, was not a literary rival. Fitzgerald maintained his literary friendships—with Edmund Wilson, John Peale Bishop, Ring Lardner—and preserved the forms of friendship with Hemingway.

The three principal sources of evidence about the Fitzgerald/Hemingway friendship are the letters they exchanged; their comments in other correspondence—especially with their editor Maxwell Perkins; and Hemingway's posthumously published Paris memoir, *A Moveable Feast.* The last has been the most influential and has largely shaped readers' impressions of the relationship.

Hemingway wrote *A Moveable Feast* more than thirty years after the events he reports. The well-publicized discovery of trunks of Hemingway's papers from the Twenties at the Paris Ritz Hotel in 1956 is supposed to reinforce the authority of the memoir, but there is no evidence that the Paris sketches were salvaged from those trunks.* Nonetheless, the recovery of material from his early Paris days may have had a catalytic effect on the composition of the recollections written between 1957 and 1960 that became *A Moveable Feast.*

*Mary Hemingway's account of the event states that the Ritz trunks contained ''the blue-and-yellow covered penciled notebooks and sheaves of typed papers, ancient newspaper cuttings, bad water colors done by old friends, a few cracked and faded books, some musty sweatshirts and withered sandals'' (''The Making of the Book: A Chronicle and a Memoir,'' *New York Times Book Review* [10 May 1964], 26–27). See Jacqueline Tavernier-Courbin, *Ernest Hemingway's* A Moveable Feast: *The Making of Myth* (Boston: Northeastern University Press, 1991).

The published version of *A Moveable Feast* is not what it purports to be: it is not a straight reminiscence, and it is not printed as Hemingway left it. Thus, no page of manuscript or typescript corresponding to the published "Preface" has been located; its concluding paragraph is not in the drafts: "If the reader prefers, this book may be regarded as fiction. But there is always the chance that such a book of fiction may throw some light on what has been written as fact." The draft passage corresponding to these sentences reads "This book is fiction but there is always a chance that such a work of fiction may throw some light on what has been written as fact." Another preface draft states that "No one can write true facts in reminiscence."[2]

The published text of *A Moveable Feast* is not trustworthy. Mary Hemingway's "Note" states that "He finished the book in the spring of 1960. . . ." Apart from the questionable accuracy of that date, Hemingway cannot be said to have "finished" *A Moveable Feast;* it survives in drafts as a work in progress. Moreover, Mrs. Hemingway's description of her editorial procedure is not entirely reliable:

> . . . I went over the book and gave it the same hardheaded editing I would have done if I had been copying from Ernest's original typing and hand script as I used to do in Cuba. Working toward lucidity I put in or removed commas, checked spelling, sometimes but rarely cut out repetitious words or phrases which I felt sure were accidental rather than intentional or for phonetic or poetic effect. With Harry Brague, Ernest's editor at Scribner's, I made a few further cuts when we went over the manuscript together, and we switched about a couple of the chapters for continuity's sake. No one added any word to the book ["The Making of the Book"].

Collation of Hemingway's latest working drafts against the book establishes that the editorial process went beyond Mrs. Hemingway's description: sentences and paragraphs were formed by combining verbal pieces of the drafts.

The published epigraph to the Fitzgerald chapters in *A Moveable Feast* does not survive in manuscript or typescript and is a conflation of working drafts.

Printed Text	*Secretarial Typescript**
	CHAPTER SEVENTEEN (Foreword to Scott)
His talent was as natural as the pattern that was made by the dust on a butterfly's wings. At one time he understood it no more than the butterfly did and he did not know when it was brushed or marred. Later he became conscious of his damaged wings and of their construction and he learned to think and could not fly any more because the love of flight was gone and he could only remember when it had been effortless.	*His talent was as natural as the pattern that was made by the dust on a butterfly's wings. At one time he understood it no more than the butterfly did and he did not know when it was brushed or marred. Later he became conscious of his damaged wings and of their construction and he learned to think. He was flying again and I was lucky to meet him just after a good time in his writing if not a good one in his life.*

*This TS has Hemingway's MS note ''Italics''—indicating that he had approved it.

The chronology in the epigraph is unclear. The transition ''Later'' at the start of the third sentence of the TS indicates that Fitzgerald's talent was damaged before Hemingway met him, but that he had made a recovery to write *The Great Gatsby* (''He was flying again'')—a conclusion that is not supported by the evidence of Fitzgerald's writing before 1925. The third sentence of the published version can be understood to refer to the writing of *Tender Is the Night.*

The book published as *A Moveable Feast* represents a revised text of an unfinished autobiographical novel. Hemingway's other Paris novel, *The Sun Also Rises*, is a roman à clef. *A Moveable Feast* is a roman à clef that retains the characters' real names.

Introduction

1. *Esquire*, 6 (August 1936), 27, 194-201.
2. The working drafts for *A Moveable Feast* (New York: Scribners, 1964) are with the Ernest Hemingway Papers at the John Fitzgerald Kennedy Library, Boston, Mass.

I

Fitzgerald and Hemingway dramatized themselves—acting out their own mythologies. One played the ruined writer; the other played the titan. Both roles met with public acceptance.

Writers become identified with their material. Since failure is a major theme in Fitzgerald's fiction, readers have become conditioned to regard him as the embodiment of defeat. The concerns of Hemingway's fiction are endurance-courage-cojones, which he embodied in his well-publicized nonliterary life. It became increasingly difficult to differentiate the public Papa from the private writer. He provided good newspaper copy; his photos show the ebullient Hemingway engaging in sport or war, or the bearded patriarchal Hemingway looking wise and indomitable. Hemingway's photos present a man enjoying himself because he is getting all there is out of life. The most frequently reproduced photos of Fitzgerald are of the young man doing a dance step with his wife and daughter—or the middle-aged man at forty with gray skin and unhappy eyes, wearing a checked jacket and a knit club tie, looking like the ghost of F. Scott Fitzgerald.

"Scott Fitzgerald was a failure as a success—and a failure as a failure," remarked restaurateur Prince Michael Romanoff.[1] He did not know Fitzgerald well, but the observation epigrammatizes the standard approach to Fitzgerald's career. Yet Fitzgerald's achievements would constitute a triumphant career for most writers. In a twenty-year period he published four novels, a play, some 160 short stories, a score of essays—and left a novel unfinished at his death. Although Fitzgerald denigrated his stories as hackwork, they include

14 rue de Tilsitt, Paris, 1925.

some of the best in American literature: "The Rich Boy," "May Day," "The Diamond as Big as the Ritz," "Babylon Revisited," "The Last of the Belles," "Winter Dreams." He was not a quick and sloppy writer who dashed off an occasional masterpiece between benders. His manuscripts show that even for the disparaged *Saturday Evening Post* stories there were layers of careful revision. For his novels Fitzgerald was accustomed to rewriting—not just polishing—in proof. He was as much a craftsman as Hemingway was. Yet Hemingway's name evokes literary dedication, whereas Fitzgerald's evokes irresponsibility. The publicly drunk Fitzgerald was an embarrassment, but the working Fitzgerald was unobserved. Hemingway occupied his nonwriting time with sport and made it clear that hunting and fishing were related to his aesthetic. He had the ability to make everything he did seem to have something to do with literature. Hemingway radiated confidence. Fitzgerald became identified with failure—largely through his own public statements. A shrewd careerist would not have published the "Crack-Up" essays. Hemingway attributed Fitzgerald's public humiliations to a love of defeat. A better explanation is provided by Fitzgerald's exemplary quality, for he seemed to embody the national mood. So intense was his identification with his times that he assumed the roles that the prevailing mood required. During the Jazz Age he symbolized ebullience and confidence. During the Depression he symbolized thwarted expectations and remorse.

Fitzgerald wrote in his 1937 essay "Early Success" that "The compensation of a very early success is a conviction that life is a romantic matter."[2] For the romantic sensibility the value of an experience is inseparable from the circumstances that attend it: the meaning of the moment is the moment itself. In *This Side of Paradise* Amory Blaine dreams of "being made the youngest general in the world"; and Fitzgerald observes that "It was always the becoming he dreamed of, never the being."[3] It is hyperbolic to claim that Fitzgerald threw away his early success, but he was unable to shape a career from it. Neither could he embrace failure. At the end of his life he was incapable of fading out as a Hollywood hack.

In "The Crack-Up" Fitzgerald refers to his once-held conviction that "Life was something you dominated if you were any good."[4] The obvious irony is that he was not a dominator. Indeed, he was a born hero-worshiper who sought models for his conduct. The greatest hero Fitzgerald found was life-dominating Ernest Hemingway. A key to Fitzgerald's feelings about Hemingway is provided by the phrase "Ernest who was an equal and my kind of idealist."[5]

That Fitzgerald saw Hemingway as someone who shared his values is puzzling at first. Fitzgerald was a great believer, with a "heightened sensitivity to the promises of life."[6] Hemingway confronted an antagonistic world in which there was nothing to believe except courage: stay around and they would kill you. The Hemingway code provided a method for enduring in the absence of traditional beliefs. *Il faut d'abord durer* became his chief commandment. There is a malevolent presence in Hemingway's work, and the Hemingway hero copes with it by substituting courage and discipline for the lost faiths. The concern of Hemingway and his heroes with craftsmanship provided a way of imposing controls over life: the value of the experience is in how well it is performed. The apparent absence of emotion in Hemingway's early work fooled many readers into classifying him as an anti-romantic writer. But the insistence on personal standards, the self-testings against private gauges, the courage required to confront a hostile world, and the controlled despair formulate an anti-romantic romanticism in Hemingway.

Fitzgerald was able to identify with Hemingway as "my kind of idealist" in literature. At every stage of his career, from obscure apprentice to graybeard master, Hemingway spoke with conviction about his dedication to his craft—as well as about the irresponsibility of other writers. Fitzgerald responded to the intensity of Hemingway's commitment because Fitzgerald believed in the aristocracy of literature. As an artist Hemingway embodied the standards of discipline and dedication that Fitzgerald aspired to. One of the many paradoxes of Fitzgerald is that he cherished high goals for his work while dissipating his creative energies. As a Princeton undergraduate he had remarked that he wanted to be one of the greatest writers that ever lived. So did Hemingway, whose ambitions manifested themselves in competition with all writers, living or dead. When he spoke about beating Stendhal or retaining his championship, he meant it: "I won the title in the twenties and defended it in the thirties and forties. I am not afraid to defend it in the fifties."[7] Hemingway did not progress from strength to strength. His best fiction was written before he was thirty, and he produced only one major novel—*For Whom the Bell Tolls*—after 1929. Nonetheless, he spoke with the authority of success. Everything he did, everything he wrote, became important because he was Ernest Hemingway.

At the time of their first meeting in the spring of 1925 Fitzgerald was at the peak of his powers, having developed from the inconsistent brilliance of *This Side of Paradise* and *The Beautiful and Damned* to the control of *The Great Gatsby.* In July 1922 he had announced to Maxwell Perkins: "I want to write something *new*—something extraordinary and beautiful and simple + intricately patterned."[8] *The Great Gatsby*—published before Fitzgerald was twenty-nine—fulfilled that ambition. Instead of building on the achievement of *Gatsby,* Fitzgerald was unable to concentrate on sustained work for the next seven years. Despite his well-earned playboy image, Fitzgerald suffered guilt over his dissipations. The example of Hemingway made Fitzgerald feel both more and less guilty. If Hemingway's dedication to writing shamed Fitzgerald, it also allowed him to feel that he shared it.

Fitzgerald and Hemingway discussed problems of technique and the aims of fiction, but it requires ingenuity to detect evidence of imitation. By the time they met, their styles and material had been fixed. The literary relationship between Fitzgerald and Hemingway existed on the basis of shared ideals about the value of literature. Their work was utterly dissimilar in style, themes, material, and technique.

Fitzgerald was a traditional stylist who wrote a modulated lyrical prose. Although some of his social material seemed sensational in the early Twenties, Fitzgerald was an old-fashioned moralist with conventional standards of conduct. He was an intrusive author in the sense that he was a storyteller who commented on the story as he told it. When he employed narrators in *The Great Gatsby* and *The Love of the Last Tycoon,* they function as novelists. Fitzgerald's stance as a storyteller required an authorial voice. Hemingway had difficulty breaking away from the first-person narrative of *The Sun Also Rises* and *A Farewell to Arms.* His early fiction tries to eliminate the authorial presence, conveying the impression of experience reported as directly as possible. At the start of his career Hemingway was regarded as an experimental stylist in his abrupt rhythms, understatement, and objectivity.

One thing shared by the work of Fitzgerald and Hemingway—although achieved by different methods—is a concern with "the way it was." Writing to Perkins in 1934 about Hemingway, Thomas Wolfe, and himself, Fitzgerald observed: "What family resemblance there is between we three as writers is the attempt that crops up in our fiction from time to time to recapture the exact feel of a moment in time and space exemplified by people rather than things. . . ."[9] Hemingway utilized factual details much more than Fitzgerald. There is a reportorial quality in his work that is absent from Fitzgerald's fiction. Hemingway's technique—in his early work, at least—was to let the observed detail convey emotion with no authorial comment. Fitzgerald was more concerned with evoking and analyzing the feeling of an experience than with recording detail, although he used selected detail meaningfully. As he advised his daughter, "But when in a freak moment you will want to give the low-down, not the scandal, not the merely *reported* but the *profound* essence of what happened at a prom or after it, perhaps that honesty will come to you—and then you will understand how it is possible to make even a forlorn Laplander *feel* the importance of a trip to Cartier's!"[10]

The Fitzgerald-Hemingway friendship was lopsided, but it was not one-sided. *A Moveable Feast*—probably does not present an accurate view of Hemingway's feelings about Fitzgerald during the early years of their friendship. *Feast* is not the young Hemingway's diary; it is not a record of the way it was at the time. The mood is that of an aging giant looking back from the perspective of what he has become. His letters to Fitzgerald in the Twenties are more trustworthy, for *Feast* was written during Hemingway's dark years. While his letters do not show that Hemingway respected Fitzgerald, they do reveal his high opinion of Fitzgerald's talent: "He is the great tragedy of talent in our bloody generation."[11]

Greatness or disgrace may be a function of the liver's capacity to process alcohol. American literature is crowded with bad drinkers, and Fitzgerald was among the worst. Alcohol turned him foolish, destructive, truculent, childish. His drinking behavior exhausted the patience of friends. The response was especially strong in the case of Hemingway, who had developed drinking conduct as a test of manhood. Another Hemingway test of manhood that Fitzgerald failed was the ability to control women. Distrusting the castrating power of women, Hemingway was appalled by what he regarded as Zelda Fitzgerald's domination of her husband. He was particularly disgusted by her interference with Fitzgerald's work. Hemingway's work came before all things.

At the same time that Fitzgerald was capable of exasperating conduct, he possessed authentic charm and had the ability to make people believe he was really interested in them—because he was. Looking back at himself as he had been in the Twenties, Fitzgerald commented, "Once I believed in friendship, believed I *could* (if I didn't always) make people happy and it was more fun than anything."[12] Fitzgerald had a compulsion to help people. He was characteristically generous to other writers and did not manifest any sense of competition with them. It could be argued that his generosity was a form of ego gratification; but his benefactions were real. When they first met, Hemingway welcomed Fitzgerald's help in advancing his reputation, and Fitzgerald joined the cadre of writers who were promoting Hemingway's career. Not only was Fitzgerald's interest in Hemingway's career helpful, but Fitzgerald—sober—was an extremely attractive friend. "Endearing" is the word Hemingway applies to him at this time in *A Moveable Feast.*

Hemingway was ruthless in his judgment of people. As a man who proclaimed a strict code of conduct, he had no empathy for weakness. Yet he needed friends and made close friendships easily—

possessing the ability to draw people to him and make them feel that they had been accorded membership in an exclusive club. Membership did not carry tenure, for the friends of Hemingway were subject to permanent banishment. As he grew older he found it better to have nonliterary friends. He was more comfortable with stooges than with equals. Nonetheless, in the Twenties Hemingway made allowances for Fitzgerald, mending breaks in the friendship. After Hemingway became in his thirties the most famous living American author, Fitzgerald's friendship became an expendable bother. As Archibald MacLeish wrote of Hemingway, "Fame became of him."[13]

Chapter 1

1. In conversation with M.J.B.
2. *American Cavalcade*, 1 (October 1937), 74-79; collected in *The Crack-Up* (New York: New Directions, 1945).
3. New York: Scribners, 1920; p. 19.
4. *Esquire*, 5 (February 1936), 41, 164; collected in *The Crack-Up.*
5. Letter to Zelda Fitzgerald, *F. Scott Fitzgerald: A Life in Letters*, edited by Bruccoli with the assistance of Judith S. Baughman (New York: Scribners, 1994), p. 187-189. Unless otherwise cited, all Fitzgerald letters quoted here are in *A Life in Letters.*
6. *The Great Gatsby* (New York and Cambridge: Cambridge University Press, 1991), p. 6.
7. Lillian Ross, "How Do You Like it Now, Gentlemen?" *New Yorker*, 24 (13 May 1950), 36-62.
8. *Correspondence of F. Scott Fitzgerald*, edited by Bruccoli and Margaret M. Duggan (New York: Random House, 1980), p. 112.
9. 30 July 1934. Princeton University Library.
10. *The Crack-Up*, edited by Edmund Wilson (New York: New Directions, 1945), p. 304.
11. *Ernest Hemingway: Selected Letters*, edited by Carlos Baker (New York: Scribners, 1981), p. 365. Unless otherwise cited, all Hemingway letters quoted here are in *Selected Letters.*
12. To Maxwell Perkins, 20 May 1940. *A Life in Letters*, pp. 445-446.
13. "Years of the Dog," *Collected Poems, 1917–1952* (Boston: Houghton Mifflin, 1952), pp. 134–135.

II

The first written mention of either writer by the other came in Fitzgerald's October 1924 letter to Maxwell Perkins from the Riviera, where he was finishing *The Great Gatsby.* Acting as a volunteer literary scout for Scribners, Fitzgerald wrote: "This is to tell you about a young man named Ernest Hemmingway, who lives in Paris, (an American) writes for the transatlantic Review + has a brilliant future. Ezra Pount published a collection of his short pieces in Paris, at some place like the Egotist Press, I havn't it hear now but its remarkable + I'd look him up right away. He's the real thing."[1] It is characteristic of Fitzgerald that although his letter of recommendation is peppered with errors—he required years to master the spelling of *Hemingway*—it is right about the crucial matter: Hemingway was "the real thing." The publication to which Fitzgerald reacted so enthusiastically was *in our time*, published in March 1924 by the Three Mountains Press of Paris in the series "*The Inquest* into the state of contemporary English prose" edited by Pound. This thirty-two-page pamphlet bound in stiff covers was limited to 170 copies and consisted of eighteen vignettes. The connection between Fitzgerald and Hemingway was probably provided by Edmund Wilson, Fitzgerald's Princeton friend who was establishing himself as an influential literary critic. Wilson receptively reviewed Hemingway's first two Paris publications, *Three Stories & Ten Poems* (Contact Press, 1923) and *in our time,* in the October 1924 issue of *The Dial*—the month that Fitzgerald alerted Perkins to "Hemmingway."

By October 1924 Hemingway had achieved two nonjournalistic appearances in American little magazines: a fable and a poem in *The*

Villa Marie
Valescure
St Raphael, France

Dear Max:

The royalty was better than I'd expected. This is to tell you about a young man named Ernest Hemmingway, who lives in Paris, (an American) writes for the transatlantic Review & has a brilliant future. Ezra Pount published a a collection of his short pieces in Paris, at some place like the Egotist Press. I havn't it hear now but its remarkable & I'd look him up right away. He's the real thing.

Fitzgerald recommended Hemingway to Perkins in October 1924—before they had met.
(SCRIBNERS ARCHIVES, PRINCETON UNIVERSITY LIBRARY)

Double Dealer and six poems in *Poetry. The Best Short Stories of 1923* (published January 1924) included "My Old Man" in a volume dedicated "TO ERNEST HEMENWAY." His luck was better in Paris, where he was developing a reputation as a young writer of exceptional promise in a city populated by expatriate American writers. In addition to his two small Paris books, Hemingway had published one story, "Indian Camp," and two articles in the *transatlantic review,* and a poem and six vignettes in the *Little Review* by the fall of 1924.

Fitzgerald does not appear to have read *3 & 10* when he wrote to Perkins. If he had, his recommendation might have been even stronger, for the three stories were "Up in Michigan," "Out of Season," and "My Old Man." Fitzgerald's prediction of Hemingway's "brilliant future" was prescient, for it was apparently based on the vignettes of *in our time,* which provided no more than samples of Hemingway's style and tone:

> We were in a garden in Mons. Young Buckley came in with his patrol from across the river. The first German I

Fitzgerald at the time of The Great Gatsby.

saw climbed up over the garden wall. We waited till he got one leg over and then potted him. He had so much equipment on and looked awfully surprised and fell down into the garden. Then three more came over further down the wall. We shot them. They all came just like that.[2]

The hallmarks of Hemingway's prose are here: the clear diction, the abrupt rhythm, the absence of transitions between sentences, the "and" constructions, the reliance on simple declarative sentences, the controlled understatement, the violent material. Nonetheless, Fitzgerald's prediction was reckless, for the longest of the eighteen vignettes was 655 words.

During the fall and winter of 1924-1925 Fitzgerald reminded Perkins about Hemingway while revising *The Great Gatsby* in Rome and Capri. Perkins was unable to obtain a copy of *in our time* until February 1925, when he wrote Hemingway expressing interest in publishing him; but the letter went astray because Perkins did not have Hemingway's current address.[3] The first Paris meeting between Fitzgerald and Hemingway occurred before May 1, 1925; on that date Fitzgerald wrote Perkins that Hemingway had signed with Boni & Liveright for a volume of short stories.

In the spring of 1925 Ernest Hemingway, who was not yet twenty-six, was living with his wife Hadley and their son John ("Bumby") on the Left Bank. Born in 1899 the son of a doctor in Oak Park,

Fitzgerald's initial recognition of Hemingway's genius probably resulted from reading this collection of vignettes.

Illinois, Hemingway grew up in a middle-class, conservative, pious family. After graduation from Oak Park High School in 1917, he worked for six months as a cub reporter on the *Kansas City Star* before going to Italy in 1918 as an ambulance driver with the American Red Cross. He was wounded on July 8 and spent the rest of the war in the hospital. After returning to America he unsuccessfully tried to write fiction before resuming journalism in Toronto and Chicago. In September 1921 Hemingway married Hadley Richardson, who was seven years older than he.

By Christmas the Hemingways were in Paris, where he wrote articles for the *Toronto Star* at space rates. He was not on salary; the paper paid him for what it printed. In Paris he made literary friends easily, for at every stage of his career he possessed vitality and magnetism. His dedication to writing was real and convincing. Among his Paris friends and benefactors were Ezra Pound, Gertrude Stein, and two publishers, Robert McAlmon (Contact Press) and William Bird (Three Mountains Press). Sylvia Beach, proprietress of the Shakespeare & Co. bookshop on the rue l'Odéon and publisher of James Joyce's *Ulysses*, remained a lifelong friend. Although she did not publish Hemingway, Beach was a widely respected figure in the Paris literary community, and her good will promoted his career. When the Hemingways returned to Toronto in September for the birth of their child, *Three Stories & Ten Poems* had been published by McAlmon and *in our time* had been accepted by Bird. Hemingway worked for the *Toronto Star* until December 1923, when he quit his job because his boss was abusing him and because he couldn't get on with his own writing in Toronto. In January 1924 the Hemingways were back in Paris, living over a sawmill at 113 rue Notre Dame des Champs off the Boulevard du Montparnasse.

Hemingway's account of his Paris apprenticeship from 1922 to 1926 are full of dedication and poverty. The dedication was authentic, but the poverty was illusory. At the time of their marriage Hadley had an income of $3,000 a year from her trust fund. Americans with dollars could live comfortably in Paris during the Twenties, for the rate of exchange was favorable. Although Hadley's income was reduced by the mismanagement of her trustee, the Hemingways were never paupers and did not have to rely on his sporadic earnings for eating or drinking money. Their apartment lacked plumbing, but there was always money for the things he wanted to do. "Hunger was good discipline," he claimed in *A Moveable Feast;* nonetheless, they had a cook. The Hemingways could afford trips to Spain for the bullfights and vacations in Switzerland and Austria when he found it difficult to write during the rainy Paris winters. There was even money to bet on the horses—surely a losing proposition despite Hemingway's confidence in his handicapping skill.

In the spring of 1925 Francis Scott Key Fitzgerald, who was not yet twenty-nine, was living with his wife Zelda and their daughter Scottie at 14 rue de Tilsitt, near the Arc de Triomphe on the Right Bank. Born in 1896, Fitzgerald had grown up in St. Paul, Minnesota. His father was an unsuccessful businessman, and the family lived on Mrs. Fitzgerald's inheritance. Although Fitzgerald was sensitive about his position as a relatively poor boy at rich-boy schools, the family could afford to send him to expensive schools. After Newman, a Catholic prep school in New Jersey, he entered Princeton with the class of 1917. In constant academic difficulties because he neglected studies to write for college publications and the Triangle Club musical productions, he repeated his junior year. He left Princeton in 1918 to take an army commission. After his discharge—he never saw combat, to his lasting regret—Fitzgerald tried to make a quick success in New York advertising in order to marry Zelda Sayre, the Alabama belle he had met while stationed near Montgomery. When she proved unwilling to wait or to live on his small salary, Fitzgerald quit his job and rewrote the novel he had written in the army. Published by Scribners, *This Side of Paradise* was a surprise success in 1920, selling 40,000 copies in its first year. Money poured in as Fitzgerald became a skilled writer of short stories for the slick magazines. His income for 1920, his first full year as a professional writer, was $18,500—which had the purchasing power of more than $100,000 in 1994. Fitzgerald needed it. He and Zelda were married in April 1920 and embarked on an extravagant life—the variety of extravagance that has nothing to show for money spent. Fitzgerald became a celebrity for his talent, handsome looks, and ebullient behavior. In the spring of 1924 the Fitzgeralds went to the Riviera—at that time unfashionable in the warm months—to live quietly and economize while he wrote *The Great Gatsby.* They were incapable of economizing, but Fitzgerald hoped that his novel would make enough money to permit him to give up commercial short stories and concentrate on writing novels. Published in April 1925, *Gatsby* sold fewer than 23,000 copies by the end of the year. Nonetheless Fitzgerald knew that *Gatsby* marked an advance in his work and intended to surpass it. On the first of May—in the letter that reports on Hemingway—Fitzgerald communicated his confidence to Perkins: "The happiest thought I have is of my new novel—it is something really NEW in form, idea, structure—the model for the age that Joyce and Stien are searching for, that Conrad didn't find.''

When F. Scott Fitzgerald entered the Dingo—with or without Duncan Chaplin—that April day in 1925, he was the author of *This Side of Paradise, The Beautiful and Damned, The Great Gatsby, Flappers and Philosophers,* and *Tales of the Jazz Age.* Ernest Hemingway was the author of two virtually privately published volumes that totaled eighty-eight printed pages and 470 copies. Yet from the inception of their friendship there was a role reversal. The famous author was awed by the apprentice. In addition to his admiration for Hemingway's talent, Fitzgerald was impressed—even intimidated—by two aspects of the already-evolving Hemingway legend: by his reputations as a war hero and as an athlete.

Fitzgerald, who did not get overseas in World War I, felt that he had missed a test of manhood and brooded about how he would have behaved in battle. He studied books about the Great War and collected photos of the battlefields. Hemingway was reputedly a war hero who had been wounded while serving with the Red Cross and then fought with the Arditti, an elite Italian corps. In actuality he had never been in combat. He was wounded by a mortar shell while distributing candy and tobacco and had been hit by machine-gun fire while carrying another wounded man. At the time of the Armistice he was still undergoing treatment in Milan. Nonetheless, Hemingway was known in Paris as a battle veteran, a reputation he did not discourage.

Fitzgerald was a disappointed athlete who admitted that he sought literary recognition to compensate for his failure at football. At five feet seven inches Fitzgerald was too small for football. Although he won his letter at Newman, he was cut from the Princeton freshman squad after the first day of practice because they didn't need 140-pound halfbacks. Hemingway looked like an athlete; he seemed bigger than he was at six feet and 190 pounds. In point of fact, the only athletic event in which Hemingway had distinguished himself at Oak Park High School was the plunge—a flat distance dive. He won a football letter but was not on the starting team. In Paris he assiduously promoted his reputation as a pugilist, which enhanced the burgeoning Hemingway image, as it was reported that, disgusted with the conduct of a fighter in a professional match, Hemingway had climbed into the ring and knocked him out. He said that he had been trained by professionals in Chicago as a boy, that he had worked as a sparring partner, and that he had been a bouncer in tough joints. There is no evidence to support these claims. Hemingway boxed for exercise in Paris—often with inexperienced men like Ezra Pound—and set himself up as a boxing master. On October 19, 1925, he reported to his mother that he was earning extra money by giving boxing lessons and that Fitzgerald was one of his pupils[4]; but there is no supporting evidence.

A Moveable Feast is the only source for their first meeting at the Dingo. In the published account Hemingway describes Fitzgerald as "between handsome and pretty" and makes an ominous comment: "The mouth worried you until you knew him and then it worried you more." Hemingway notes that he himself was with "some completely worthless characters"; presumably it was permissible for him to drink with "completely worthless characters" because he knew that they were "completely worthless." Fitzgerald compliments his work, which annoys Hemingway because "praise to the face is open disgrace." Instead of listening to Fitzgerald, Hemingway studies his appearance and notices that he is wearing a Brooks Brothers button-down collar and a Guards tie. (This tie has one-inch diagonal stripes of blue and dark red; it can be legitimately worn by all ranks of the British Brigade of Guards, which consists of the five regiments of Foot Guards and the Household Cavalry.) Hemingway considers warning Fitzgerald that the tie might cause him embarrassment with Britishers: "there were two there at the time." Later in the chapter it develops that they were probably Duff Twysden and Pat Guthrie, the Lady Brett and Mike Campbell of *The Sun Also Rises,* whom Fitzgerald refers to as " 'That girl with the phony title who was so rude and that silly drunk with her.' " Did it matter that a couple of "completely worthless characters" might have been offended by Fitzgerald's tie? It was uncharacteristic for Hemingway to be punctilious about dress; in those days he made a point of being superior to clothes, wearing sweatshirts and patched pants.

Fitzgerald orders champagne in the Dingo and annoys Hemingway by asking whether he had slept with his wife before they were married: there is confirmation that he asked this question of new acquaintances. Then Fitzgerald passes out. One of the renowned alcoholics of American letters, Fitzgerald actually had a low tolerance for alcohol. Hemingway was a functioning alcoholic with a large capacity for alcohol.

A Moveable Feast does not drop the matter of Fitzgerald's tie—which Hemingway remembers after thirty years as having been purchased in Rome. At their next meeting a few days later in La Closerie des Lilas café on the Boulevard du Montparnasse, Fitzgerald claims that he left the Dingo because he was fed up with Hemingway's British friends, but Hemingway insists that there hadn't been any British there; but then he provides a puzzling correction:

> "Oh," I said. He had gone back to the Dingo later. Or he'd gone there another time. No, I remembered, there had been two British there. It was true. I remembered who they were. They had been there all right.
>
> "Yes," I said. "Of course."

The function of this quasi-stream of consciousness passage is apparently to demonstrate Hemingway's truthfulness—his readiness to admit an error in 1925 and in 1957. But the tone also suggests that Hemingway is humoring Fitzgerald. These are devices of fiction. The Fitzgerald chapters of *A Moveable Feast* may or may not be trustworthy reportage, but they are convincing as fiction.

Hemingway then asks if his British friends had been rude about Fitzgerald's tie. Fitzgerald replies: " 'Why should they have been rude about my tie? I was wearing a plain black knitted tie with a white polo shirt.' " No matter what the tie was, the image of Fitzgerald wearing a tie with a polo shirt is ludicrous. A polo shirt is a cotton knit sport shirt, usually open at the neck; it is not worn with a tie. However, at that time Brooks Brothers shirts had three collar styles called golf, tennis, and polo. The polo collar was the classic button-down collar, which Fitzgerald wore. Hemingway, by conflating polo shirt with polo collar, indicates that Fitzgerald was absurdly dressed and, worse, wearing a Guards tie and therefore running the risk of offending Duff Twysden and Pat Guthrie.*

Fitzgerald behaves well at La Closerie des Lilas, and Hemingway finds him endearing—"even if you were careful about anyone becoming endearing." He is impressed by Fitzgerald's "non-conceited" pride in *The Great Gatsby,* which Hemingway hasn't yet read; but he undercuts Fitzgerald's achievement by belittling Gilbert Seldes's

*In his review of *Scott and Ernest* Nelson Algren ridiculed the absurdity of discussing this material: "The confrontation of Scott and Ernest, in a bar called the Dingo on the Rue Delambre in 1925, marks the high tide of American literature at its most trivial" (*Chicago Tribune Book World* [2 April 1978], 5F). But Hemingway regarded it as important; he was the one who remembered the tie and shirt and wrote about them. The things a writer knows about are important to him. As Algren insisted elsewhere, the meaning of fiction is in the details.

strong review of the novel: "It could only have been better if Gilbert Seldes had been better." This review in the August 1925 *Dial* placed Fitzgerald ahead of all the writers "of his own generation and most of his elders." Seldes praised *Gatsby* for "regarding a tiny section of life and reporting it with irony and pity and a consuming passion,"[5] which rankled Hemingway. When he wrote *The Sun Also Rises* later that year Hemingway built in a scene in which Bill Gorton sings a nonsense lyric[6]: "Irony and Pity. When you're feeling . . . Oh, Give them Irony and Give them Pity. Oh, give them Irony. When they're feeling . . . Just a little irony. Just a little pity . . ."* Something more than simple envy was involved. *The Dial* was on Hemingway's shit list, and he nurtured a lasting grudge against Seldes because the magazine had rejected his work while Seldes was its managing editor.†

After Fitzgerald has shown that he can behave himself at La Closerie des Lilas, Hemingway accepts his invitation to go with him to Lyons to pick up Fitzgerald's car—at Fitzgerald's expense. Hemingway is looking forward to instructive conversations with a successful writer but is "shocked" when Fitzgerald admits that he changes his good stories for submission to *The Saturday Evening Post.* Hemingway protests against this "whoring," but Fitzgerald assures him that it does not damage his talent because he writes the good story first. There is no evidence in the extensive Fitzgerald manuscript archive of a story in which this process occurred, and there is no other report of this admission; but it is possible that Fitzgerald made the claim to Hemingway. Fitzgerald regretted the expenditure of creative energy that went into his commercial stories and frequently disparaged them.

*The obvious rhyming word *shitty* troubled Maxwell Perkins, even though it was not printed, and he attempted to persuade Hemingway to delete the song.

†Another version of their first encounter survives with the *Moveable Feast* material. The setting is the Dingo, where Hemingway and Hadley are eating supper with friends. When Fitzgerald becomes drunk, his unnamed college friend and Hemingway walk him to the Select café and put him in a cab. The second meeting of Fitzgerald and Hemingway is again at the Dingo (not La Closerie des Lilas). Zelda is present; Hemingway finds her unattractive and has trouble following her conversation. (Nonetheless, he has an erotic dream about Zelda that night, and she is pleased when he tells her.) The two couples go to the Fitzgeralds' apartment, where everything is wrong. Fitzgerald insists on showing Hemingway the record of his earnings and his collection of stereopticon war photos. The visit is terminated when Bumby chugalugs a glass of Burgundy.

When Hemingway reluctantly reads the copy of *The Great Gatsby* that Fitzgerald gives him, he is surprised that it is good. But Hemingway dislikes the dust jacket, which, he notes, had been suggested by Fitzgerald. Hemingway asks him to correct the statement that Gatsby was a Lake Superior salmon fisherman, but Fitzgerald insists that he checked the detail in the *Encyclopædia Britannica.*

A Moveable Feast recounts the Lyons trip in detail. At the start Fitzgerald fails to show up at the train station, and Hemingway goes to Lyons alone, expecting to meet him there.* Fitzgerald arrives the next morning. The Citroën had been abused by Fitzgerald, who drove it without adding oil or water. They start for Paris and are soaked by rain because Zelda had the convertible top removed.

At the hotel in Châlon-sur-Saône Fitzgerald insists that he is in danger of dying from lung congestion. Hemingway nurses him and fakes taking his temperature with a large bath thermometer. The reader is required to believe that Fitzgerald accepts Hemingway's explanation: " 'You multiply by the square of the size of the thermometer.' " Fitzgerald tells Hemingway about Zelda's 1924 affair with a French aviator at St. Raphaël, a story that Fitzgerald would retell him in other versions: "Scott was very articulate and told a story well. He did not have to spell the words nor attempt to punctuate and you did not have the feeling of reading an illiterate that his letters gave you before they had been corrected." (Hemingway exaggerated the extent to which Fitzgerald was orthographically impaired. His letters are as literate as Hemingway's, which resemble the writing or typing of a child.) At dinner in the hotel Fitzgerald passes out from drink.

The next day they drive to Paris while Fitzgerald discourses on Michael Arlen's novels, and Hemingway invents a pretext to limit Fitzgerald's drinking. Fitzgerald later listed the Lyons excursion as among "Most Pleasant Trips" in his *Notebooks* (see Appendix, #1528). In June he wrote to Gertrude Stein: "Hemmingway and I went to Lyon . . . to get my car and had a slick drive through Burgundy. He's a peach of a fellow and absolutely first-rate."[7]

A few days after their trip Fitzgerald brings Hemingway a copy of *The Great Gatsby:* "It had a garish dust jacket and I remember being embarrassed by the violence, bad taste and slippery look of it. It looked the book jacket for a book of bad science fiction." But Fitzgerald explains that the jacket "had to do with a billboard along a highway in Long Island that was important to the story." *Gatsby* has become the most valuable American dust jacket in the rare-book

*Fitzgerald's failure to meet Hemingway is documented by a book owned by Fitzgerald. A rear blank page has the blind impression of this message: "MADAME FITZGERALD 14 RUE DE TILSITT PARIS SCOTT MISSED TRAIN PLEASE WIRE HIM CARE GARAGE I WILL BE AT HOTEL BRISTOL LYON WIRE ME ADDRESS OF GARAGE THERE HEMINGWAY". Apparently Hemingway had this copy of Ernest Boyd's *Portraits: Real and Imaginary* with him and utilized a blank page to write the telegram. See *F. Scott Fitzgerald: Inscriptions* (Columbia, S.C.: Bruccoli, 1988), #35.

Hemingway ridiculed this dust jacket.

market; it is greatly admired as an example of jacket art, which is ultimately a matter of taste. What is not disputable is what it illustrates. The jacket has a woman's face over an amusement park nightscape; it does not depict the symbolic billboard of Dr. T. J. Eckleburg. After removing the offensive jacket, Hemingway reads *Gatsby* and is so favorably impressed that he vows to forgive Fitzgerald's foolish behavior: "When I had finished the book I knew that no matter what Scott did, nor how he behaved, I must know it was like a sickness and be of any help I could to him and try to be a good friend."

''Hawks Do Not Share,'' the second Fitzgerald-inspired sketch in *A Moveable Feast,* introduces Zelda Fitzgerald at ''a very bad lunch'' in the Fitzgeralds' ''gloomy'' apartment. Their daughter Scottie speaks ''with a strong Cockney accent'' because the Fitzgeralds have hired an English nanny they erroneously believe has an upper-class accent. They are obviously unable to do anything properly. From the start there was mutual distrust between Hemingway and Zelda—which developed into antipathy. Hemingway had lost his respect for his father as Dr. Hemingway yielded to a dominating wife, and he compensated for his father's weakness in his own marriage. The Hemingways did what Ernest wanted to do, and his work came first. He was disgusted by Zelda's influence over Fitzgerald and by what he regarded as her deliberate interference with Fitzgerald's writing. Zelda Fitzgerald may not have regarded Hemingway as a threat to her dominion, but she was immune to his charm and had reservations about his character. ''Bogus'' was one of her judgments, amplified with ''materialistic mystic,'' ''phony he-man,'' and ''pansy with hair on his chest.''[8]

Hemingway became convinced that Zelda Fitzgerald encouraged her husband's drinking to keep him from writing. Moreover, Hemingway reports that she was seeking out lesbian company as part of her scheme to impede Fitzgerald's ability to work: ''Scott was afraid for her to pass out in the company they kept that spring and the places they went to. . . . Zelda did not encourage the people who were chasing her and she had nothing to do with them, she said. But it amused her and it made Scott jealous and he had to go with her to the places. It destroyed his work, and she was more jealous of his work than anything.'' Hemingway states that he realized Zelda Fitzgerald was deranged in 1926 and that ''everything was all right and was going to turn out well in the end'' when she asked, '' 'Ernest, don't you think Al Jolson is greater than Jesus?' ''

There were some good times during the spring of 1925. When Dean Christian Gauss of Princeton was in Paris, Fitzgerald took pleasure in arranging lunches at which he discussed literary topics with Hemingway and Gauss. Hemingway took Fitzgerald to 27 rue de Fleurus, where he charmed Gertrude Stein, who later stated in *The Autobiography of Alice B. Toklas:* ''Fitzgerald was the only one of the younger writers who wrote naturally in sentences. . . . She thinks Fitzgerald will be read when many of his well-known contemporaries are forgotten.''[9]

Chapter 2

1. 10 October 1924. *A Life in Letters*, p. 82.
2. "Chapter 4," *in our time* (Paris: Three Mountains Press, 1924), p. 12.
3. *A Life in Letters*, p. 97. See also Hemingway to Perkins, 15 April 1925, *Selected Letters*, pp. 156–157.
4. Bruccoli Collection.
5. "Spring Flight," Vol. 79, 162–164.
6. New York: Scribners, 1926; p. 116.
7. *A Life in Letters*, p. 115.
8. Sara Mayfield, *Exiles From Paradise: Zelda and Scott Fitzgerald* (New York: Delacorte, 1971), p. 141.
9. New York: Harcourt, Brace, 1933; p. 268.

III

On the evidence of their correspondence, Hemingway emerges as a better friend than his self-portrait in *A Moveable Feast* shows—until 1936. Both men were savers and preserved most of their letters to each other. Fifty-seven letters or telegrams have been located: twenty-eight from Fitzgerald, and twenty-nine from Hemingway.

Fitzgerald and Hemingway functioned differently as letter writers. Fitzgerald's letters are carefully written and have his characteristic warmth of expression; they have no direct connection with his literary work. Hemingway's letters are informal and discursive. In addition to imparting information, his letters document the Hemingway image. They had a literary function: Hemingway was an almost compulsive letter writer and used correspondence as warm-up or cooling-off exercises for his literary work.

The first two letters set the tone for much of their correspondence. Hemingway dominates; Fitzgerald defers. On July 1, 1925, Hemingway writes from Spain en route to the fiesta of San Fermin.

Burguete, Navera.
July 1—

Dear Scott—

We are going in to Pamplona tomorrow. Been trout fishing here. How are you? And how is Zelda?

I am feeling better than I've ever felt—havent drunk any thing but wine since I left Paris. God it has been wonderful country. But you hate country. All right omit description of country. I wonder what your idea of heaven would be—

A beautiful vacuum filled with wealthy monogamists. All powerful and members of the best families all drinking themselves to death. And hell would probably an ugly vacuum full of poor polygamists unable to obtain booze or with chronic stomach disorders that they called secret sorrows.

To me a heaven would be a big bull ring with me holding two barrera seats and a trout stream outside that no one else was allowed to fish in and two lovely houses in the town; one where I would have my wife and children and be monogamous and love them truly and well and the other where I would have my nine beautiful mistresses on 9 different floors and one house would be fitted up with special copies of the Dial printed on soft tissue and kept in the toilets on every floor and in the other house we would use the American Mercury and the New Republic. Then there would be a fine church like in Pamplona where I could go and be confessed on the way from one house to the other and I would get on my horse and ride out with my son to my bull ranch named Hacienda Hadley and toss coins to all my illegitimate children that lined the road. I would write out at the Hacienda and send my son in to lock the chastity belts onto my mistresses because someone had just galloped up with the news that a notorious monogamist named Fitzgerald had been seen riding toward the town at the head of a company of strolling drinkers.

Well anyway were going into town tomorrow early in the morning. Write me at the / Hotel Quintana
Pamplona
Spain

Or don't you like to write letters. I do because it's such a swell way to keep from working and yet feel you've done something.

So long and love to Zelda from us both—

Yours,
Ernest[1]

The first extant letter from Fitzgerald—postmarked November 30, 1925—is, characteristically, an apology.

14 Rue de Tilsit

Dear Ernest: I was quite ashamed of the other morning. Not only in disturbing Hadly, but in foistering that "Juda Lincoln" alias George Morgenthau apon you. However it is only fair to say that the deplorable man who entered your apartment Sat. morning was not me but a man named Johnston who has often been mistaken for me.

Zelda, evidences to the contrary, was not suffering from lack of care but from a nervous hysteria which is only releived by a doctor bearing morphine. We both went to Bellau Wood next day to recuperate.

For some reason I told you a silly lie—or rather an exageration, silly because the truth itself was enough to make me sufficiently jubilant. The Sat. Eve. Post. raised me to $2750.00 and not $3000. which is a jump of $750. in one month. It was probably in my mind that I could now get $3000. from the smaller magazines. The *Post* merely met the Hearst offer, but that is something they seldom do.

What garbled versions of the McAlmon episode or the English orgy we lately participated in, I told you, I don't know. It is true that I saved McAlmon from a beating he probably deserved and that we went on some wild parties in London with a certain Marchioness of Milford Haven whom we first met with Telulah Bankhead. She was about half royalty, I think. Anyhow she was very nice—anything else I may have added about the relations between the Fitzgeralds and the house of Windsor is pure fiction.

I'm crazy to read the comic novel. Are you going to the Mclieshe's Tuesday? I hope Hadly is well now. Please believe that we send our

Best Wishes to
Ernest M. Hemmingway[2]

Hemingway's first American book, *In Our Time,* was published by Boni & Liveright on October 4, 1925, in a printing of 1,335 copies. This volume collected fourteen short stories and the vignettes from the Paris *in our time.* It was a highly promising first volume of stories, including seven Nick Adams stories; but story collections by unknown writers are not good publishing investments. Horace Liveright was betting on Hemingway's future. A second printing of this book was not required until March 1927—after the success of *The Sun Also Rises.* The dust jacket for *In Our Time* had a display of blurbs by Sherwood Anderson, Gilbert Seldes, Donald Ogden Stewart, Waldo Frank, Edward J. O'Brien, and Ford Madox Ford—who called Hemingway "the best writer in America." Hemingway subsequently broke with all of them except O'Brien. Fitzgerald's essay-review—which did not appear in *The Bookman*

EDWARD J. O'BRIEN

"I regard this volume of short stories as a permanent contribution to the American literature of our time—a brave book not only for us but for posterity."

SHERWOOD ANDERSON

"Mr. Hemingway is young, strong, full of laughter, and he can write. His people flash suddenly up into those odd elusive moments of glowing reality, the clear putting down of which has always made good writing so good."

IN OUR TIME

BY ERNEST HEMINGWAY

GILBERT SELDES

"Extraordinary in its vividness and its brutality, it is, for the most part, deliberately unliterary, in the modern style. I can see it being warmly admired as I admire it, and violently disliked as I dislike some of it. But it has too much character, too much vital energy and passion to leave anyone indifferent. To me that is a high recommendation."

DONALD OGDEN STEWART

"After trying to make a meal out of the literary lettuce sandwiches which are being fed to this country, it is rather nice to discover that one of your own countrymen has opened a shop where you can really get something to eat."

WALDO FRANK

"Not in a long time have I been so impressed by the work of a new American author. Mr. Hemingway can write. His stories are hard, passionate bits of life."

FORD MADOX FORD

"The best writer in America at this moment (though for the moment he happens to be in Paris), the most conscientious, the most master of his craft, the most consummate, is Ernest Hemingway."

Dust jacket for Hemingway's short story collection, his first book published in the United States.

until May 1926—was entitled ''How to Waste Material: A Note on My Generation.'' After a discussion of the failure of American writers to deal honestly with American material, Fitzgerald turns to Hemingway:

> ''In Our Time'' consists of fourteen stories, short and long, with fifteen vivid miniatures interpolated between them. When I try to think of any contemporary American short stories as good as ''Big Two-Hearted River'', the last one in the book, only Gertrude Stein's ''Melanctha'', Anderson's ''The Egg'', and Lardner's ''Golden Honeymoon'' come to mind. It is the account of a boy on a fishing trip—he hikes, pitches his tent, cooks dinner, sleeps, and the next morning casts for trout. Nothing more—but I read it with the most breathless unwilling interest I have experienced since Conrad first bent my reluctant eyes upon the sea.
>
> The hero, Nick, runs through nearly all the stories, until the book takes on almost an autobiographical tint—in fact ''My Old Man'', one of the two in which this element seems entirely absent, is the least successful of all. Some of the stories show influences but they are invariably absorbed and transmuted, while in ''My Old Man'' there is an echo of Anderson's way of thinking in those sentimental ''horse stories'', which inaugurated his respectability and also his decline four years ago.
>
> But with ''The Doctor and the Doctor's Wife'', ''The End of Something'', ''The Three Day Blow'', ''Mr. and Mrs. Elliot'', and ''Soldier's Home'' you are immediately aware of something temperamentally new. In the first of these a man is backed down by a half breed Indian after committing himself to a fight. The quality of humiliation in the story is so intense that it immediately calls up every such incident in the reader's past. Without the aid of a comment or a pointing finger one knows exactly the sharp emotion of young Nick who watches the scene.
>
> The next two stories describe an experience at the last edge of adolescence. You are constantly aware of the continual snapping of ties that is going on around Nick. In the half stewed, immature conversation before the fire you watch the awakening of that vast unrest that descends upon the emotional type at about eighteen. Again there is not a single recourse to exposition. As in ''Big Two-Hearted River'', a picture—sharp, nostalgic, tense—develops before

your eyes. When the picture is complete a light seems to snap out, the story is over. There is no tail, no sudden change of pace at the end to throw into relief what has gone before.

Nick leaves home penniless; you have a glimpse of him lying wounded in the street of a battered Italian town, and later of a love affair with a nurse on a hospital roof in Milan. Then in one of the best of the stories he is home again. The last glimpse of him is when his mother asks him, with all the bitter world in his heart, to kneel down beside her in the dining room in Puritan prayer.

Anyone who first looks through the short interpolated sketches will hardly fail to read the stories themselves. "The Garden at Mons" and "The Barricade" are profound essays upon the English officer, written on a postage stamp. "The King of Greece's Tea Party", "The Shooting of the Cabinet Ministers", and "The Cigar-store Robbery" particularly fascinated me, as they did when Edmund Wilson first showed them to me in an earlier pamphlet, over two years ago.

Disregard the rather ill considered blurbs upon the cover. It is sufficient that here is no raw food served up by the railroad restaurants of California and Wisconsin. In the best of these dishes there is not a bit to spare. And many of us who have grown weary of admonitions to "watch this man or that" have felt a sort of renewal of excitement at these stories wherein Ernest Hemingway turns a corner into the street.[3]

After *In Our Time* Hemingway decided that Boni & Liveright was not the right publisher for him. Fitzgerald wanted him for Scribners, and Hemingway continued to correspond with Maxwell Perkins after signing with Boni & Liveright. But Hemingway seemed tied up. The contract for *In Our Time* gave Boni & Liveright the option on three books, which would lapse if the publisher declined the book submitted after *In Our Time.*

In the summer of 1925—while awaiting publication of *In Our Time*—Hemingway began writing a novel based on events at the recent fiesta of San Fermin. For the July trip to Pamplona he had organized his own entourage. In addition to Hadley, he brought along Duff Twysden, an alcoholic and promiscuous English remittance woman; Pat Guthrie, an alcoholic Scottish remittance man who was her fiancé-lover; Harold Loeb, an American writer who had recently had an affair with Duff; Bill Smith, Hemingway's boyhood friend from Michigan; and American humorist Donald Ogden Stewart. The Twysden-Guthrie-Loeb mix was potentially awkward. Hemingway became disgusted by Loeb's behavior toward Twysden and turned nasty. Whether Hemingway was resentful because Loeb had slept with Twysden remains a matter for speculation. These people are all clearly identifiable in *The Sun Also Rises:* Duff Twysden is Brett Ashley; Pat Guthrie is Mike Campbell; Harold Loeb is Robert Cohn; Smith and Stewart are amalgamated in Bill Gorton.[4]

Hemingway began writing the novel in Spain on July 21, 1925—his twenty-sixth birthday—and finished the first draft in Paris on September 21. Before revising it, he wrote in one week during November a book-length parody of Sherwood Anderson, *The Torrents of Spring,* which he submitted to Boni & Liveright in December 1925 as the second book under his option contract.

Anderson's short stories had impressed Hemingway during his apprenticeship. The two men had been friendly in Chicago in 1921, before the Hemingways went to Paris, and Anderson had encouraged the aspiring writer. One of Hemingway's first good stories, "My Old Man," shows Anderson's influence. But Hemingway regarded Anderson's 1925 novel, *Dark Laughter,* as pretentious and faked. In *The Torrents of Spring* he undertook to provide corrective parody—as Henry Fielding had done in the eighteenth century by writing *Shamela* in response to Samuel Richardson's *Pamela.* Since Anderson was a star Boni & Liveright author, the suspicion that Hemingway wrote *Torrents* as a contract breaker is inescapable; but he denied the allegation. Related to this point is the question of whether Fitzgerald was a co-conspirator, for he wanted Hemingway to join Maxwell Perkins's stable at Scribners. A Fitzgerald communication to Liveright and to editor T. R. Smith indicates that he was innocent of involvement in such a scheme—or that he was a master of the disingenuous letter.

14 Rue de Tilsitt
Paris

Dear Horace and Tom:

Ernest Hemminway showed me his new book the other day (the satiric book: *The Torrents of Spring*) and seemed a bit in doubt as to how you were going to receive it. I don't know how much value, if any, you attach to my opinion but it might interest you to know that to one rather snooty reader, at least, it seems about the best comic book ever written by an American. It is simply devastating to about seven-eighths of the work of imitation Andersons, to facile and "correct" culture and to this eternal looking beyond appearances for the "real," on the part of people who have never even been conscious of appearances. The thing is like a nightmare of literary pretensions behind which a certain hilarious order establishes itself before the end—so it hasn't that quality of leaving a painful passionate *funnyness* as the last taste in your mouth. Like Alice in Wonderland it sends you back to the sane world above cant and fashion in which most of us flatter ourselves that we live—sometimes.

Beyond that it is absorbingly interesting—the failure to be that is the one unforgivable sin. Frankly I hope you won't like it—because I am something of a ballyhoo man for Scribners and I'd some day like to see all my generation (3) that I admire rounded up in the same coop—but knowing my entheusiasm and his own trepidation Ernest agreed with me that such a statement of the former might break the ice for what is an extraordinary and unusual production.

With Best Wishes to you Both
Your friend
F. Scott Fitzg—[5]

Hemingway submitted *Torrents* to Liveright on December 7 with a cover letter mentioning Fitzgerald's high opinion of the work. Fitzgerald appears in *Torrents* in a ponderously facetious "Author's Note to the Reader":

> It was at this point in the story, reader, that Mr. F. Scott Fitzgerald came to our home one afternoon, and after remaining for quite a while suddenly sat down in the fireplace and would not (or was it could not, reader?) get up and let the fire burn something else so as to keep the room warm. I know, reader, that these things sometimes do not show in a story, but, just the same, they are happening, and think what they mean to chaps like you and me in the literary game. If you should think this part of the story is not as good as it might have been remember, reader, that day in and day out all over the world things like this are happening. Need I add, reader, that I have the utmost respect for

Mr. Fitzgerald, and let anybody else attack him and I would be the first to spring to his defence! And that includes you too, reader, though I hate to speak out bluntly like this, and take the risk of breaking up a friendship of the sort that ours has gotten to be.[6]

Fitzgerald's reaction of this passage is not known; but he was probably not greatly amused, for it shows him as helplessly drunk. Hemingway presumably regarded the material as friendly joking, for he presented the carbon-copy typescript of *Torrents* to the Fitzgeralds, inscribed "To Scott and Zelda with love from Ernest."[7] Whatever Hemingway intended in *Torrents,* it should have served as a warning to Fitzgerald: the effect of later appearances of Fitzgerald in Hemingway's published work would be unequivocal.*

In December 1925 Hemingway wrote Fitzgerald from Schruns in the Austrian Alps, providing avuncular literary advice:

Dear Scott-

I hope you and Zelda are well again. Did Pauline bring the books? I gave her the Ludendorff, Brig. Young and Mr. Farrar's Spot Light. I was pretty sick too with my damned throat and especially so after reading the whole of the Torrents of Spring book out loud to them the Murpheys as an act of bravado after not being able to talk all day. Jesus Christ some time I'd like to grow up. I've had hell with it now for a week. Suppose it will be all right in a couple of days.

We had a good trip down here. No other foreigniers in the town. I've been staying in bed, shooting pool with the natives and ski-ied twice but haven't any strength, consequently no legs, consequently no guts. Hadley and Bumby are in swell shape. I used to give Hadley a handicap of 200 in Billiards. Now she beats me level.

It has snowed for two days. About 2½ feet of snow.

*A manuscript for *The Sun Also Rises*—then titled "The Lost Generation"—opens with a foreword explaining the title: "There is only this then to say that this generation that is lost has nothing to do with any Younger Generation about whose outcome much literary speculation occurred in times past. This is not a question of what kind of mothers will flappers make or where is bobbed hair leading us." The last sentence alludes to syndicated newspaper articles Fitzgerald wrote in 1924: "Why Blame It on the Poor Kiss if the Girl Veteran of Many Petting Parties is Prone to Affairs After Marriage" and "What kind of Husbands Do 'Jimmies' Make?"—the latter having appeared in the *Toronto Star Weekly,* Hemingway's former venue.

THE TORRENTS OF SPRING

A Romantic Novel In Honor of The Passing Of A Great Race.

By ERNEST HEMINGWAY.

To Scott and Zelda
with love from Ernest.

And perhaps there is one reason why a comic writer should of all others be the least excused for deviating from nature, since it may not be always so easy for a serious poet to meet with the great and the admirable; but life everywhere furnishes an accurate observer with the ridiculous.

Henry Fielding.

Fitzgerald kept this typescript, which is now with his papers at the Princton University Library.

Cold and the air nice and tight. The mountains are damned nice to see again.

Have read Fathers and Children by Turgenieff and the last Vol. of Buddenbrooks by Thomas Mann. Fathers and Chi-en isn't his best stuff by a long way. Some swell stuff in it but it can never be as exciting again as when it was written and that's a hell of a criticism for a book.

You're write about the Murphy's. They're grand people. Nice people are so damned nice.

Buddenbrooks is a pretty damned good book. If he were a good writer it would be swell. When you think a book like that was published in 1902 and unknown in English until last year it makes you have even less respect, if you ever had any, for people getting stirred up over Main Street, Babbitt and all the books your boy friend Menken has gotten excited about just because they happened to deal with the much abused Am. Scene.

Did you ever read The Growth of the Soil? and then for Christ sake to read Thomas Boyd.

I think you should learn about writing from everybody who has ever written that has anything to teach you. But what all these bastards do is learn certain concrete ideas that are only important as discoveries. Like if I were now, suddenly to discover the law of gravitation.

Like me to write you a little essay on The Importance of Subject? Well the reason you are so sore you missed the war is because war is the best subject of all. It groups the maximum material and speeds up its action and brings out all sorts of stuff that normally you have to wait a lifetime to get. What made 3 Soldiers a swell book was the war. What made Streets of Night a lousy book was Boston. One as well written as the other. I can hear you telling me I'm all wrong. Maybe I am. Love is also a good subject as you might be said to have discovered. Other major subjects are money from which we get riches and poores. Also avarice. Gentlemen the boy lecturer is tired. A dull subject I should say would be impotence. Murder is a good one so get a swell murder into yr. next book and sit back. And don't for Christ sake feel bad about missing the war because I didnt see or get anything worth a damn out as a whole show, not just as touching myself, which is the cheap, romantic view point, because I was too young. Dos, fortunately, went to the war twice and grew up in between. His first book was lousy.

Now dont be a lousy crut and not answer this because letters are worth million of dollars down here.

Best love to Zelda.
Yrs. always
Ernest/
Hotel Taube,
Schruns,
Vorarlberg,
Austria
December 15, 1925

How did your plan of having Harold Stearns make good in two weeks- after all these years- turn out?

Dear Zelda and Scott:—

Taty says if I want to send my love I must do it myself with my little pen! So here it is and in great quantities. I hope you are both feeling fine by now?

Hadley[8]

Fitzgerald's reply to this letter does not survive, but shortly before Christmas 1925 Hemingway wrote referring to a lost letter in which Fitzgerald had ranked the *In Our Time* stories:

Dear Scott-

Have sent the 400 dollars (dollars) to your concierge.* You can keep it yourself or give it to Harold Stearns. You write a swell letter. Glad somebody spells worse than I do.

Sure, I know Hank Wales. He was once a bartender in Goldfields, got to be a newspaper man some way, came over in 1918 when any newspaper man could work anywhere, got all smashed up, in a motorcycle accident I think, taught himself to read, write and speak French and is a hell of a good newspaper man. I used to hate him when I first knew him and now I am fonder of him than any other newspaper man except Bill Bird and Guy Hickock. Hank used to send amazing and beautiful stories during the Peace Conference and one day Col. House said to him "Wales where do you get your facts?" Hank had just given the Yugo Slav oil fields to Japan or somebody else. "Col.

*Repayment of a loan. M.J.B.

House,'' Hank says. ''What the Chicago Tribune wants isnt facts. It's news.''

Why did you ask about Hank? He hasn't got a pleasant manner and he certainly looks and acts like hell. I suppose the reason I like him so much is because he likes me. Any dope about him being ex bartender etc. is confidential. He also managed pugs.

Your rating of I.OT. stories very interesting. The way I like them as it seems now, without re-reading is grade I (Big 2 hearted. Indian Camp. 1st ¶ last ¶ of Out of Season Soldier's Home)

Hell I cant group them. Why did you leave out My Old Man? That's a good story, always seemed to me, though not the thing I'm shooting for. It belongs to another categorie along with the bull fight story and the 50 grand. The kind that are easy for me to write.

Cat in the Rain wasnt about Hadley. I knew you and Zelda always thought it was. When I wrote that we were at Rapallo but Hadley was 4 months pregnant with Bumby. The Inn Keeper was the one at Cortina D'Ampezzo and the man and girl were a Harvard Kid and his wife that I'd met at Genoa. Hadley never made a speech in her life about wanting a baby because she had been told various things by her doctor and I'd—. No use going into all that.

The only story in which Hadley figures is Out of Season which was an almost literal transcription of what happened. Your ear is always more acute when you have been upset by a row of any sort, mine I mean, and when I came in from the unproductive fishing trip I wrote that story right off on the typewriter without punctuation. I meant it to be tragic about the drunk of a guide because I reported him to the hotel owner—the one who appears in Cat In The Rain—and he fired him and as that was the last job he had in the town and was quite drunk and very desperate hanged himself in the stable. At that time I was writing the In Our Time chapters and I wanted to write a tragic story <u>without</u> violence. So I didn't put in the hanging. May be that sounds silly. I didn't think the story needed it.

I'm sorry as hell for H.S. but there's nothing anybody can do for him except give him money and be nice to him. There's nothing to be achieved. No solution. And again I'm fond of him. Probably as in the case of Hank, because he likes me.

There's nothing you can do for him except give him

money and you've done that and naturally can't assume the continuance of it as an obligation. He lives altogether in his imagination. The poor old bastard. I always get awfully sorry for people and especially for liars, drunks, homely whores, etc. Never get very sorry for worthy cases. after all. Panhandling is no damned fun. A glut who's drinking himself to death ought not to be constantly having to raise the funds to do it with. I do think Harold had a pretty damned good head. Also think he destroyed it or completely coated it with fuzz by drinking. You've done your part toward him. Just dont give him any more dough. But don't, for Christ sake ever let him think that I don't absolutely believe in him. Because there's nothing to be done about him and therefore it's pretty sad and I couldn't sleep if I hurt his feelings. Christ nose that when I cant sleep I have enough sons of bitching things I've done to look back on without adding any ornamental ones.

The ear that get's pulled is the stump. Referring Battler.

McAlmon is a son of a bitch with a mind like an ingrowing toe nail. I'm through defending that one. I still feel sorry for him but damned little. After I called him on you he went around for two nights talking on the subject of what a swine I was, how HE had done everything for me, started me off etc. [I.E. sold out an edition each of that lousy little book and In Our Time at 15 francs and 40 francs a copy. I not receiving a sou. The only books he ever sold of all the books he's published) and that all I did was exploit people emotionally. I've defended the lousy little toenail paring for 3 years against everybody because I knew his horribly unhappy English arrangement etc. But am through now. Am going to write a Mr. and Mrs. Elliot on him. Might as well give his emotional exploitation story some foundation.

Seem to be in a mood of Christ like bitterness this A.M. Have swell piano in her room for Hadley and she's practicing. Played poker last night and drank too much beer. 7 bottles. Won 158,000 Kroner. Makes about $2.35.

No fairies in Vorarlberg anyway.

Will report on full on Dostoevsky.

I think MacLeishes and Murphy's are swell. Also Fitzgeralds.

God I hope Zelda gets all right at the bains place. Pain's such an awful thing. It's such a rotten shame for her to be sick. I do think she'll get better down South and you will both be a damned sight better off on the Riviera than in Paris. You both looked so damned well when you came up last fall and Paris is poisonous for you. We'll see you there too.

God I wish I hadn't drunk so much beer. Going to buy Bumby a rocking horse for 80,000 Kroner though. The presents will go swell with it. Please thank Scotty for Bumby.

There was a Chinook yest. and day before and then it rained and now it is bright and cold and the snow ruined.

I am buying you 2 illustrated German war books. The swell illustrated ones are just beginning to come out. One on the mountain fighting Italian Front. And the other the history of the Wurtenburg Artillery. Am sending to Frankfort. Have seen the mountain book It's swell. When you get them if the pictures outweigh the German text I'll get you some more. There's going to be one on the Sturmtrupper. The mountain pictures are swell.

We went in to Bluderiz and heard Herr Kapitan Leutenant Mumm lecture on the battle of Skagguak with movies. You'd have liked it. Hadley hated the Kapt. Leut. so that she was very thrilled. He was an awful man.

Review of In Our Type from Chicago Post says all of it obviously not fiction but simply descriptive of passages in life of new Chicago Author. God what a life I must have led.

Am reading Peter Simple by Capt. Marryat. Havent read it since I was a kid. Great book. He wrote 4 great books. Frank Mildmay or the Naval Officer. Midshipman Easy. Peter Simple and Snarleyaw or the Dog Fiend. He wrote a lot of Kids books in later life and people get them mixed up. You ought to read Peter Simple.

If you want to read about war read any of those 1st 3.

Pauline Pfeiffer gets here tomorrow to stay for Xmas and New Years.

Know you will be glad to read in N.Y. Herald that 2 men died of cold in Chalons Sur Saone where you nearly died same. Good thing we got out in time. By the way, where the hell is your car?

Hadley, Bumby and I or me send our love and Merry Christmas to Zelda, Scotty and yourself.

This might have been a good letter if it hadnt been for the beer.

Original ending of story had dose } referring to
clapp instead of gonoreaha but I } Very Short Story

didn't know whether clap had two ps or one so changed it to gonoccoci. The hell I did. Try and get it. (This is a piece of slang I invented down here)

Hope you have a swell Christmas.
Yrs. always.
Yogi Liveright
Please write even at $400 a letter. Will raise you to $435 but dont get drunk to celebrate.

[*left margin*] You know what Austria (Osterreich) means? The Eastern Kingdom. Isn't that swell? Tell Zelda.[9]

Harold Stearns—who appears in *The Sun Also Rises* as Harvey Stone—was an alcoholic American writer Fitzgerald was trying to help in Paris. Robert McAlmon was an American writer who was the publisher of the Paris-based Contact Editions. Upon his marriage-of-convenience to the English writer Bryher, McAlmon received money from her father, Sir John Ellerman. Much of it went into the Contact Editions, which published McAlmon's work and that of other writers. Contact became Hemingway's first publisher with *Three Stories & Ten Poems,* and *in our time* was jointly dedicated to McAlmon and William Bird. Hemingway's complaint that he didn't get anything for the "books" McAlmon published is weak, for there was little to be made from 300 copies of a $2 booklet—$60 at a 10 percent royalty. McAlmon had meaningfully aided Hemingway's career at a time when his stories were unsalable but grew resentful of Hemingway's success. Moreover, McAlmon had a reputation as a troublemaking gossiper. Their feud became increasingly vitriolic and involved Fitzgerald.

Horace Liveright predictably declined *The Torrents of Spring* by cable on December 30, 1925: ". . . who on earth do you think would buy it? Apart from the fact that it is a bitter, and I might say almost vicious caricature of Sherwood Anderson, it is so entirely cerebral. . . . we disagree with you and Scott Fitzgerald and Louis Bromfield and Dos Passos, that it is a fine and humorous American Satire."[10] Liveright asked to see Hemingway's novel.

Hemingway reported to Fitzgerald from Schruns on his negotiations with Boni & Liveright, Knopf, and Harcourt, Brace:

December 31, 1925

Dear Scott—

Have just received following cable from Liveright—Rejecting Torrents of Spring Patiently awaiting manuscript Sun Also Rises Writing Fully—

I asked them in the letter I sent with the Ms. to cable me their decision. I have known all along that they could not and would not be able to publish it as it makes a bum out of their present ace and best seller Anderson. Now in 10th printing. I did not, however, have that in mind in any way when I wrote it.

Still I hate to go through the hell of changing publishers etc. Also the book should come out in the late Spring at latest. That would be best. Later would not be bad but Spring would be ideal.

My contract with Liveright—only a letter—reads that in consideration of they're publishing my first book at their own expense etc. they are to have an option on my first three books. If they do not exercise this option to publish within 60 days of receipt of Ms. it lapses and if they do not exercise their option on the 2nd book it lapses for 3rd book. So I'm loose. No matter what Horace may think up in his letter to say.

As you know I promised Maxwell Perkins that I would give him the first chance at anything if by any chance I should be released from Liveright.

So that is that.

In the meantime I have been approached by Bradley (Wm Aspenwell) for Knopf.

In the meantime I have the following letter from Louis Bromfield.

Dear Ernest—

Appropos of "Torrents of Spring" I received a letter today from Alfred Harcourt who replied at once to a line I had written (taking the liberty after talking with you) regarding the chances of your shifting publishers. He is very eager to see the Anderson piece and is thoroly familiar with your stuff—both in the magazines and In Our Time. In this connection he writes - "Hemingway is his own man and talking off his own bat. I should say, Yea Brother, and we shall try to do the young man as much credit as he'll do us, and that's considerable. I'd like to see his Anderson piece. It's a chance for good fun, if not for too much money for either of us. Hemingway's first novel might rock the country.

He also stands ready to advance money in case you need it, as soon as you like, provided you are free of Liveright and want to go to Harcourt. I was pleased to have so prompt and interested an answer, though, of course, it was to be expected, etc.

So that's that.

In any event I am not going to Double Cross you and Max Perkins to whom I have given a promise.

I will wire Liveright tomorrow a.m to Send Manuscript to Don Stewart care of the Yale Club, New York (only address I can think of tonight) and summarize by cable any propositions he may be making me in his letter.

It's up to you how I proceed next. Don I can wire to send Ms. to Max Perkins. You can write Max telling him how Liveright turned it down and why and your own opinion of it. I am re-writing The Sun Also Rises and it is damned good. It will be ready in 2-3 months for late fall or later if they wish.

As you see I am jeopardizing my chances with Harcourt by first sending the Ms. to Scribner and if Scribner turned it down. It would be very bad as Harcourt have practically offered to take me unsight unseen. Am turning down a sure thing for delay and a chance but feel no regret because of the impression I have formed of Maxwell Perkins through his letters and what you have told me of him. Also confidence in Scribners and would like to be lined up with you.

You, however, are an important cog in the show and I hate to ask you to write even one letter when I know you are so busy getting away and all.

However there is the situation.

I dont know exactly what to write to Bromfield. Perhaps you will suggest something. In any event say nothing to Bromfield who has been damned decent, nor to anybody else in Paris till you hear from me.

I will wire Liveright in the morning (to send Ms. to Don at Yale Club.) Then when I hear from you I can wire Don to send Ms. to Maxwell Perkins. Write me Scribners' address.

Today is Thursday. You will get this letter on Saturday (perhaps) The mail boats leaving are the President Roosevelt on Tuesday and the Majestic and Paris on Wednesday. Mark your letter via one of the latter 2 ships and it will go fastest.

Have been on a long trip all day. Tired as hell. Chinook for 10 days. Snow all gone to slush. Suppose that I will spend all my advance royalties on cables again this year.

Oh yes. That reminds me that the advance I want is $500. The advance I had on the Short Stories was $200.

God it feels good to be out from Liveright with the disturbing reports I have had from Fleischman etc. Liveright supposed to have dropped $50,000 in last venture. Has sold ½ business sold Modern Library etc. They ought to get someone like Ralph Barton or Held or Covarrubias to illustrate the Torrents. It has 5,000 more words than Don's first Parody Outline of History.

Well so long. I'm certainly relying on your good nature in a lousy brutal way.

Anyway. So long again and best love to Zelda and to you both from Hadley and

Ernest/

New Years Morning P.S.

Got to worrying last night and couldnt sleep. Do you think I ought to go to N.Y.? Then I would be on the spot and could settle things without a six week lapse between every proposition. Also could be on hand to make or argue any excisions on Torrents. If Liveright wants to hang onto me as his cable indicates could settle that. Also should get In Our Time plates if I change publishers. Etc. Meantime I have to wait at least 2 weeks more for my new passport. Old one ran out Dec. 20. Applied for new one Dec. 8 or 9—takes 5 weeks for it to come.

Well so long anyway. Bumby's very excited about going to get his new jockey cap, whip etc. I'm going down to get them through the Customs today

Best to you always,
Ernest/[11]

At this point Fitzgerald became actively engaged as Hemingway's go-between with Perkins, although it is not clear how much authority he really had. Early in January 1926 Fitzgerald sent Perkins a report on the status of the parody:

(2.) Hemmingways book (not his novel) is a 28,000 word satire on Sherwood Anderson and his imitators called The *Torrents of Spring*. I loved it, but believe it wouldn't be popular, + Liveright have refused it—*they are backing Anderson* and the book is almost a vicious parody on him. You see I agree with Ernest that Anderson's last two books have let everybody down who believed in him—I think

> they're cheap, faked, obscurantic and awful. Hemmingway thinks, but isn't yet sure to my satisfaction, that their refusal sets him free from his three book (letter) agreement with them. In that case I think he'll give you his novel (on condition you'll publish satire first—probable sale 1000 copies) which he is now revising in Austria. Harcourt has just written Louie Bromfield that to get the novel they'll publish satire, sight unseen (utterly confidential) and Knopf is after him via Aspinwall Bradley.
>
> He and I are very thick + he's marking time until he finds out how much he's bound to Liveright. If he's free I'm *almost* sure I can get satire to you first + then if you see your way clear you can contract for the novel *tout ensemble.* He's anxious too to get a foothold in your magazine—one story I've sent you—the other, to my horror he'd given for about $40 to an "arty" publication called *This Quarter,* over here.
>
> He's *dead set* on having the satire published first. His idea has always been to come to you + his only hesitation has been that Harcourt might be less conservative in regard to certain somewhat broad scenes. His address is:
>
> Herr Ernest Hemmingway
> Hotel Taube
> Schrunns
> Vorarlburg
> Austria
>
> Don't even tell him I've discussed his Liveright + Harcourt relations with you.
>
> As soon as he has definate dope I'll pass it on to you I wanted a strong wire to show you were as interested, and more, than Harcourt. Did you know your letter just missed by two weeks getting *In Our Time.* It had no sale of course but I think the novel may be something extraordinary—Tom Boyd and E.E. Cummings + Biggs combined.

Fitzgerald cabled Perkins on January 8, 1926: YOU CAN GET HEMINGWAYS FINISHED NOVEL PROVIDED YOU PUBLISH UNPROMISING SATIRE HARCOURT HAS MADE DEFINITE OFFER WIRE IMMEDIATELY WITHOUT QUALIFICATIONS. Perkins replied the same day: PUBLISH NOVEL AT FIFTEEN PERCENT AND ADVANCE IF DESIRED ALSO SATIRE UNLESS OBJECTIONABLE OTHER THAN FINANCIALLY. And on the eleventh Perkins cabled Fitzgerald: CONFIDENCE ABSOLUTE KEEN TO PUBLISH HIM.

Perkins was ready to accept Hemingway's first novel and his uncommercial satire sight unseen, largely on the basis of Fitzgerald's enthusiasm. But Fitzgerald had not read the novel he was recommending. Although Hemingway had a complete draft of *The Sun Also Rises,* he would not let Fitzgerald read it. CONFIDENCE ABSOLUTE expressed Perkins's confidence in Fitzgerald's instinct as well as his confidence in Hemingway's future.

On January 13, 1926, Perkins wrote Fitzgerald explaining his position:

> I did my best with that cable, but there was a fear that this satire—although in the hands of such a writer it could hardly be rightly so upon any theory—might be suppressible. . . . But I believe that as compared with most others [publishers], Hemingway would be better off in our hands because we are absolutely true to our authors and support them loyally in the face of losses for along time, when we believe in their qualities and in them. It is that kind of a publisher that Hemingway probably needs, because I hardly think he could come into a large public immediately.

While Hemingway was making plans to go to New York for meetings with publishers, Fitzgerald prepared the way for him with Perkins: "To hear him talk you'd think Liveright had broken up his home and robbed him of millions—but thats because he knows nothing of publishing, except in the cucoo magazines, is very young and feels helpless so far away. You won't be able to help liking him—he's one of the nicest fellows I ever knew."

Hemingway arrived in New York aboard the *Mauretania* on February 9, 1926. His first call was at Boni & Liveright, where he and Horace Liveright agreed to terminate their contract. The next day Hemingway called on Perkins. By this time Perkins had almost certainly read *The Torrents of Spring*; Donald Ogden Stewart had recovered the typescript from Boni & Liveright and delivered it to Scribners before Hemingway's visit. Hemingway brought the working draft of *The Sun Also Rises* to New York, but there is no indication that Perkins read it before making his offer of $1,500 advance on both works against a 15 percent royalty. These terms were generous for the properties. Perkins liked *Torrents,* but it was not commercial. The property was Ernest Hemingway, and Perkins was betting on him. After his meeting at Scribners, Hemingway broke off discussions with Alfred Harcourt of Harcourt, Brace.

Perkins was forty-one in 1926. After graduating from Harvard, he had joined Scribners in 1910. From New England stock, Perkins was

The Hemingways, 1926.

The Torrents of Spring *was the first Hemingway book published by Charles Scribner's Sons.*

reserved and conservative. Nonetheless, he was responsible for shifting Scribners from an old-line house to a publisher of the best young writers. His first exciting find was F. Scott Fitzgerald, and Perkins's authors eventually included Ring Lardner, Ernest Hemingway, Thomas Wolfe, and James Jones. Perkins's relationships with his authors were close, as they came to rely on him for aid beyond editorial guidance. He was attracted to Hemingway by more than a recognition of genius, for he was a drinker and enjoyed masculine company. Perkins was the father of five daughters, and his authors became surrogate sons. Yet Perkins was sometimes embarrassed by

Maxwell E. Perkins

Hemingway's vocabulary. A favorite anecdote in American publishing involves Perkins's reluctance to speak the obscenities he was trying to persuade Hemingway to delete. On one occasion Hemingway got him to write "fuck" on his desk calendar. Later, while Perkins was out of his office, Charles Scribner came looking for him and was surprised to find the calendar notation. The punch line in one version of the anecdote is that when Perkins returned, Scribner solicitously said, "Don't you want to take the rest of the day off, Max? You must be exhausted."

597 Fifth Avenue

While Hemingway was in New York he saw Owen Davis's dramatization of *The Great Gatsby* on Broadway. Fitzgerald's third story collection, *All the Sad Young Men,* was also published in February. This strong volume included "The Rich Boy" and "Winter Dreams." The first printing of 10,000 copies sold rapidly, and two more printings of 3,000 each were required.

Fitzgerald was out of touch in the Pyrenees, where Zelda was taking a cure for colitis. Before the first of March—but probably

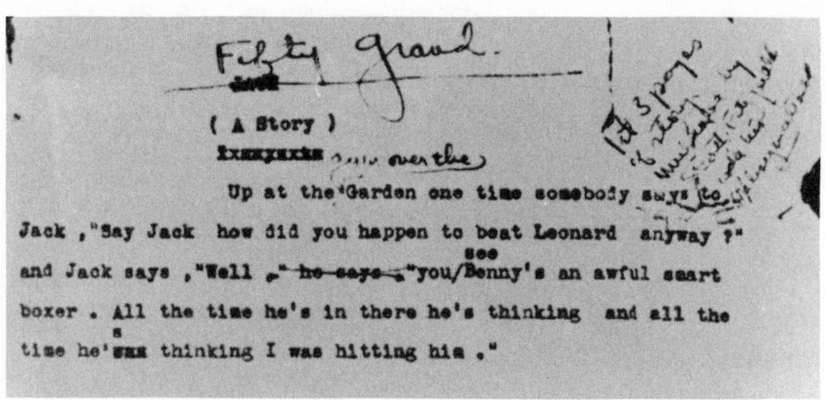

Fifty Grand.

(A Story)

Up at the Garden one time somebody says to Jack ,"Say Jack how did you happen to beat Leonard anyway ?" and Jack says ,"Well ," you see Benny's an awful smart boxer . All the time he's in there he's thinking and all the time he's thinking I was hitting him ."

(JOHN F. KENNEDY LIBRARY)

after Hemingway had left New York—Fitzgerald sent Perkins practical advice on dealing with Hemingway: "In any case he is temperamental in business made so by these bogus publishers over here. If you take the other two things *get a signed contract* for The *Sun Also Rises* (novel) Anyhow this is my last word on the subject—confidential between you + me. Please destroy this letter." "The other two things" were *Torrents* and the short story "Fifty Grand" that Fitzgerald had urged Hemingway to submit to *Scribner's Magazine.* Perkins asked Hemingway to cut the story for space reasons, not content. He was unable to cut it, and "Fifty Grand" was published by *The Atlantic Monthly* in July 1927. "Fifty Grand" triggered a Hemingway grudge against Fitzgerald after Fitzgerald persuaded him to delete the opening anecdote about Jack Brennan's bout with Benny Leonard because it was too well known.* When asked how he beat Leonard, Britton replied that Benny was a smart fighter: "All the time he's in there he's thinking and all the time he's thinking I was hitting him."[12] Hemingway regarded this comment as a key piece of boxing metaphysics and came to believe that Fitzgerald had damaged the story. In one of his typescripts of "Fifty Grand" Hemingway noted "1st 3 pages of story [mutilated] by Scott Fitzgerald with his [ ]"

The three surviving typescript pages for the deleted opening of

*Hemingway's character Jack Brennan was based on Jack Britton, welterweight champion from 1919 to 1922. Benny Leonard was lightweight champion from 1917 to 1924. Britton beat Leonard on a foul in 1922.

''Fifty Grand'' do not substantiate the charge that Fitzgerald spoiled the story. After the Benny Leonard anecdote, Jack Brennan remarks that Kid Lewis is a kike, but Benny is a Jewish boy. Brennan, Soldier Bartlett, and narrator Jerry go to Hanley's saloon, where Bartlett continues to needle Brennan. Two thirds down page three there is the opening sentence of the published story: '' 'How are you going yourself, Jack?' I asked him.'' In the margin next to this line appears the only notation in Fitzgerald's hand; the faint writing appears to read ''D. yourself.''

The story is not damaged by the excision. Bartlett's irritating remarks are lost, but the point about his kidding is made early in the published story. The description of the saloon is not important. In the introduction to his unpublished volume, ''The Art of the Short Story and Nine Stories to Prove It,'' written in 1959—thirty years later—Hemingway recalled the bad advice of ''My loyal and devoted friend Fitzgerald, who was truly more interested in my own career at this point than in his own. . . .''[13]

In the first week of March 1926 Hemingway stopped off in Paris on his way back to his family in Schruns and reported to Fitzgerald on his meeting with Perkins. Hemingway's real purpose for being in Paris was to see Pauline Pfeiffer, with whom he was having a clandestine affair; she became his second wife in 1927.

The *Moveable Feast* manuscripts include an eight-page account of Hemingway's conversations with Bumby in Paris and their meeting with Fitzgerald at which Bumby orders a beer to ''make an example'' of proper drinking conduct for Fitzgerald. Since it indicates that Hemingway and Hadley were still married, the time of this encounter had to have occurred before Fitzgerald left Paris in March 1926—before Bumby (born October 10, 1923) was three years old.

Chapter 3

1. ALS, 3 pp. *Selected Letters*, pp. 165–166.
2. ALS, 2 pp. *A Life in Letters*, pp. 130-131.
3. ''How to Waste Material—A Note on My Generation,'' *The Bookman*, 63 (May 1926) 262–265; collected in *F. Scott Fitzgerald in His Own Time*, edited by Bruccoli and Jackson R. Bryer (Kent, Ohio: Kent State University Press, 1971).
4. *Hemingway and the SUN Set*, edited by Bertram Sarason (Washington, D.C.; NCR/Microcard Books, 1972).

5. *Correspondence of F. Scott Fitzgerald*, p. 183.
6. *The Torrents of Spring* (New York: Scribners, 1926), pp. 119–120.
7. Princeton University Library.
8. C. 15 December 1925; ALS, 3 pp. *Selected Letters*, pp. 176–177.
9. C. 25 December 1925; ALS, 6 pp. *Selected Letters,* pp. 180–183.
10. 30 December 1925, Alderman Library, University of Virginia. Walker, Gilmer, *Horace Liveright: Publisher of the Twenties* (New York: David Lewis, 1970), p. 124.
11. ALS, 5 pp. *Selected Letters*, pp. 183–185.
12. John F. Kennedy Library.
13. *Paris Review*, 79 (1981), 85-102; collected in *New Critical Approaches to the Short Stories of Ernest Hemingway*, edited by Jackson J. Benson (Durham, N.C.: Duke University Press, 1990).

IV

While Hemingway was writing and revising *The Sun Also Rises,* Fitzgerald was not getting on with his fourth novel. In 1926 he wrote only two unremarkable stories, "Your Way and Mine" and "The Dance," but his earnings for the year topped $25,000 from his share of the play and movie rights to *The Great Gatsby.* In Fitzgerald's *Ledger* he described 1925–1926 as "Futile, shameful useless but the $30,000 rewards of 1924 work. Self disgust. Health gone."[1] At this point in his career he needed to consolidate the achievement of *Gatsby.* He planned to write a novel about the destruction of a young American man by the influence of expatriate life in France. The novel was to involve matricide; the working titles were "Our Type," "The World's Fair," "The Melarky Case," and "The Boy Who Killed His Mother." He worked on this plot, with many interruptions, from 1925 to 1930 and accumulated five incomplete drafts before he abandoned it to write *Tender Is the Night.*

Fitzgerald had discussed the material for his novel with Hemingway. In April 1926 Hemingway wrote from Paris to Fitzgerald on the Riviera, including a burlesque of Fitzgerald's work in progress:

> Dear Scott—
>
> Had a letter from Curtis Browne that Jonathan Cape wants to publish In Our Time and will pay 25 pounds advance and 10% a copy and 3 D. for British Empire rights not including Canada. Liveright wouldn't sell them sheets—they are going to set it up themselves.
>
> Curtis Browne is going to be my Contintental and British

agents and say they are dickering with a German publisher that wants I.O.T.

I've returned the proofs of Torrents to Scribners a week or so ago. It looks very good.

Sun Also Rises is all done and back from the typists 1085 francs total typing charges. So I guess I'll send it off. I've cut it to about 90,000 words.

May dedicate it like this.

To My Son
John Hadley Nicanor
This Collection of Instructive Anecdotes

I'm hoping to hell you'll like it. You'll see it in August. I think may be it is pretty interesting. Later—You won't like it.

Chink is in town for 2 weeks. He and I are going to walk from Sarogossa across the Pyrenees by way of Andorra the end of July. I've had a rotten cold. Been being very social and am god damn tired of it. Do you know any thing about the girl Don's marrying? We go to Spain the 12th of May. Hadley's playing the piano very well. Where are you on your book? Write to me. Rousseau asks about you at the bank. He had us to lunch. We went. Went 5 of the 6 days to the bike race. It was swell gat. Went with Chink and many generals etc to see Sandhurst play Saint Cyr.

Yr. letter just to hand and Walsh's poem on coming in his pants or whatever you want to call it made me vomit again seen on the envelope. But unlike the dog which returns to his vomit I tore up the envelope—Just as I tore out the original poem and just as threw away This Quarter after tearing out my story to keep it.

Havent seen Archie MacLeish on acct his absense in Persia. Seen Bromfield's once. Glad to see you're feeling better as understand that stimulates literary production.

Glad to hear you see further than Tarkington. Sorry to hear you see not as far as Hemingway. How far do the French women see?

Very glad if you realize criticizim to be horse shit without horse shits pleasant smell nor use as fertilizer. Have not seen Bookman.

Nevertheless I thank you for services rendered. Havent seen the New Fiction except Gents Prefer which seemed 2nd rate Lardner and very dull. Perkins sent Thomason's book which seemed very juvenile. I'd thought it would be much better. There wasnt that much hand to hand fighting in 100 years of the Crusades. Have not seen Sherwood Anderson's note book though I believe I should in order to get a lot of new ideas.

Fifty Grand is, I believe, in the hands of some agent. I could ask the 250 I could have gotten by cutting it for Scribners. Am thoroly disgusted with writing but as there is nothing else I care as much for will continue writing.

Paul Nelson* would be good story for you to write if you knew anything about it.

I'm glad as hell you got the money for the movie rights of Gatsby. With that and Gatsby in person at the Ambassador you sh'd be able to write a pretty good novel with the franc around 30. Maybe someday you'll get the Nobel Prize. Understand it's not yet been given to an American. Am recommending to Mr. Walsh that he give you This Quarter's $2000 bucks and have just called in my attorney to make you my heir. So Don't Worry About Money. Chink says he'll leave you Bellamont Forest too if you like. Pauline Pfeiffer says you can have her job on Vogue. I've written Scribner to send all my royalty checks to you.

It makes no difference your telling G. Murphy about bull fighting statement except will be careful about making such statements. Was not referring to guts but to something else. Grace under pressure. Guts never made any money for anybody except violin string manufacturers.

Your friend Ring is hampered by lack of intelligence, lack of any aesthetic appreciation, terrible repressions and bitterness. Any one of those is a terrible load for any writer to carry no matter how talented. He is, of course, 100 times as intelligent as most U.S. writers.

Bumby has the whooping cough. Hadley has had a rotten cough now for over 6 weeks. I expect they give it back and forth to each other.

We go to Spain May 12. If Bumby is not well then I'll go on ahead and Hadley come later. We go to U.S.A. in End of Sept. Antibes in August. I'll have a copy of Sun etc. there and w'd welcome your advising me on anything about it. Nobody's read any amount of it yet. If you are worried it is not a series of anecdotes—nor is it written very much like either Manhattan Transfer nor Dark Laughter. I

*One of Fitzgerald's Princeton classmates, who was living in France, M.J.B.

have tried to follow the outline and spirit of The Great Gatsby, but I feel I have failed somewhat because of never having been on Long Island. The hero, like Gatsby, is a Lake Superior Salmon Fisherman. (There are no salmon in Lake Superior) The action all takes place in Newport, R.I. and the heroine is a girl named Sophie Irene Loeb who kills her mother. The scene in which Sophie gives birth to twins in the death house at Sing Sing where she is waiting to be electrocuted for the murder of the father and sister of her, as then, unborn children I got from Dreiser but practically everything else in the book is either my own or yours I know you'll be glad to see it. The Sun Also Rises comes from Sophie's statement as she is strapped into the chair as the current mounts.

Well why not write?
Regards to all yr. family
Herbert J. Wesshit[2]

Hemingway regarded Fitzgerald's financial problems as ridiculous, and on April 24—right after mailing the typescript of *The Sun Also Rises*—he wrote to Perkins, recycling the joke about donating his royalties to Fitzgerald. This letter mentions an unlocated "long letter from Scott a few days ago" saying that he was on the wagon and working hard on his novel.[3] From this time Hemingway's letters to Perkins often involve concerned or patronizing observations on Fitzgerald, as though an older brother were advising his father about a worrisome younger son.

On the 4th of May 1926 Hemingway wrote to Fitzgerald from Paris:

May 4.

Dear Scott-

Don't you write anymore? How are you going? I have finished a story—short—and am sending it to Scribners tomorrow. We go to Spain a week from Thursday. Maxwell Perkins writes that Torents will be out at latest May 21st. I sent them The Sun etc. about 10 or 12 days ago. It's rained here everyday for 3 weeks. I feel low as hell. Havent seen Bromfields, Edith Wharton, Comrade Bercovinci or any other of the little literary colony for some time. May be there will be a literary colony in Madrid.

Dotty Parker, Les Seldes and Seward Collins—you remember, the man who shot Lincoln—all went to Spain and of course hated it.

Murphys arrived yest, and it isn't Dos that's marrying. It's Don. If I said Dos it was a slip of the ink. I'll pour that ink out. Oh Jesus it is such foul weather and I feel too low to write. I wish to hell you had come up with Murphys—I've not had one man to talk to or bull shit with for months. In Spain of course I don't talk at all—am in for 3 mos. of listening and reading the papers.

Write to me. I dont even get letters How are you feeling? Are you really working on your novel? Is it true that you are swiping my big death house scene? Is it true that you have become blind through alcoholic poisoning and had to have your pancreas removed? I have just given 200,000 francs to save the franc. Harold Stearns is giving the same amount.

I am thinking of going out, in a few minutes, and getting very cock eyed drunk.

Love to yr. family,
Yrs.
Ernest
(Christ what a name)[4]

Hemingway's late May letter from Madrid confirms that pieces of their correspondence have not survived; he apologizes for his "snooty" letter that seemed to dismiss Fitzgerald's *Bookman* article on *In Our Time* and refers to an unlocated Fitzgerald letter:

Dear Scott:

I was glad to hear from you and glad to note that you were on the "Waggon." Sorry my letter was snooty—I didn't mean it that way. You were saying how little you valued critical articles unless they were favourable for practical purposes and I was just agreeing. Thats was all the Services rendered was about. Youll be seeing Hadley today. Wish the hell I were. Madrid is fine and cold and dry with a very high sky and lots of dust blowing down your nose—or up my nose. Corrida called off for today by the veterinaries who wouldn't pass the bulls (sic) because they were too small and sick. I was out when they turned them down and it was a collection of animals Harold Stearns could have killed while drunk—with a jack knife.

Didnt Ford say I was the great writer of English? Tomorrow they have a lad from Seville with a dose of clapp—a local boy (who was admired by Gilbert Seldes if that means anything to you) and one of the lousiest bull fighters on Earth—named Fortuna—And I might just as easily—a damn sight easier be seeing you at Juan les Pins. I missed the big fight on the 13th—of course—todays called off—tomorrow's a lot of cruts and Monday maybe a good one.

Mencken is noble all right I wish to hell I had your letter to answer. Herschel Brickel is in Paris. He read Torrents and was crazy about it. If that means anything. He's a nice guy personally anyway nothing about Seldes. We met Seldes and a lot of other 2nd class passangers at Noel Murphys where we were invited by 2 pneumatiques 2 telegrams and a personal call. I hadnt seen so many 2nd class passengers since I crossed on the Mauretania.

I dont want to look up my Spanish friends because then I'll have to be talking Spanish, if I can talk Spanish, and going around and I'd like to work. Yeah you were right about generalties about Ring. All such are the bunk. You were wrong about Paul Nelson—way way wrong. I was referring to a very special exciting and dramatic story that you don't know. No scandal. Neither, however, was it the simple minded uneducated young writer having the wool pulled over his eyes by the smooth Irish chameleon as you suggested. That isnt snooty. Why the hell should we have to pull our punches writing?

I'm glad as hell that your book is going and that it is so swell. That's not kidding. I'll be glad to hear from Max Perkins what they think of Sun etc. It is so obviously not a collection of instructive anecdotes and is such a hell of a sad story—and not one at all for a child to read—and the only instruction is how people go to hell—(Doesn't it sound terrible, I can hear you say) that I thought it was rather pleasant to dedicate it to Bumby—If you're right I won't put in the anecdote part—but I'll dedicate it to him for reasons that will be obvious when you read the book and also for another reason. Ive a carbon with me and you can read it at Juan les Sapins if there aren't proofs before then.

The 2 bottle men drank port and the best were 3 <bottle men> but I understand the bottles were small. Did you ever read the Encyclopaedia Brit. on Lawn Tennis in America? There are a hell of a lot more Salmon in Encyclopaedia Brit. than in Lake Superior. Besides it doesnt make any difference because look at Shakespere and the seacoast of Tchecoslovakia etc. Nouvelle Revue Francaise is going to publish 50 grand as Cinquante Grosse Billetes. in July or Aug.

No news here. Write me and I swear to god I'll write a good letter next time. I know this is lousy but I'm lonesome as hell.

Best to Zelda. Hadley will greet you all fully.

Always your co-worker for the Clean Books Bill.

Ernest M. Shit.[5]

Glenway Wescott wrote after Fitzgerald's death that during 1925 or 1926 Fitzgerald tried to persuade him to help promote Hemingway's career. Wescott—who would be travestied in *The Sun Also Rises* as Robert Prentiss—was impressed by Fitzgerald's assumption that he shared the desire to aid another writer who, according to Fitzgerald, was "inimitably, essentially superior." Wescott came to believe that Fitzgerald's admiration for Hemingway's genius damaged him because it culminated in the conviction that he could abandon his own literary responsibilities to Hemingway.[6] This analysis is hyperbolic, for it discounts Fitzgerald's ambition for fame and even literary immortality; nonetheless, Wescott's testimony indicates the intensity of Fitzgerald's commitment to Hemingway at that time.

Fitzgerald did not read the typescript of *The Sun Also Rises* until June 1926, when the Hemingways (joined by Pauline Pfeiffer) came to the Riviera. The Fitzgeralds had leased the Villa Paquita at Juan-les-Pins; but it did not suit them, and they turned it over to the Hemingway menage.

The Fitzgeralds' closest friends in Europe were Gerald and Sara Murphy, a wealthy American couple who devoted themselves to living well. Gerald was an artist whose paintings have been recognized as precursors of the pop art school. Their expatriate friends included John Dos Passos, Philip Barry, and Archibald MacLeish. Fitzgerald had introduced Hemingway to the Murphys in 1925, and Gerald became his strong admirer. Indeed, Murphy regarded Hemingway as a much more serious figure than Fitzgerald. The Hemingway-Murphy relationship was close for a decade, but Hemingway came to believe that the Murphys had corrupted him with their praise and had encouraged the dissolution of his first marriage. In *A Moveable Feast* he denounced the Murphys (without naming them) as "the rich" who,

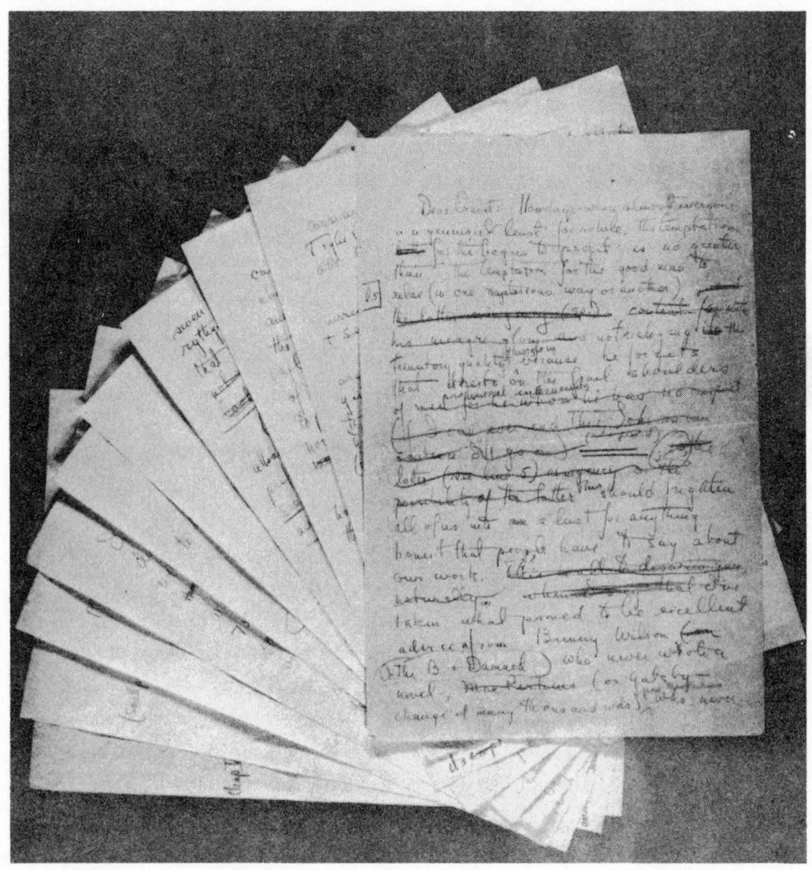

Fitzgerald's vetting report on The Sun Also Rises. (JOHN F. KENNEDY LIBRARY)

aided by their "pilot fish" Dos Passos (also unnamed), had violated his innocence in 1926.[7]

When Hemingway arrived at Juan-les-Pins in early June, the Murphys gave a champagne party at the casino to welcome him; Fitzgerald spoiled it with his drunken behavior. This summer was supposed to be devoted to sobriety and hard work, but Fitzgerald drank steadily and made no progress on his novel. Zelda Fitzgerald remarked that it "goes so slow it ought to be serialized in the Encyclopedia Britannica."[8]

Hemingway states in *Feast* that "Scott did not see it [*The Sun Also Rises*] until after the completely rewritten and cut manuscript had been sent to Scribners at the end of April.''* This statement is both true and misleading, for it implies that Hemingway did not avail himself of Fitzgerald's editorial advice. Fitzgerald read a carbon copy before June 5 while proof was being set by Scribners. His undated ten-page critique—which Hemingway preserved—establishes that Hemingway acted on Fitzgerald's recommendations in cutting the novel in galleys:

> Dear Ernest: Nowdays when almost everyone is a genius, at least for awhile, the temptation for the bogus to profit is no greater than the temptation for the good man to relax (in one mysterious way or another)—not realizing the transitory quality of his glory because he forgets that it rests on the frail shoulders of professional entheusiasts. This should frighten all of us into a lust for anything honest that people have to say about our work. I've taken what proved to be excellent advice (On the B. + Damned) from Bunny Wilson who never wrote a novel (on Gatsby—change of many thousand wds) from Max Perkins who never considered writing one, and on T. S. of Paradise from Katherine Tighe (you don't know her) who had probably never read a novel before.
>
> [This is beginning to sound like my own current work which resolves itself into laborious + sententious preliminaries].
>
> Anyhow I think parts of <u>Sun Also</u> are careless + ineffectual. As I said yestiday (and, as I recollect, in trying to get you to cut the 1st part of 50 Grand) I find in you the same tendency to envelope or (and as it usually turns out) to <u>embalm</u> in mere wordiness an anecdote or joke thats casually appealed to you, that I find in myself in trying to preserve a piece of ''fine writing.'' Your first chapter contains about 10 such things and it gives a feeling of condescending <u>casuallness</u>
>
> P. 1. ''highly moral story''
>
> ''Brett said'' (O. Henry stuff)
>
> ''much too expensive
>
> ''something or other'' (if you don't want to tell, why waste 3 wds, saying it. See P.23—''<u>9 or 14</u>'' and ''or how many years it was since 19XX'' when it would take

*The MS for *Moveable Feast* reads ''Scott did not see it until the completed manuscript had been sent to Scribners. I think I showed it to him first in the first proofs in which I made several cuts.''

two words to say That's what youd kid in anyone else as mere "style"—mere horseshit I can't find this latter but anyhow you've not only got to write well yourself but you've also got to scorn not-do what anyone can do and I think that there are about 24 sneers, superiorities, and nose-thumbings-at-nothing that mar the whole narrative up to p. 29 where (after a false start on the introduction of Cohn) it really gets going. And to preserve these perverse and willfull non-essentials you've done a lot of writing that honestly reminded me of Michael Arlen.

[You know the very fact that people have committed themselves to you will make them watch you like a cat. + if they don't like it creap away like one]

For example.

Pps. 1 + 2. Snobbish (not in itself but because the history of English Aristocrats in the war, set down so verbosely so uncritically, so exteriorly and yet so obviously inspired from within, is shopworn.) You had the same problem that I had with my Rich Boy, previously debauched by Chambers ect. Either bring more thot to it with the realization that that ground has already raised its wheat + weeds or cut it down to seven sentences. It hasn't even your rhythym and the fact that may be "true" is utterly immaterial.

That biography from you, who allways believed in the superiority (the preferability) of the *imagined* to the seen not to say to the merely recounted.

P. 3. "Beautifully engraved shares" (Beautifully engraved 1886 irony) All this is O.K. but so glib when its glib + so profuse.

P. 5 Painters are no longer real in prose. They must be minimized. [This is not done by making them schlptors, backhouse wall-experts or miniature painters]

P. 8. "highly moral urges" "because I believe its a good story" If this paragraph isn't maladroit then I'm a rewrite man for Dr. Cadman.

P. 9. Somehow its not good. I can't quite put my hand on it—it has a ring of "This is a true story ect."

P. 10. "Quarter being a state of mind ect." This is in all guide books. I havn't read Basil Swoon's but I have fifty francs to lose.

[About this time I can hear you say "Jesus this guy thinks I'm lousy, + he can stick it up his ass for all I give a Gd Dm for his 'criticism.' " But remember this is a new departure for you, and that I think your stuff is great. You were the first American I wanted to meet in Europe—and the last. (This latter clause is simply to balance the sentence. It doesn't seem to make sense tho I have pawed at it for several minutes. Its like the age of the French women.

P. 14. (+ thereabout) as I said yesterday I think this anecdote is flat as hell without naming Ford which would be cheap.

It's flat because you end with mention of Allister Crowly. If he's nobody its nothing. If he's somebody its cheap. This is a novel. Also I'd cut out actual mention of H. Stearns earlier.

- - - - - - - - - - - - - - -

Why not cut the inessentials in Cohens biography? His first marriage is of no importance. When so many people can write well + the competition is so heavy I can't imagine how you could have done these first 20 pps. so casually. You can't play with peoples attention—a good man who has the power of arresting attention at will must be especially careful.

From here Or rather from p. 30 I began to like the novel but Ernest I can't tell you the sense of disappointment that beginning with its elephantine facetiousness gave me. Please do what you can about it in proof. Its 7500 words—you could reduce it to 5000. And my advice is not to do it by mere pareing but to take out the worst of the scenes.

I've decided not to pick at anything else, because I wasn't at all inspired to pick when reading it. I was much too excited. Besides this is probably a heavy dose. The novel's damn good. The central theme is marred somewhere but hell! unless you're writing your life history where you have an inevitable pendulum to swing you true (Harding metaphor), who can bring it entirely off? And what critic can trace whether the fault lies in a possible insufficient thinking out, in the biteing off of more than you eventually cared to chew in the impotent theme or in the elusiveness of the lady character herself. My theory always was that she dramatized herself in terms of Arlen's dramatatization of somebody's dramatizating of Stephen McKenna's dramatization of Diana Manner's dramatization of the last girl in Well's Tono Bungay—who's original probably liked more things about Beatrix Esmond than about Jane Austin's Elizibeth (to whom we owe the manners of so many of our wives.)

Appropos of your foreward about the Latin quarter—suppose you had begun your stories with phrases like: "Spain is a peculiar place—ect" or "Michigan is interesting to two classes—the fisherman + the drummer."

Pps 64 + 65 with a bit of work should tell all that need be known about Brett's past. (Small point) "Dysemtry" instead of "killed" is a clichês to avoid a clichê. It stands out. I suppose it can't be helped. I suppose all the 75,000000 Europeans who died between 1914–1918 will always be among the 10,000,000 who were killed in the war.

God! The bottom of p. 77 Jusque the top p. 78 are wonderful, I go crazy when people aren't always at their best. This isn't picked out—I just happened on it.

The heart of my criticism beats somewhere apon p. 87. I think you can't change it, though. I felt the lack of some crazy torturing tentativeness or insecurity—horror, all at once, that she'd feel—and he'd feel—maybe I'm crazy. He isn't like an impotent man. He's like a man in a sort of moral chastity belt.

Oh, well. It's fine, from Chap V on, anyhow, in spite of that—which fact is merely a proof of its brilliance.

Station Z.W.X. square says good night. Good night all.[9]

In the typescript and galley proof of *The Sun Also Rises*, Chapter One recounts Brett Ashley's marital history and her life with Mike Campbell, who has only "beautifully engraved" stock certificates left from his failed business venture. Both are alcoholics, and their drinking habits are analyzed. Brett frequently sits for portrait painters. The second chapter opens with Jake Barnes's intrusive address to the reader about the necessity of writing in the first person although he had wanted to maintain his objectivity in order to achieve "irony and pity."[10] He explains that the novel is not the product of "highly moral urges." Jake then summarizes his journalistic career and describes his life in the Quarter—the Left Bank Latin Quarter. Robert Cohn and Braddocks (Ford Madox Ford) are introduced, setting up the anecdote about mistaking Aleister Cowley for Hilaire Belloc—which Hemingway recycled thirty years later for *Moveable Feast.* Jake explains that it is necessary to include Braddocks because "he was a great friend of Robert Cohn and Cohn is the hero." At the end of galley three

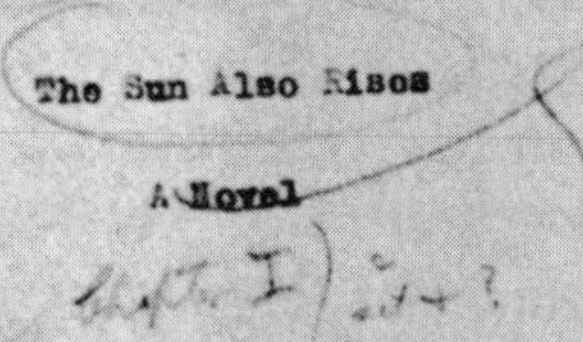

The Sun Also Rises

A Novel

This is a novel about a lady. Her name is Lady Ashley and when the story begins she is living in Paris and it is Spring. That should be a good setting for a romantic but highly moral story. As every one knows Paris is a very romantic place. Spring in Paris is a very happy and romantic time. Autumn in Paris, although very beautiful, might give a note of sadness or melancholy that we shall try to keep out of this story.

Lady Ashley was born Elizabeth Brett Murray. Her title came from her second husband. She had divorced one husband for something or other, mutual consent; not until after he had put one of those notices in the papers stating that after this date he would not be responsible for any debt, etc. He was a Scotchman and found Brett much too expensive, especially as she had only married him to get rid of him and to get away from home. At present she had a legal separation from her second husband, who had the title, because he was a dipsomaniac, he having learned it in the North Sea commanding a mine-sweeper, Brett said. When he had gotten to be a proper thorough going dipsomaniac and found that Brett did not love him he

The discarded opening. (UNIVERSITY OF VIRGINIA LIBRARY)

appear the opening words of the published novel: "Robert Cohn was once middleweight boxing champion of Princeton."

Hemingway acted on Fitzgerald's urging to delete the first two chapters, though *Feast* conveys the impression that he regarded Fitzgerald's editorial judgment as worthless. Fitzgerald's other major criticism (page 87—the scene in Chapter VII of the published novel when Brett comes to Jake's flat) was that Hemingway had not properly conveyed Jake's feelings about his sexual predicament—a serious reservation in the case of a character who has had his penis shot off. The passage that Fitzgerald singled out for praise ("God! The bottom of p. 77 Jusque the top p. 78 are wonderful") occurs in Chapter VI, where Frances Clyne berates Cohn for discarding her.

It is not strange that Fitzgerald would have written a ten-page memo to a friend he was seeing every day. As his preamble shows, he was aware that he was running a risk in criticizing the novel at all. Hemingway never responded mildly to criticism, and Fitzgerald was obviously concerned about angering or alienating his greatly admired friend. A document was required to prepare for discussions in which Hemingway was to be persuaded to kill the first two chapters. On June 5 Hemingway informed Perkins:

> I believe that, in the proofs, I will start the book at what is now page 16 in the Mss. There is nothing in those first sixteen pages that does not come out, or is explained, or re-stated in the rest of the book—or is unnecessary to state. I think it will move much faster from the start that way. Scott agrees with me. He suggested various things in it to cut out-in those first chapters—which I have never liked—but I think it is better to just lop that off and he agrees.

Fitzgerald's report to Perkins on *The Sun Also Rises* was delayed until about June 25 because of a trip to Paris for Zelda's appendectomy:

> First as to Ernests book. I liked it but with certain qualifications. The fiesta, the fishing trip, the minor characters were fine. The lady I didn't like, perhaps because I don't like the original. In the mutilated man I thought Ernest bit off more than can yet be chewn between the covers of a book, then lost his nerve a little and edited the more vitalizing details out. He has since told me that something like this happened. Do ask him for the absolute minimum of necessary changes, Max—he's so discouraged about the previous reception of his work by publishers and magazine editors. (Tho he loved your letter) From the latter he has

> had a lot of words and until Bridges offer for the short story <"Fifty Grand"> (from which he had even before cut out a thousand words on my recommendation) scarcely a single dollar. From the *Torrents* I expect you'll have little response. Do you think the Bookman article did him any good?

Zelda Fitzgerald was less impressed by *The Sun Also Rises* than her husband was. When she remarked that Hemingway's novel was about "Bullfighting, bullslinging, and bull——," Fitzgerald cut her off, telling her not to disparage Hemingway."[11] Sara Mayfield, Zelda's childhood friend from Montgomery, visited the Fitzgeralds on the Riviera that summer; her book *Exiles From Paradise* reports that Zelda was disturbed by Hemingway's influence on Fitzgerald. Zelda blamed Hemingway for encouraging the drinking bouts that interfered with Fitzgerald's work and was repelled by Hemingway's "morbid preoccupation with offbeat sex and the sadism and necrophilia that go with it."[12]

The Fitzgeralds did not join the Hemingways, Pauline Pfeiffer, and the Murphys on their July trip to the fiesta of San Fermin. Fitzgerald never attended a bullfight with Hemingway. After Pamplona the Hemingways returned to the Riviera for the rest of the summer. Having succeeded in bringing Hemingway to Scribners, Fitzgerald attempted to have him represented by Harold Ober, who handled Fitzgerald's magazine work at the Paul Revere Reynolds literary agency. Fitzgerald hoped that Ober would be able to place Hemingway's stories in high-paying American magazines. Until 1927 all of Hemingway's stories were published in little magazines, which made token payments. Short stories provided most of Fitzgerald's income, and he felt that Hemingway should be receiving high prices, as well as American visibility, for his stories. Fitzgerald's efforts to make a connection between Hemingway and Ober were unsuccessful. Hemingway was suspicious of agents and never employed one in America, except for the sale of movie rights.

In early September 1926, after Hemingway had left the Riviera, Fitzgerald reported that he was hard at work on his novel. This claim would become a refrain over the next years as Fitzgerald endeavored to assure Hemingway that he was a serious writer—and as Hemingway encouraged him to stick with the novel.

Dear Ernest-Sorry we missed you + Hadley. No news. I'm on the wagon + working like hell. Expect to sail for N.Y Dec 10th from Genoa on the Conte Biancamo. Will be here till then. Saw Bullfight in Frejus. Bull was euneuch (sp.). House barred + dark. Front door chained. Have made no new enemies for a week. Hamilton domestic row ended in riot. Have new war books by Pierrefeu. God is love.

Signed
Ernestine Murphy.

Did you read in the N.Y. Herald about—
"... Henry Carpenter, banker, and Willie Stevens, half-wit, ..."

S[13]

Fitzgerald's note was written on the bottom of a letter from Harold Ober reporting his inability to place "Fifty Grand" and asking for other Hemingway stories.

While awaiting publication of *The Sun Also Rises* Hemingway wrote Fitzgerald from Paris reporting his separation from Hadley and confirming that he had cut the opening of *Sun*:

69 Rue Froidevaux
Paris 14.

Dear Old Fitz—

Glad to hear again from the Master. How goes the work, Fitz? Glad to hear it. Glad to hear it. Keep it up old boy. I had exactly the same experience myself when I started writing. Then one day I met George Horace Lorimer in the Petit Chaumiere and from then on things simply slipped along.

How the hell are you anyway? I decided to give away all my stories when I got here so as to clear away all the stuff I was counting on selling and that would force me to write some more. So I gave Today Is Friday to some pamphlet organization that had written asking for an essay to be published with a drawing by Cocteau and sent the Alpine Idyll to the New Masses which is the most peurile and shitty house organ I've ever seen—they also having requested a contribution—and just to see what the alibi would be sent The Killers—which I'd just finished to Scribners. So right away back I get a cable from Max

Perkins saying Killers grand bridges writing offer Sun proofs received Perkins.

So even cynical little boys like Ernest get pleasant surprises. Only now I only wait to hear of the sudden death of Bridges, the losing of his job by Perkins and the suspension of Scribner's magazine. Otherwise may get published.

Since then have completed a new story, yest. and am starting another one. Thanks a lot for the letter from Reynolds and for your sterling attitude on the censorship question. All France is proud of you. Don't listen to any of the subversive element of Juan les Pins exemplified by the police or other bureaucratic classes, that may try to nullify this. The author of Gatsby le Magnifique will be backed by at least as many people as went to bat for Dreyfuss. Don't let them jail you. Just don't let them. The real France is backing you.

Hadley and I are still living apart. I am thinking of riding down to Marseilles on my bike in Oct. and living in Marseilles for a month or so and working. Will ride over and see you when you get the book finished. Our life is all gone to hell which seems to be the one thing you can count on a good life to do. Needless to say Hadley has been grand and everything has been completely my fault in every way. That's the truth, not a polite gesture. Still having been in hell now since around last Christmas with plenty of insomnia to light the way around so I could study the terrain I get sort of used to it and even fond of it and probably would take pleasure in showing people around. As we make our hell we certainly should like it.

I cut The Sun to start with Cohn—cut all that first part. made a number of minor cuts and did quite a lot of rewriting and tightening up. Cut and in the proof it read like a good book. Christ knows I want to write them a hell of a lot better but it seemed to move along and to be pretty sound and solid. I hope to hell you'll like it and I think maybe you will.

Have a swell hunch for a new novel. I am calling it the World's Fair. You'll like the title.

Give my love to Zelda and tell her how sorry we were not to see you when we came around to say goodbye. I haven't been drinking, haven't been in a bar, haven't been at the Dingo, Dome nor Select. Haven't seen anybody. Not going to see anybody. Trying unusual experiment of a writer writing. That also will probably turn out to be vanity. Starting on long semi-permanent bike trip to last as long as the good weather lasts as soon as my present piles go down. Then will get a lot of work done, all the stories I want to write, probably working in Marseilles. Then we'll see.

The world is so full of a number of things I'm sure we should all be as happy as kings. How happy are kings?

Stevenson.

Yrs always,

Ernest

Walsh, author of the Soldier drugfiend bullbaiter poem is attacking me to the extent of several columns in the next This Quarter charging Hemingway has sold out to the vested interests. I wrote him a postcard saying his poem made me vomit when This Q. came out. Now it seems from a flawless knight of LITERATURE I have become a hack writer in the pay of SCRIBNERS earning these vast sums. I saw a copy of this which he is circulating largely in carbons before publication. Gentlemen I give you the Irish.

[*upside down at the bottom of page three*] Write if you fell like it. I get lonesome.[14]

Like others, Fitzgerald—who was rather puritanical when sober—tried to emulate Hemingway's bawdy humor. A September 1926 letter to Hemingway included a scatological parody of the *In Our Time* vignettes.

We were in a back-house in Juan-les-Pins. Bill had lost controll of his splincter muscles. There were wet Matins in the rack beside the door. There were wet Eclairers de Nice in the rack over his head. When the King of Bulgaria came in Bill was just firing a burst that struck the old limeshit twenty feet down with a splat-tap. All the rest came just like that. The King of Bulgaria began to whirl round and round.

"The great thing in these affairs—" he said.

Soon he was whirling faster and faster. Then he was dead.

At this point in my letter my 30th birthday came and I got tight for a week in the company of such facinating

gents as Mr. Theodore Rousseau + other ornaments of what is now a barren shore.

Ernest of little faith I hope the sale of The Killers will teach you to send every story either to Scribners or an agent. Can't you get "Today is Friday" back? Your letter depressed and rather baffled me. Have you and Hadley permanently busted up, and was the nessessity of that what was on your soul this summer. Don't answer this unless you feel like it. Anyhow I'm sorry everything's such a mess and I do want to see you if you come to Marseitte in October.

We saw the Murphys before they left, got stewed with them (at their party)—that is we got stewed—and I believe there was some sort of mawkish reconciliation. However they've grown dim to me and I don't like them much any more. Mclieshes too have grown shadowy—he's so nice but she's a club woman at heart and made a great lot of trouble in subtle ways this summer. We saw Marice the day she left + the huge Garoupe standing desolate, and her face, and the pathetic bales of chiclets for the Garoupe beach in her bedroom are the strongest impression I have left of a futile and petty summer. It might all have happened at Roslynn Long Island.

Swimmings almost over now. We have our tickets for America Dec. 10th on the Conte Biancamo—we'll spend the winter in New York. Bishop was here with his unspeakably awful wife. He seems aenemic and washed out, a memory of the past so far as I'm concerned.

Im glad as hell about the story and I hope its the first of many. I feel too much at loose ends to write any more tonight. Remember—if I can give you any financial help let me know.

Always Your Friend

Scott—

I had a lot more to say but its 3:30 A.M. and I've been working since 11 this morning and its very hazy. Have you read

The Spanish Farm
+
Sixty four—ninety four } by Mottram ?

Wonderful war books. Much better than Ford Maddox Ford. In fact the best thing I've read this summer. Met your cousin from Princeton![15]

Late in 1926, after the October publication of *The Sun Also Rises,* Hemingway wrote from Paris expressing euphoria and self-castigation:

Dear Scott:

Ive been trying every week to get down to see you before

you leave—Mike Ward was getting a car to drive down but first he was sick—then the cars were always full; then the guy who was to take his place in the bank was sick and that brings us to this Wednesday which was today and the last time we were to start.

How are you and how have you been–? Have you worked and how is the novel. I'll bet it will be a damned good novel once you settled down to writing it—and you must have had plenty of time at Juan les Pins for writing lately.

I've had a grand spell of working; sold another story to Scribners—making two—and have sent them another that I am sure they will buy—a hell of a good story about Milan during the war—and just finished a better one that I should be typing now. Have two other stories that I know can't sell so am not sending them out—but that will go well in a book

This is a bloody borrowed typewriter—my own busted. I see by an ad in the World that The Sun etc. is in 2nd printing and Heywood Broun in the same paper Nov. 19 a full col. on it etc. Reviews have been good although the boys seem divided as to who or whom I copied the most from you or Michael Arlen so I am very grateful to both of you—and especially you, Scott, because I like you and I don't know Arland and have besides heard that he is an Armenian and it would seem a little premature to be grateful to any Armenian. But I am certainly grateful to you and I am asking Scribners to insert as a subtitle in everything after the eighth printing THE SUN ALSO RISES (LIKE YOUR COCK IF YOU HAVE ONE)

A greater Gatsby
(Written with the friendship of F. Scott FitzGerald
(Prophet of THE JAZZ AGE)

God I wish I could see you. You are the only guy in or out of Europe I can say as much for (or against) but I certainly would like to see you. I haven't enough money to come down on the train and so have been at the mercy of these non leaving free motors. The bad weather has made biking impossible. I started once that way but had a hell of a spill and luxe-ed my epaule. How the hell are you anyway.

What does 2nd printing mean in numbers? Book was published Oct. 22 thst was in the ad of Nov. 19. Max Perkins wrote the first of Nov. that the advance orders hadn't been much but that re-orders were coming in. He didn't mention any figures. Has he written to you?

College Humor has written asking me to write them essays, pieces, shit or long fiction and I turned the letter over to Max to give to Reynolds. Sometimes I have funny stuff and I think Reynolds might be willing to sell it as somebody told me Cowedge Humour paid large prices. They said they were reviewing Sun Also etc, in January issue. Hope it goes better at Princeton than the Lampoon.

As for personal life of the noted, notedby who, author, Hadley is divorcing me. Have turned over to her all existing finances and all received and future royalties from Sun. Cape and Heinemann have both made offers for British rights. Do you think Reynolds might sell it to the Movies or some such place. I'm going to take a cut on those if there are any. Have been eating one meal a day and if I get tired enough sleeping—working like hell lately—find starting life poorer than any time since I was 14 with an earning capacity of what stories I sell to Scribners very interesting. I suppose everybody's life goes to hell and anyway have been very healthy and, lately, able to use the head again. If anybody in N.Y. asks about me don't tell them a god damned thing. I would tell you all about things but don't seem able to write about them and am not very good at talking about them. Anyway so many people seem to talk so well about one's affairs that there doesn't seem ever any necessity to speak about them oneself.

Anyway I'm now all through with the general bumping off phase and will only bump off now under certain special circumstances which I don't think will arrise. Have refrained from any half turnings on of the gas or slitting of the wrists with sterilized safety razor blades. Am continuing my life in original role of son of a bitch sans peur et sans rapproche. The only thing in life I've ever had any luck being decent about is money so am very splendid and punctilious about that. Also I have been sucked in by ambition to do some very good work now no matter how everything comes out. I think some of the stuff now is good. Have learned a lot.

It is now time to cut this off and mail it.

Write to me and tell me all the dirt. What do you hear from N.Y.? Where are you going to live? How are Zelda?

and Scotty? Bumby and Hadley are damned well. I had Bumby for ten days while Hadley wzs on a trip and one morning I took him to a cafe and got him a glace and a new harmonica and holding the harmonica and eating the glace he said, "La vie est beau avec papa." He is very fond of me and when I ask him what does papa do, hoping to hear him say Papa is a great writer like the clippings. He says Papa does nothing. So then I taught him to say, "Bumby will support Papa," so he says that all the time. What will Bumby do? Bumby will support papa en espagne avec les taureaux.

Love to you all
Ernest.[16]

Before departing the Riviera in December Fitzgerald sent Hemingway a note offering assistance:

Villa St. Louis
Juan-les-Pins

Dear Ernest:

We leave this house Tuesday for Genoa + New York. I hope everything's going better for you. If there is anything you need done here or in America—anything about your work, or money, or human help under any head, remember you can always call on

Your Devoted Friend
Scott[17]

Fitzgerald followed this note with a letter written aboard the *Conte Biancamano* but mailed from Washington on December 23, 1926.

Dear Ernest=

Your letter depressed me—illogically because I knew more or less what was coming. I wish I could have seen you + heard you, if you wished, give some sort of version of what happened to you. Anyhow I'm sorry for you and for Hadley + for Bumby and I hope some way you'll all be content and things will not seem so hard and bad.

I can't tell you how much your friendship has meant to me during this year and a half—it is the brightest thing in our trip to Europe for me. I will try to look out for your interests with Scribner in America, but I gather that the

Ernest and Pauline Hemingway at the time of their wedding in 1927.

need of that is past now and that soon you'll be financially more than on your feet.

I'm sorry you didn't come to Marseille. I go back with my novel still unfinished and with less health + not much more money than when I came, but somehow content, for the moment, with motion and New York ahead and Zelda's entire recovery*—and happy about the amount of my book that I've already written.

I'm delighted with what press I've already seen of The Sun ect. Did not realize you had stolen it all from me but am prepared to believe that its true + shall tell everyone. By the way I liked it in print even better than in manuscript.

1st Printing was probably 5000. 2nd Printing may mean that they've sold 4,500 so have ordered up 3000 more. It may mean any sale from 2500 to 5000 tho.

College Humor pays fine. No movie in Sun Also unless book is big success of scandal. That's just a guess.

We all enjoyed "La vie est beau avec Papa". We agree with Bumby.

Always Yours Affectionately,
Scott

Write me care of Scribners.[18]

*From colitis, appendicitis, and an ovarian problem. M.J.B.

Fitzgerald's letter does not mention Hemingway's forthcoming marriage to Pauline Pfeiffer, but it is highly unlikely that he did not know about it. Fitzgerald and Pauline did not find each other attractive.

The Sun Also Rises was widely and respectfully reviewed. The first printing of 5,000 sold fast, and it was reprinted in November, December, January 1927, February (twice), March. By November 1929 it was in its tenth printing, and Hemingway had replaced Fitzgerald as the brightest star in Perkins's constellation. Hemingway did not receive the royalties at this time because he had assigned the novel to Hadley as a divorce settlement; but he subsequently recovered all the rights.

Chapter 4

1. *F. Scott Fitzgerald's Ledger* (Washington, D.C.: NCR/Microcard Books, 1972), p. 180.
2.. ALS, 6 pp. *Selected Letters*, pp. 199–201.
3. *Selected Letters*, p. 202.
4. ALS, 2 pp. *Selected Letters*, p. 203.
5. ALS, 5 pp. *Selected Letters*, pp. 204–205.
6. "The Moral of Scott Fitzgerald," *New Republic*, 104 (17 February 1941), 213–217; collected in *The Crack-Up*.
7. *A Moveable Feast*, p. 207.
8. Sotheby Parke Bernet sale # 3966 (29 March 1977), # 117.
9. AL, 10 pp. See Philip Young and Charles W. Mann, "Fitzgerald's *Sun Also Rises*: Notes and Comment," *Fitzgerald/Hemingway Annual 1970*, pp. 1–9.
10. The typescript of the opening chapters is at the Alderman Library, The University of Virginia. See *The Sun Also Rises: A Facsimile Edition*, 2 vols., edited by Bruccoli. Detroit: Manly/Omnigraphics, 1990.
11. Mayfield, p. 112.
12. Mayfield, p. 113.
13. ALS, 1 p. *A Life in Letters*, p. 146.
14. TLS, 3 pp. *Selected Letters*, pp. 216–218.
15. ALS, 3 pp. *A Life in Letters*, p. 146–147.
16. TLS, 3 pp. *Selected Letters*, pp. 231–233.
17. ALS, 2 pp. John Fitzgerald Kennedy Library.
18. ALS, 2 pp. *A Life in Letters*, p. 1480.

V

Early in 1927 Fitzgerald was visiting his parents in Washington, D.C., and trying to remedy a one-sided grudge Hemingway was nurturing against H. L. Mencken, editor of *The American Mercury* and the most influential American critic in that era, whom Fitzgerald greatly respected.

Address Scribners

Dear Ernest:

A line in terrible haste. Lunched with Mencken in Baltimore yesterday. He is just starting reading The Sun ect—has no recollection of having seen Big Two Hearted River + admits confusion about two *In Our* Times. Got him to say he'd pay you $250. for anything of yours he could use. So there's another market.

Told him about how you were going to beat him up. He's a "peach of a fellow" (no irony, just a slip of the pen. He's thoroughly interested + utterly incapable of malice. Whole thing was rather sloppy, as he's one of the busiest men in America.

The Killers was fine.

Yr. Devoted Friend
Scott[1]

Mencken had not reviewed *In Our Time* or *The Sun Also Rises*—which may have been what was bothering Hemingway. However, the *Mercury* had ridiculed the Paris *in our time* with an unsigned brief notice in August 1925 under the heading "Quackery":

> The sort of brave, bold stuff that all atheistic young newspaper reporters write. Jesus Christ in lower case. A hanging, a carnal love, and two disembowelings. Here it is set forth solemnly on Rives hand-made paper, in an edition of 170 copies, and with the imprimatur of Ezra Pound.[2]

The style is straight Mencken.

By 1927 Mencken had ignored two salvos from Hemingway which were invitations to counterattack. *The Torrents of Spring* was satirically dedicated "TO H. L. MENCKEN AND S. STANWOOD MENCKEN IN ADMIRATION." Since S. Stanwood Menken (the correct spelling) was a reformer who represented some of the things H. L. Mencken ridiculed, the coupling of their names was intentionally incongruous. *The Sun Also Rises* included a reference to Mencken in Bill Gorton's nonsense speech: " 'Remember the woods were God's first temples. Let us kneel and say: 'Don't eat that Lady—that's Mencken.' "[3] It is a fair inference that Hemingway—who had not had any contact with Mencken—was using a ploy of ambitious young writers by attacking a prominent literary figure. If so, it didn't work because Mencken did not retaliate.

After a California trip Fitzgerald reported from the Roosevelt Hotel in Washington:

> Dear Ernest:
>
> Where are you? You can have this hotel if you will only send for it. I have told you that before. It was formerly the warehouse where Theodore Roosevelt kept his jock straps—you remember, of course, how balls kept growing on him after the Spanish-American war until—poor wounded heart—he scarcely knew where to turn.
>
> God! So much has happened. An extraordinary thing. I'd give my orange tie to see you for two minutes. I'm so damn glad the book has been such a brilliant success, and also that its selling. I've been a month in Hollywood—the Goddamndest experience I've had in seven years—for God's sake come and visit us this summer. Book nearly done.
>
> Always Your Devoted Friend
> Scott
>
> Address Scribners[4]

"Book nearly done" was an exaggeration. Fitzgerald did not regard authorship as a process of rivalry, but he was concerned about retaining Hemingway's respect.

On March 31, 1927, Hemingway wrote from Paris expressing affection and admiration for Fitzgerald. This letter includes Hemingway's repeated story about providing Harold Loeb with an opportunity to retaliate for the Robert Cohn characterization in *Sun*.*

March 31 - toujours care of the
Guaranty Trust co.

Dear Scott

And you are my devoted friend too. You do more and work harder and oh shit I'd get maudlin about how damned swell you are. My god I'd like to see you. I got the two letters from the Roosevelt hotel and the cable about Vanity Fair this week. In principle I'd decided to not write any articles stories to order serials etc. because I don't work very easily and can't throw it off but only throw it out and then it's used up and gone. But you thought up a swell subject that wouldn't be any form of jacking off for me to write on at all. You're a hell of a good guy. Wrote something for them yest. morning in bed. Will look at it tomorrow and then fic it up and send it on. Some crap about bull fights. I think it's interesting maybe.

How the hell have you been? How nearly done is the book really? How do you feel?

Hadley and Bumby are sailing for N.Y. April 16. Bumby was down in Switzerland with me for a while and was grand. I'm to have him vacations according french law and whenever I want him according to Hadley. She is in grand shape, very happy and very much in love. None of this to tell anybody. I told Scribners to turn all the Sun royalties over to her directly a Did the same with Cape. It comes out in England this month. I went over the proofs so they didn't re-write and garble it like In Our Time. Have a couple of stories you'll see in April Scribners. Have written four since. Max perkins will have told you the Atlantic took fifty grand. Don't know whether they plan to print it on special easily inflammable paper with punctures along the edge so it will detach so that subscribers can detach it and hurl it into the fire without marring their files of the

*See Loeb's *The Way It Was* (New York: Criterion, 1959).

Atlantic *[upside down at the bottom of page one]* They were too gentlemanly to mention money. As yet I've heard nothing about money for it. Do the Atlantic pay?]

Isn't it fine about Mencken. Well well well pitcher that. That last is the Sinclair Lewis influence. That's the way his characters talk. You can write this book you're working on at random without even keeping track or remembering which characters are whom and still not be in danger of anyccompetition from the other boys. Don has taken to automatic writing and his wife assures him it is better and finer than ever. Bloomfield's next book is about a preacher (unlike Somerset Maugham or S. Lewis) Bloomfield will probably make him a decayed old new england preacher named Cabot Cabot Cabot and naturally he talks only with God - to rhyme with Cod. But sooner or later I can see that the decayed French aristocracy will come into the book and they will all be named the Marquis Deidre de Chanel and will be people whom Louis Bromfield the most brilliant and utterly master of his craft of all the younger generation of decayed french aristocracy novelists will have studied first hand himself at the Ritz and Ciros - doubtless at great expense to his friends. I went out there to dinner one night and they had a lot of vin ordinaire and cats kept jumping on the table and running off with what little fish there was and then shitting on the floor. Bloomfield, in the effort to make me feel at home did everything but put his feet on the table. I thought to show I felt at home perhaps I had better piss in the finger bowls. We talked about what fine books we each wroteband how we did it. Personally I do mine on a Corona Number 4. And when I wash it my dear I simply can't do a thing with it.

Have been broke now for a couple of months. Happily at present it coincides with Lent. I will have piled up so much credit above that will be able to get you, Zelda and (We sat at the table in the shade of the station) this the start of something or other

Scotty all out of purgatory with no more strain than a bad cold. Pat has left Duff and taken to living with Lorna Lindsay or linslay. A guy named Loeb was in town and was going to shoot me so I sent word around that I would be found unarmed sitting in front of Lipp's brasserie from two to four on saturday and Sunday afternoon and everybody who wished to shoot me was to come and do it then or else for christ sake to stop talking about it. No bullets whistled. There was a story around that I had gone to switserland to avoid being shot by demented characters out of my books. Pauline is fine and back from America. I've been in love with her for so damned long that it certainly is fine to see a little something of her.

Haven't been in the quarter nor seen anyone—Murphie's came through enroute to Central Europe with the MacLeish's. Had a card from Gerald from Berlin giving me conge on his studio where I've been living for May ist. Someone else is going to use it for something else. It was swell of them to let me use it and a hell of a lot better than under, say, the bridges. They have been swell. Also MacLeishes.

If you don't mind, though, you are the best damn friend I have. And not just-oh hell—I can't write this but I feel very strongly on the subject.

Give my love to Zelda and remember Mr. Hemingway to Scotty. Yours always,

Ernest

What about The Sun also and the movies? Any chance?[5]

In the spring of 1927 the Fitzgeralds settled at Ellerslie, a mansion near Wilmington, Delaware, they rented until March 1929. On April 18, 1927, Fitzgerald wrote to Hemingway—who was in Paris awaiting his May marriage to Pauline Pfeiffer—praising "Canary for One" and "In Another Country," quoting the opening sentence of the latter story:

God! Those terrible Bromfields! I recognized the parsimonious dinner

Dear Ernest:

Your stories were great (in April Scribner). But like me you must beware Conrad rythyms in direct quotation from characters especially if you're pointing a single phrase + making a man live by it.

"In the fall the war was always there but we did not go to it any more" is one of the most beautiful prose sentences I've ever read.

So much has happened to me lately that I despair of ever assimilating it—or for forgetting it which is the same thing.

I hate to think of your being hard up. Please use this if it would help. The Atlantic will pay about $200, I suppose. I'll get in touch with Perkins about it when he returns from

(JOHN F. KENNEDY LIBRARY)

vacation (1 wk.). Won't they advance you all you need on the bk of stories? Your title* is fine by the way. What chance of yr. crossing this summer?

My novel to be finished July 1st
With eager + anxious good wishes
Scott

Adress for a year
Ellerslie Mansion
Edge Moor
Delaware

Huge old house on
Delaware River

Pillars ect. I am called "Colonel." Zelda "de old Missus"[6]

Fitzgerald enclosed a check, but Hemingway would not need loans after his second marriage. Pauline Pfeiffer was the daughter of a wealthy Arkansas landowner; in addition to her own financial prospects, she enjoyed the generosity of her uncle, Gustavus Adolphus Pfeiffer, the controlling stockholder of Richard Hudnut cosmetics. After their marriage Hemingway's lifestyle expanded considerably. Although his books sold well, the royalties did not support the way the Hemingways lived: the house in Key West, hunting and fishing in Wyoming and Montana, following the bullfights in Spain, an African safari. Pauline was a devout Catholic, and Hemingway became a practicing Catholic when he married her—claiming that he had been baptized by a priest when he was wounded in 1918.

Hemingway did not acknowledge Fitzgerald's April 1927 letter until summer, when he wrote from Spain:

*_Men Without Women._ M.J.B.

Dear Scott,

I got your check cashed it like a son of a bitch without writing and never wrote. All of which if you study your bank account I don't have to tell you. But don't think of me as having become an Hecht or a Bodenheim or one of those literary gents that thinks writing books gives a gent license to larceny etc. because I am now writing and I will pay you the one hundred bucks as soon as the new monumental work entitled Men Without Women comes out. Not later than October let us both hope.

How the hell are you? What do you think of Men Without Women as a title? I could get no title, Fitz, run through Ecclesiastics though I did. Perkins, perhaps you've met him, wanted a title for the book. Perkins's an odd chap, I thought, what a quaint conceit! He wants a title for the book. Oddly enough he did. So, I being up in Gstaad at the time went around to all the book stores trying to buy a bible in order to get a title. But all the sons of bitches had to sell were little carved brown wood bears. So for a time I thought of dubbing the book The Little Carved Wood Bear and then listening to the critics explanations. Fortunately there happened to be a church of England clergyman in town who was leaving the next day and Pauline borrowed a bible off him after promising to return it that night because it was the bible he was ordained with. Well, Fitz, I looked all through that bible—it was in very fine print and stumbling on that great book Ecclesiastics—read it aloud to all who would listen. Soon I was alone and began cursing the bloody bible because there were no titles in it—although I found the source of practically every good title you ever heard of. But the boys, principally Kipling, had been there before me and swiped all the good ones so I called the book Men Without Women hoping it would have a large sale among the fairies and old Vassar Girls.

If you think that paragraph is dull revert to the first paragraph where I promised to pay you back the hundred dollars. There's gold in that paragraph, Fitz.

How is your novel? Have you finished it? When is coming out? I know you will be glad to hear that I am calling my new novel The World's Fair. So is Brommy as I call dear Louis. Did you see how Fanny—Butcher the woman with the Veal Brains called Brommy the American Fielding. Jesus Christ. It was this that moved me to write again. Due to climate, temperature, upbringing, lack of experience education, and tripas there isn't and won't be any American Fielding but I am resolved that son of a bitch—oh hell. It is funny though for a guy to set out to be the American Galsworthy and be dubbed the American Fielding.

I myself, Fitz, have had the splendid experience of being regraded as the tightest man in the world on acct. of never loosening up and spending any of my Sun Also Rises takings while having lived for five months on yr. 100 and $750 I got from Maxwell Perkins in the meantime having turned down large sums of dough from Hearsts including sending back a check for $1000 bucks sent as an advance on a contract for Io stories at 1000 the first five 1250 the second five—15,000 for the serial etc. Doubtless it would seem more practical to an impartial observer for me to have taken a thousand off Hearst rather than a hundred off of Fitzgerald andnI darsesay it would. The only trouble is that I cant absolutely cant write a damned thing under contract.

However am now going to write a swell novel—will not talk about it on acct. the greater ease of talking about it than writing it and consequent danger of doing same.

Got a sheet to fill out from Who's Who and my life has been so fuckingly complicated that I was only able to answer two of the questions and did not know but what they might be used against me.

Hadley and Bumby are fine and have been out on the Pacific slopes where you were too so you know what the hell they are like. Hadley plans to sail from N.Y. on the Lancastria Oct. 22 will be in N.Y. for three or four days beforehand—her address is care of the Guaranty Trust N.Y. If you were around town and could see her I know she would be cockeyed pleased and I would appreciate it.

Pauline is fine. We were going to come over to the states thism fall but as I am starting working well I better keep on and get the stuff done and then come over in the Spring. Where will you be. Please Scott forgive me for being such a turd about not not writing or acknowledging the check. I had a note from Northrup in Santiago enclosing a card of yours—it came just as he was sailing. So I wrot him in Chicago.

Love to Zelda and Scotty—write me all the dirt. The Murphies have been in Antibes all summer I think. Have heard nothing from Don Stewart since he left last fall. Nothing from Benchley. Letters from Dos pretty often. MacLeishes are in America. Pat Guthrie after Duff got her divorce wouldn't marry her because she had lost her looks and now lives with Lorna Lindsley who saved him from jail on a bad check and who can let him go to jail at any time. Duff is on the town. She kidnapped her kid from England and has no money to keep him—all her small amt. of income goes to keep the kid and nurse in south of france in reduced style of titled youngsters. I ran into her one night—she wasn't sore about the Sun—said the only thing was she never had slept with the bloody bull fighter. That was only night I was in the quarter for a year. Been in Spain since first of July—just bumming went all over Galicia.

What the hell. Please write. I would like to hear all about Literary Affairs—wish I could see you and talk.

Yours
Ernest[7]

Through the fall of 1927 Perkins shared with Hemingway his concern about Fitzgerald's nervous state and his inability to get on with his novel. After visiting Ellerslie he worried that Fitzgerald might have a nervous and physical breakdown. Perkins persuaded him to switch to Sano, a brand of low-nicotine cigarettes—making the misdiagnosis that "tobacco was hurting him more than drink."[8] Hemingway told Perkins that he would like to be able to come to America and get Fitzgerald back in shape.[9]

In October Fitzgerald wrote congratulating Hemingway on *Men Without Women,* his second collection of stories.

Dear Ernest:

Thousands will send you this clipping.* I should think it would make you quite conscious of your public existence. Its well meant—he praised your book a few days before.

The book is fine. I like it quite as well as The Sun, which doesn't begin to express my entheusiasm. In spite of all its geographical + emotional rambling its a unit, as much as Conrad's books of Contes were. Zelda read it with facination, liking it better than anything you've written. Her favorite was Hills Like White Elephants, mine, barring The Killers was Now I Lay Me. The one about the Indians was the only one that left me cold and I'm glad you left out

*A parody of Hemingway in F.P.A.'s "Conning Tower" column. M.J.B.

Up in Michigan.† They probably belong to an earlier + almost exhausted vein.

"In the fall the war was always there but we did not go to it anymore." God, what a beautiful line. And the waking dreams in Now I Lay me and the whole mood of Hills Like.

Did you see the pre-review by that cocksucker Rascoe who obviously had read only three stories but wanted to be up to the minute?

Max says its almost exhausted 7500—however that was five days ago. I like your title—All the Sad Young Men Without Women—and I feel my influence is beginning to tell. Manuel Garcia is obviously Gatsby. What you havn't learned from me you'll get from Good Woman Bromfield and soon you'll be Marching in the Van of the Younger Generation.

No work this summer but lots this fall. Hope to finish the novel by 1st December. Have got nervous as hell lately—purely physical but scared me somewhat—to the point of putting me on the wagon and smoking denicotinized cigarettes. Zelda is ballet dancing three times a week with the Phila symphony—painting also. I think you were wise not jumping at Hearsts offer. I had a contract with them that, as it turned out, did me unspeakable damage in one way or another. Long is a sentimental scavenger with no ghost of taste or individuality, not nearly so much as Lorimer for example. However, why not send your stories to Paul Reynolds? He'll be glad to handle them + will get you good prices. The Post now pays me $3500.—this detail so you'll be sure who's writing this letter.

I can't tell you how I miss you. May cross for 6 wks in March or April. The Grandmothers was respectable but undistinguished, and are you coming home. Best to Pauline. With good wishes + Affection Scott[10]

Fitzgerald presented Mencken with an inscribed copy of Men Without Women when it was published in 1927:

Dear Menk:

Please read this—at least read The Killers Pursuit Race + Now I lay me

†On May 10, Perkins had asked Fitzgerald's advice about publishing "Up in Michigan," the story that Liveright had earlier declined to publish in *In Our Time*. Fitzgerald replied on the 12th: "One line *at least* is pornographic, though *please* don't bring my name into the discussion. The thing is—what is a seduction story with the seduction left out. Yet if that is softened it is quite printable." M.J.B.

He's really a great writer, since Anderson's collapse the best we have I think. Ever yours

Scott Fitzg—[11]

Fitzgerald's efforts may have prompted Mencken to review *Men Without Women* in the May 1928 *American Mercury.* Pairing Hemingway with Thornton Wilder, he commented, "It is technical virtuosity that has won them attention; it is hard work and fundamental thinking that must get them on, if they are to make good their high promise."[12]

During Christmas 1927 Hemingway and Pauline were skiing at Gstaad, and he sent Fitzgerald a letter with "enclosed scraps." The scraps do not survive, but there is a one-page fragment from Hemingway to Fitzgerald with the upper left corner torn off dated 18 December.

Dear Scott—

The enclosed scraps—if pieced together—will form a fine letter containing all the news, which I wrote—tore up—as too bloody dull to send but havent pep or anything else enough to write over. Wish the hell I could see you Nobody to talk about writing or the literary situation with. Why the hell dont you write yr novel?
Best to Zelda and Scotty.
Max Perkins says M Without W is selling like a book by Fitzgerald (you know the guy who wrote Omar Kayam) We are coming to America in March or April—land at San Antonio Texas if its on the coast.

At moment of writing I have
1 Blindness—
2. Piles
3 A bad case of grippe
4 A toothache—
Merry Christmas to all and to all a Happy New Year like this one wasnt—yr affect disciple in the literary game

HEM[13]

Hotel Rossli
Gstaad-Suisse
Dec 18
letter about six
o lousy to send.
Glad you s How the hell are you

anyway? I started a novel early in the fall and had 20 chapters done—about 55–60,000 words then got sick (nothing) just grippy in the head so I couldnt write—then came down here with Bumby and Pauline to get healthy—and at Montreux on the way down Bumby when I picked him up in the night to put him on the pot stuck one of his fingers in my right eye and the nail went in and cut the pupil—just a little place like this *[drawing, resembling an arc]*—like a fishscale or something. But it was my one good eye and I've been in bed and shot to hell in one way or another ever since. So that's all the news except its been 30 below zero here.

This is no letter because I cant see yet so I'm sorry as[14]

The twenty chapters that he had written were for a "modern Tom Jones," which he abandoned to start *A Farewell to Arms* in 1928.

Fitzgerald's December letter included a confident—but untrue—report on his novel as "almost through." Again he disparages his commercial stories while noting that his *Post* price has been raised. (His story price in 1927 was $3,500—not $4,000.)

Ellerslie
Edgemoor
Delaware

Dear Ernest:

Perkins sent me the check for 800 bits (as we westerners say), indicating I hope, that you are now comfortably off in your own ascetic way. I am almost through my novel, got short and had to do three Post stories but as I am now their pet exhibit and go down on them to the tune of 32,000 bits per felony it didn't take long to come to the surface.

(This tough talk is not really characteristic of me—its the influence of All the Sad Young Men Without Women in Love.) Louis Golding stepped off the boat + said you and I were the hope of American Letters (if you can find them) but aside from that things look black, "old pard"—Brommy is sweeping the west, Edna Ferber is sweeping the east and Paul Rosenfeld is sweeping what's left into a large ornate wastebasket, a gift which any Real Man would like, to be published in November under the title: The Real Liesure Class, containing the work of one-story Balzacs and poets so thin-skinned as to be moved by everything to exactly the same degree of mild remarking.

Lately I've enjoyed Some People, Bismark (Ludwig's), Him (in parts) and the Memoirs of Ludendorff. I have a new German war book, Die Krieg against Krieg, which shows men who mislaid their faces in Picardy and the Caucasus—you can imagine how I thumb it over, my mouth fairly slithering with fascination.

If you write anything in the line of an ''athletic'' story please try the Post or let me try them for you, or Reynolds. You were wise not to tie up with Hearsts. They are absolute bitches who feed on contracts like vultures, if I may coin a neat simile.

I've tasted no alcohol for a month but Xmas is coming.

Please write me at length about your adventures—I hear you were seen running through Portugal in used B.V.Ds, chewing ground glass and collecting material for a story about Boule players; that you were publicity man for Lindberg; that you have finished a novel a hundred thousand words long consisting entirely of the word ''balls'' used in new groupings; that you have been naturalized a Spaniard, dress always in a wine-skin with ''zipper'' vent and are engaged in bootlegging Spanish Fly between St. Sebastian and Biaritz where your agents sprinkle it on the floor of the Casino. I hope I have been misformed but, alas! it all has too true a ring. For your own good I should be back there, with both of us trying to be good fellows at a terrible rate. Just before you pass out next time think of me.

This is a wowsy country but France is swehw and I hope to spend March and April, or April and May, there and elsewhere on the continent.

How are you, physically and mentally? Do you sleep? Now I Lay Me was a fine story—you ought to write a companion piece, Now I Lay Her. Excuse my bawdiness but I'm oversexed and am having saltpetre put in my Pâté de Foie Gras au Truffles Provêncal.

Please write news. My best to Pauline—Zelda's also to you both. God will forgive everybody—even Robert McAlmon and Burton Rascoe.

Always Afftly

Scott[15]

Hemingway replied from Gstaad later in December:

Dear Scott -

Always glad to hear from a brother pederast. You ask for the news. Well I have quit the writing game and gone into the pimping game. They have been purifying Paris and running all the former and well known pimps out and it has left a big lack and a fine opportunity both of which I am trying to fill. I have lined up a fine lot of girls "les girls" a french word and when you and the Mrs. Come over in the Spring I will be able to offer you some very interesting reductions.

Old Brommy has certainly swept the women's clubs. It was a sure thing that he would encounter my mother. "Mother of Four Takes Up Painting at 52" and he did. He told her he was certain he had recognized her although he couldn't place her because Ernest was his best friend and how wouldn't he know Ernest's mother. Now my mother has a new cause to weep because I don't write like Brommmy.

Are you keeping little Scotty off of the hop any better? We hear many happy anecdotes over here about how she jammed H.L.Menken with her own little needle the last time he visited at the Mansions and that that was how the American Mercury came to be written.

Teddy Chandler the boy whom if I am not mistaken once killed your mother is over here.* Also Bill Bullitt or Bull Billet a big Jew from Yale and fellow novel writer., Pat Guthrie who once lived with Duff Twizden is now being kept by Lorna Lindsley who is looking even fresher and lovelier. None of these people I ever see but will be glad to look them up for you.

My son Bumby is following in his father's footsteps and makes up stories. Hearsts have offered him 182,000 bits for a serial about Lesbians who were wounded in the war and it was so hard to have children that they all took to drink and running all over Europe and Asia just a wanton crew of wastrels. I have introduced him to a lot of them and he is writing hard and I am helping him a little now and then with the spelling and Pauline reads aloud to him your stories out of the Post so he will get an idea of the style which is going to be the same as that of the latest poems by MacLeish only trimmed with Persian Lamb. Bumby is calling the thing

*Theodore Chanler, an American composer, was a source for the Francis Melarky character in Fitzgerald's matricide novel. M.J.B.

lesbos Lesbos LESBOS

I see few people except Mike Ward the ex Banker who had an amazing adventure the other night in the Club Daunau where he hit a man standing at the bar because he said something about me that he, Mike, did not hear but didn't like the sound of. He asked the man if he was a friend of mine and when the man said no Mike hit him. Later it turned out that the man had not mentioned me at all but Mike said that the man was no friend of mine he could tell.

You ought to have loyal friends like that Fitz.

There was no money in Spanish fly so I gave up the Spanish Fly game. My eye is all right now and we are hoping it will snow. Jinny has been here since the 1st of December hopingit will snow too. We have only been hoping since the 14th of December. I have a sore throat and am in bed. I gues you will agree we got Lindberg a nice lot of publicity. Would you like me to be publicity man for either Scotty or Zelda. You are right about the spanish wine skin and I find it very comfortable but it has nothing so unhemanish as a zipper. I have to watch myself that way and deny myself many ofthe little comforts like toilet paper, semi-colons, and soles to my shoes. Any time I use any of those people begin to shout that old Hem is just a fairy after all and no He man ha ha. On acct. being so laid up so long started a fine beard which ia now almost rabbinical. May keep it until come to the states but doubt it.

Write me all the news and views. Love to Zelda and little Scotty if you can keep her off the stuff long enough for her to understand the message. You shouldn't let that child have Heroin Scott. I've thought it over from every angle and it can't be good for her. I know that you have to keep up appearances and I know the way things are nowadays but nobody can convince me that it really does a child of that age any good.

Write again. Now I don't owe you anything besides undying gratitude a and say i80 bottles of champagne I can write free-er.

yrs. always,

Ernest.[16]

While Hemingway was writing *A Farewell to Arms* in 1928 Fitzgerald was still stuck on his novel, which he interrupted to write twelve stories in 1927–28, ten of which were in *The Saturday Eve-*

ning Post. His earnings of $29,000 in 1927 and $25,000 in 1928 had the combined purchasing power of at least $400,000 now; Yet he lived from story to story. Fitzgerald's drinking behavior became increasingly erratic, and his domestic situation deteriorated as Zelda Fitzgerald's ambitions for a career of her own drove her to begin intense ballet training at twenty-seven.

In March 1928 Hemingway was hit by a falling skylight in the toilet of his Paris apartment; nine stitches were required, leaving a permanent scar on his forehead. Fitzgerald was in America when the accident occurred. Nonetheless, the extent of the legendizing activity that has been generated around these two figures is revealed by a false report of the event, in which Fitzgerald is the alleged perpetrator. In 1956–57 Jed Kiley, a former editor of the Paris *Boulevardier,* wrote a series of reminiscences for *Playboy,* which became a book entitled *Hemingway: An Old Friend Remembers** Kiley attributed to Fitzgerald the admission that he had deliberately pulled down the skylight in an attempt to kill Hemingway.[17] Geography renders this allegation impossible. Kiley's unverified account gained considerable currency before it was rebutted by Archibald MacLeish's letter to the London *Times Literary Supplement.* MacLeish, who took Hemingway to the hospital after the accident, stated that Fitzgerald was in no way involved.[18] Hemingway's report to Perkins on March 17, 1928, makes it clear that he was alone in the toilet when he tried to hook up a skylight cord, bringing the skylight down on his head. The Kiley fabrication continues to crop up because readers like anecdotes about Fitzgerald and Hemingway—true or untrue.

During 1928 Hemingway and Perkins exchanged concerned letters about Fitzgerald, speculating about his progress on the novel. On April 21 Hemingway wrote from Key West developing his theory that Fitzgerald had been blocked by the reviews of *The Great Gatsby*—especially Gilbert Seldes's review—which made him afraid not to write a masterpiece. The thing for Fitzgerald to do was write; he could have finished three novels in the time since *Gatsby* if he weren't trying for a masterpiece. Perkins replied that he didn't think Fitzgerald was attempting the impossible in his novel. The trouble, he felt, was Zelda's extravagance.

*New York: Hawthorn, 1965. On December 17, 1954, Hemingway informed Kiley: "A gag is a gag and a fantasy is a fantasy but the Mss. you sent me . . . entitled 'Me and Ernest Hemingway' is a long series of untruths, mis-statements and falsehoods which I could not allow you to run even if it was labelled a fictional nightmare" (University of Maryland Library).

The Fitzgeralds spent the spring and summer of 1928 in Paris, a wasted time of drinking for him while Zelda took ballet lessons. Probably in July he wrote to Hemingway, who was in America, but Fitzgerald did not mention his own work:

Teenie-weenie Corner
Sunshineville.

Precious Papa, Bull-fighter, Gourmand ect.

It has come to my ears

· That you have been seen bycling through Kansas, chewing + spitting a mixture of goat's meat + chicory which the natives collect + sell for artery-softener and market-glut

· That Bumby has won the Benjamin Altman Scholarship at Cundle School + taken first prizes in Comparitive Epistomology, Diseases of Cormorants + Small Vultures, Amateur Gyncology + Intestinal Hysterics

· That you are going to fight Jim Tully in Washdog Wisconsin on Decoration Day in a chastity belt with your hair cut á la garconne.

Is it all true?

We are friends with the Murphys again. Talked about you a great deal + while we tried to say only kind things we managed to get in a few good cracks that would amuse you—about anybody else—which is what you get for being so far away. Incidently called twice on Hadley—she was both times out but saw Bumby once + think he's the best kid I ever saw by 1000 miles.

Well, old Mackerel Snatcher, wolf a Wafer + + a Beaker of blood for me,—and when you come Shadowboxing into my life again with your new similes for "swewa" and "wousy" (which, as you doubtless notice, you've given to the world) no one will be glader than your

Devoted Friend
Scott Fitzg—

While in America don't cast any doubt on my statement that you held a bridgehead (or was it a hophead) at Caporetto for three days + utterly baffled the 2nd Austrian Army Corps. In 50 yrs all the people that could have denied it will be dead or busy holding their own bridgeheads—like

> Lawrence Stallings, who is slowly taking to himself the communal exploits of the 5th + 6th Marines. "Hebuterne—of course I know it—I took that village."
>
> Do send Lorimer a story. I read Mencken's public apology. Not bad for an old man who has had his troubles. God help us all! Have seen a good deal of Joyce. Please come back—will be here till Aug 20TH 58 Rue de Vaugirard. Then back to America for a few months.
>
> Best to Pauline![19]

This is the only letter in which Fitzgerald addresses Hemingway as "Papa."

In September or October Hemingway wrote Fitzgerald from Piggott, Arkansas, ebulliently reporting completion for the first draft of *A Farewell to Arms.* His jokes about Fitzgerald's work habits and slow progress could not have amused Fitzgerald:

> Dear Mr. Fizzgeral—
>
> A letter some time ago from MaxwellEEPerkins let me in on the little secret that you work eight hours every day—Joyce I believe worked twelve. There was some comparison between how long it took you two great authors to finish your work.
>
> Well Fitz you are certainly a worker. I have never been able to write longer than two hours myself without getting utterly pooped—any longer than that and the stuff begins to become tripe but here is old Fitz whom I once knew working eight hours every day. How does it feel old fellow? What is the secret of your ability to write for eight hours every day. I look forward with some eagerness to seeing the product. Will it be like that other great worker and fellow Celt? Have you gone in for not making sense? If I could only take the slight plunge to going in for not making sense I could work ten and twelve hours a day every day and always be perfectly happy like Gertrude Stein who since she has taken up not making sense some eighteen years ago has never known a moments unhappiness with her work.
>
> You dirty lousy liar to say you work (write) eight hours a day.
>
> Send Lorimer a story hell. I'm letting you send Lorimer stories for both of us.
>
> Finished my first draft of the bloody book a month ago—

going east now in a couple of weeks. Wanted to write some stories here but laying off writing for a month lost all impetus and now feel too healthy and at the same time mentally pooped. God I worked hard on the book. Want like hell to start re-writing but know I ought to wait a while still.

Just got back from Montana—went there from Wyo. had a grand time. Pat has doubled his weight in three months—weighed 9 something to begin with. He looks like *[three words unreadable]* never cries laughs all the time—sleeps all night built like a brick shithouse. I am thinking of advertising in the Nation or some such suitable medium Are your children Rickety, deformed, in any way unsatisfactory. See E. Hemingway (then pictures of the product—all by different Mothers) Perhaps He can help You. Mr. Hemingway understands your problem. He is the author of Mr. and Mrs. Elliott. He knows what you are up against. His own problem is different. Mr. Hemingway has to avoid children. Since the age of fourteen he has been embarrassed by a succession of perfect Little Ones. Now he has decided to make this great gift available to All. Tear off the enclosed coupon and mail it in a plain stamped envelope and you will receive his booklet Perfect Children for You All.

Just send the coupon and your photo and you will receive a personal answer from Mr. Hemingway himself.

Do not confuse Mr.Hemingway with Mr. FitzGerald. Mr. FitzGerald it is true is the fother of a very perfect child with, we must admit, a delightful English accent (a thing Mr. Hemingway cannot guarantee his clients). But Mr. FitzGerald is what is known in the profession as a 'one time performer'. You may take Mr. Fizzgerew if younwish but, in the end, you will be sorry. Mr. Dos Passos, however, we mustvstrongly counsell against. For your best interests do not take Mr. Dos Passos. Mr. Dos Passos is practically 'sterile'. You all know what that means. Mr. D.P. cannot have children. Poor Mr. D.P. It is true Mr. Hemingway sometimes envies Mr. Dos Passos but that is just another proof of Mr. Hemingway's real worth to You.

There has lately been a movement on foot to take mr. *[deleted by E.H.]* Delicacy forbids us to give Mr. *[deleted by E.H.]* first name (or last name). We cannot counsel too strongly against this. Do not press us for our reasons.

Mr. Donald Ogden Stewart has had a certain amount of

publicity lately in this connection but after mature consideration we feel that we cannot conscientiously recommend Mr. Stewart. Mr. Stewart may be a 'one timer'. There is no greater waste of money in modern social hygiene than the employment of a one timer.

Then there is the religious issue. Mr. Hemingway has enjoyed success under all religions. Even with no religion at all Mr. Hemingway has not been found wanting. In the matter of Creeds, as in Colours, he is not a Bigot.

You understand, my dear Fitz, that none of this is personal. When I say Hemingway I may mean Perkins or Bridges. When I say FitzGerald I may mean Compton MacKenzie or Stephen St. Vincent Benet the wife of the poet Eleanor Wylie. When I say *[deleted by E.H.]* I may mean Horseshit. None of this is even the slightest bit personal or 'mean'. Just good old big hearted Hem speaking. We are on the air tonight through the courtesy of the Kansas City Star and associated newspapers. Oh my this really is a fight. I wish you all could see Tommy Heeney's left eye. Now they are at it again.

Where are you going to be the end of Oct. How's to get stewed together Fitz? How about a little mixed vomiting or shold it be a "stag" party.

Write me to Piggott (Arkansas)

Ernest

glad you are friends with Murphy's.

[line deleted by E.H.]

I would rather stay friends with say, Mike Ward than be in and out of being friends with say, Saint Paul or other rich and noble characters. But then the *[deleted by E.H.]* aren't Saint Paul nor are they Minneapolis. They are figures in a ballet. A very attractive Ballet. use that some time in the Post Kid. *[this paragraph crossed out by E.H., but readable]*

[in left-hand margin] This is crossed out—Old Hem never speaks nor writes in criticism of his friends and they are my friends.

I see Glenway or Nuway (the back way) Wescott used your sailors in Villefranche scene in Goodbye to Wisconson*—In a story called The Sailor (so you wont have to read through it all.)[20]

*"The Sailor," *Good-bye Wisconsin* (1928). M.J.B.

Hemingway followed that letter with an October 11 analysis to Perkins of Fitzgerald's squandered talent:

> Instead of thinking Zelda a possible good influence (what a phrase) for Scott I think 90% of all the trouble he has comes from her.† Almost every bloody fool thing I have ever seen or known him to do has been directly or indirectly Zelda inspired. I'm probably wrong in this. But I often wonder if he would not have been the best writer we've ever had or likely to have if he hadnt been married to some one that would make him waste Every thing. I know no one that has ever had more talent or wasted it more. I wish to God he'd write a good book and finish it and not poop himself away on those lousy Post stories. I dont blame *Lorimer* I blame Zelda. I would not have Scott imagine I believed this for the world.

From this time on, Hemingway reiterated his charges against Zelda.

Fitzgerald and Hemingway had their first reunion since the summer of 1926 when the Hemingways and artist Henry Strater (the model for Burne Holiday in *This Side of Paradise*) met the Fitzgeralds at Princeton on November 17 for the Yale-Princeton game. Hemingway wrote a four-page unfinished account of this meeting intended for *A Moveable Feast.* According to this document, the two couples took the train to Philadelphia after the game and were driven by the Fitzgeralds' chauffeur in their Buick to Ellerslie. Fitzgerald got drunk on the train and annoyed strangers, including a medical student he insisted was a "clap doctor." During the drive to Ellerslie the chauffeur complained to Hemingway that Fitzgerald would not permit him to put any oil in the engine, insisting that American cars do not require additional oil. This report breaks off with the Fitzgeralds arguing about the turn-off to their house. The Hemingways spent the night at "Ellerslie" and left for Chicago by train the next day.*

†In his October 2 letter to Hemingway, Perkins had commented: "Zelda is so able and intelligent, and isn't she also quite a strong person? that I'm surprised she doesn't face the situation better, and show some sense about spending money." M.J.B.

*There is another account of this reunion in A. E. Hotchner's *Papa Hemingway* (New York: Random House, 1966), which Hotchner presents as told to him by Hemingway. In this version Hemingway went alone to dine with the Fitzgeralds in their mansion outside Baltimore. He was met at the station by the chauffeur, Pierre (his name was Philippe), with "a custom-built Hotchkiss" which Fitzgerald would not lubricate. At dinner Fitzgerald was drunk and unpleasant before passing out. There was no one to drive Hemingway to the station, so he had to spend the night instead of returning to New York to work on proofs with Perkins. The next day Fitzgerald tried to prevent Hemingway from catching the "one train a day" from Baltimore to New York. In the

After the Ellerslie visit Hemingway wrote Fitzgerald a bread-and-butter letter from the train, referring to some unexplained trouble with a policeman at the station.

Sunday
Night

Dear Scott and Zelda—
The train is bucking and pitching or bitching (but not listing anyway

We had a wonderful time—you were both grand—I am sorry I made a shall we say nuisance of myself about getting to the train on time—We were there far to too early—when you were in the hands of the cop I called on the phone from platform and explained you were a great writer—The cop was very nice—He said you said I was a great writer too but he had never heard of either of us. I told him rapidly the plots of some of your better known stories—He said—this is absolutely literal—''He seems like a Dandy Fellow''—that's the way cops talk not as they talk in Callaghan's Works.

Anyway we had a glad time and Ellersley Mansion is the most cock eyed beautiful place I've ever seen—Pauline sends her love—

Ernest

I'll write our address in Key West when I know it—
Piggott
Ark. will always reach us.[21]

On December 6, 1928, Hemingway was southbound from New York to Key West with Bumby on the Havana Special. At Trenton, New Jersey, he received a wire that his father had died in Oak Park. Hemingway wired Perkins to send $100 to the North Philadelphia

car on the way to the station Fitzgerald—petulant because Hemingway was leaving—kicked out the windshield and cut his foot. ''Scott turned savagely abusive and hysterical and I had to slap his face hard to quiet him down'' (pp. 120–122). The checkable details in Hotchner's account do not check out. In 1928 the Fitzgeralds were living at Ellerslie, near Wilmington; Hemingway never visited them at La Paix near Baltimore, where they lived during 1932–33. Fitzgerald never owned a Hotchkiss—custom-built or otherwise; at Ellerslie he had a Buick, as Hemingway correctly notes in his own account. It is uncertain whether Hotchner is a bad reporter or whether Hemingway told him a different version. A third account of the Hemingways' visit to Ellerslie is in Sara Mayfield's *Exiles from Paradise*. She reports that Zelda was disturbed by Hemingway's ''jokes with Scott about pederasty, anal eroticism, and other forms of perversion''; and that Fitzgerald and Hemingway got drunk and were jailed after a brawl (p. 133). Mayfield was not present, and there is no supporting evidence for her account. M.J.B.

station; there was no reply, so he wired both Fitzgerald and Strater. Fitzgerald delivered the cash in person to North Philadelphia.

Suffering from angina and diabetes and depressed by his bad investments in Florida real estate, Dr. Hemingway had shot himself. Hemingway believed that his mother's domination had unmanned his father. After the funeral Hemingway wrote Fitzgerald from the train en route to Key West.

> Dear Scott—You were damned good and also bloody effective to get me that money—
>
> I had like a fool only 35-40 bucks with me after Xmas shopping—plenty for Food and Tips enroute to Key West—
>
> My Father shot himself as I <suppose> you may have read in the papers.
>
> Will send you the $100 as soon as I reach Key West—or have Max Perkins send it—
>
> Thanks again like hell for your very admirable <u>performance</u> as we say in the automotive game
>
> I was fond as hell of my father and feel too punk—also sick etc.—to write a letter (but wanted to thank you—
>
> Best to Zelda and Scotty—
>
> *[unreadable]*
>
> <u>Ernest.</u>[22]

Fitzgerald replied in December, predicting completion of his novel by March 1929.

> Dear Ernest:
>
> I'm terribly sorry about your trouble. I guess losing parents is just one of the things that happens to one in the thirties—every time I see my father now I think its the last time.
>
> Thank Pauline for the really beautiful Xmas card. It was great to have you both here, even when I was intermittently unconscious.
>
> I send you what may be news, and what a nice precedent for beating up Mencken.* Saw the Murphys for an hour in New York. We're sailing March 1st + I hope to have the novel here. (Confidential about sailing though until I'm

*A newspaper clipping, "Toreador Is Barred for Beating Up Critic." M.J.B.

[ca Dec. 9, 1928]

~~Fall 1928~~

Dear Scott— you were damned good and also bloody effective to get me ~~that~~ money— I had like a fool only 35–40 bucks with me after Xmas shopping— ~~tobe~~ plenty for food and tips enroute to Key West—

~~Best love to~~

My Father shot himself as I suppose you may have read in the papers.

(PRINCETON UNIVERSITY LIBRARY)

sure—won't go unless novel's finished.) Ring thought you were fine—he was uncharacteristicly entheusiastic.

I'm bored + somewhat depressed tonight so I won't continue. Oh, yes—I met old H. Stearns just before leaving Paris and feeling drunk and Christ-like suggested a title to him: "Why I go on being poor in Paris", told him to write it as an informal letter to me and I'd sell it.* In a burst of energy he did + I sent it to Max who wrote a check for $100.00 for it. Now Harold writes me that $100 isn't very much (as a matter of fact, it isn't much of a letter either) and exhibits such general dissatisfaction that I think he thinks I held out on him. You've got to be careful who you do favors for—within a year you'll probably hear a story that what started him on his downward path was my conscienceless theft of his royalties.

Spengler's second volume is marvellous. Nothing else is any good—when will you save me from the risk of memorizing your works from over-reading them by finishing another? Remember, Proust is dead—to the great envy of

Your Crony and Gossip
Scott

Edgemoor
Delaware[23]

Chapter 5

1. ALS, 1 p. John Fitzgerald Kennedy Library.
2. *American Mercury,* 5 (August 1925), xxxviii.
3. *The Sun Also Rises*, p. 126.
4. 18 March 1927; ALS, 1 p. John Fitzgerald Kennedy Library.
5. TLS, 3 pp. *Selected Letters*, pp. 248–251.
6. ALS, 1 p. *A Life in Letters*, p. 149.
7. TLS, 2 pp. *Selected Letters*, pp. 260–262.
8. 31 October 1927.
9. c. 1 November 1927. *Selected Letters*, p. 264.
10. ALS, 3 pp. *A Life in Letters*, pp. 151–152.
11. Enoch Pratt Free Library. See also *Correspondence of F. Scott Fitzgerald*, p. 210.
12. *American Mercury*, 14 (May 1928), 127.

*"Apologia of an Expatriate," *Scribner's Magazine,* 85 (March 1929), 338–341. M.J.B.

13. ALS, 3 pp. Princeton University Library.
14. ALS, 1 p. Princeton University Library.
15. ALS, 4 pp. *A Life in Letters*, pp. 153–155.
16. TLS, 3 pp. *Selected Letters*, pp. 267–269.
17. *Hemingway: An Old Friend Remembers* (New York: Hawthorn, 1963), p. 58.
18. *Times Literary Supplement* (3 September 1964), 803.
19. ALS, 2 pp. *A Life in Letters*, pp. 157–158.
20. TLS, 2 pp. *Selected Letters*, pp. 287–289.
21. ALS, 3 pp. *Selected Letters*, p. 290.
22. ALS, 2 pp. *Selected Letters*, p. 291.
23. ALS, 1 p. *A Life in Letters*, p. 160–161.

VI

Fitzgerald's novel was not finished in March 1929, but the Fitzgeralds gave up Ellerslie and returned to France. The Hemingways were in Paris; when Hemingway heard that Fitzgerald was definitely coming, he instructed Perkins not to give Fitzgerald his Paris address. Fitzgerald had caused him to be thrown out of one apartment by fighting with the landlord, urinating on the porch, and trying to break down the door at three or four A.M. Hemingway wanted to see Fitzgerald in public places only. The news that Fitzgerald was coming to Paris gave Hemingway the horrors.[1]

Expecting to spend a great deal of time with Hemingway in Paris, Fitzgerald was hurt to learn that Hemingway's address was kept from him; he was forced to communicate with Hemingway by sending messages c/o Pauline's sister. The list of ''Snubs'' Fitzgerald entered in his *Notebooks* includes ''Ernest apartment'' (see Appendix, #728). Yet Fitzgerald endured the snub with its clear indication that their old relationship had terminated and sought Hemingway's company. Fitzgerald's eagerness to be with Hemingway is shown by this May 1929 note inviting the Hemingways to dinner:

> Dear Herr Hemophile: or ''Bleeding Boy'' as I sometimes call you.
>
> Will you take salt with us Sun. or Mon. night? would make great personal whoopee on receipt of favorable response. Send me a pneu or answer in person, save between 3 + 7, Highest references, willing to travel—gens du monde, cultivee, sympathetique cherche hote pour diman-

che ou lundi—answer because I shall prob. ask Bishop, if you can come—he is new man without frau.

God Save us, Preserve us, Bless us
Yrs. in Xt.
Fitzg—[2]

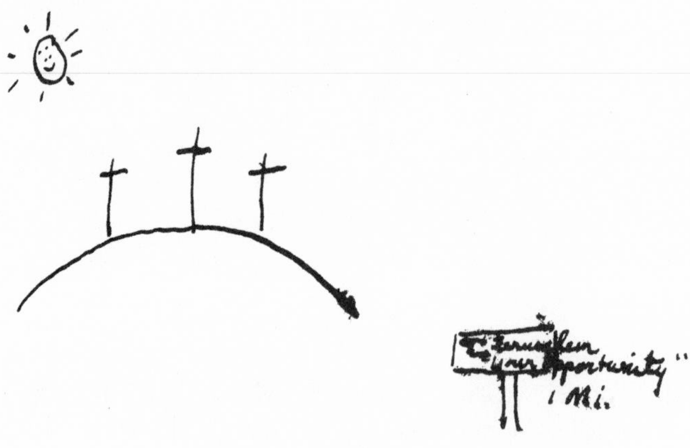

(JOHN F. KENNEDY LIBRARY)

The Paris encounters between Fitzgerald and Hemingway during spring-summer 1929 generated strains that permanently altered their friendship. Fitzgerald was drinking heavily and was defensive about his stalled novel. The animosity between Zelda and Hemingway was compounded by Pauline's disapproval of the Fitzgeralds. Fitzgerald had reasons for his unhappiness in addition to his guilt about his work. Zelda's intense ballet training in Paris left her exhausted, and her behavior became markedly erratic. Fitzgerald complained of her sexual indifference to him, and she countercharged that he was an unsatisfactory lover. It was probably at this time that Fitzgerald sought Hemingway's sexual counsel. As recounted in "A Matter of Measurements" in *A Moveable Feast,* Fitzgerald told Hemingway that Zelda complained that his penis was too small to satisfy her. Hemingway checked Fitzgerald's anatomy and assured him that his penis was normal, but Fitzgerald remained uncertain. Hemingway advised him to recover his confidence by sleeping with another woman: " 'Forget what Zelda said,' I told him. 'Zelda is crazy. There's nothing wrong with you. Just have confidence and do what the girl wants. Zelda just wants to destroy you.' " It is a gauge of Fitzgerald's anxiety and his admiration for Hemingway's masculine authority that he sought Hemingway's advice. But it is also a gauge of Fitzgerald's capacity for self-abasement that he revealed this problem to Hemingway. Although he presumably trusted Hemingway's discretion despite the evidence of his enjoyment of gossip, Fitzgerald must have known that his admission would generate Hemingway's contempt.*

After this meeting Fitzgerald departed for the Ritz bar. At this point *A Moveable Feast* reports a conversation Hemingway had with Georges, the head barman at the Ritz, some twenty-five years later. Georges was puzzled by tourists who asked him about " 'this Monsieur Fitzgerald' " whom he did not remember; but Georges told them whatever they wanted to hear. In some obscure way Hemingway connected Fitzgerald's sexual insecurity with his failure to impress himself on the Ritz barman.† It is worth noting that, Fitzgerald wrote brilliantly about the Ritz bar in *Tender Is the Night* and "Babylon Revisited."

There is no evidence that Fitzgerald revealed to Hemingway Zelda's accusation that they were engaged in a homosexual affair; Hemingway never mentioned it in writing. When Fitzgerald muttered "No more baby" in his drunken sleep after a meeting with Hemingway, Zelda had interpreted that as proof of the liaison.[3] Fitzgerald apparently began to worry about his possible latent homosexuality—or at least was concerned about acquiring that reputation. The young Canadian novelist Morley Callaghan, a member of the Perkins stable, was in Paris in 1929 and associated with Fitzgerald and Hemingway. His 1963 memoir, *That Summer in Paris,* includes this Fitzgerald statement: " 'Remember the night I was in bad shape? I took your arm. Well, I dropped it. It was like holding a cold fish. You thought I was a fairy, didn't you?"[4]

In 1930, after Zelda had been hospitalized in Switzerland, Fitzgerald wrote a long, probably unsent letter analyzing their marriage and including these observations on their return to France in 1929:

*After *A Moveable Feast* was published, Arnold Gingrich and Sheilah Graham testified in print that Fitzgerald's penis was normal. Gingrich had seen it when Fitzgerald's bathrobe fell open ("Scott, Ernest and Whoever." *Esquire*, 66 [December 1966], 188); Graham was Fitzgerald's lover during the last years of his life (*The Real F. Scott Fitzgerald* [New York: Grosset & Dunlap, 1976], 120). This controversy is unprecedented in American literary history. The discussions of Henry James's putative groin injury do not require calipers.

†The identity of the barman and the accuracy of Hemingway's report have been questioned. Stephen Watts's *The Ritz of Paris* (London: Bodley Head, 1963) notes that Georges Scheuer was a thirteen-year-old pageboy under head barman Frank Meier when the bar opened in 1921 and succeeded Meier in 1947. Watts reports Scheuer's recollections of Fitzgerald: "It was he who introduced the newer, younger, less celebrated American writer, Hemingway, to the hotel. . . . He always sat in the same place, with his back to the light" (148–149).

But somehow I felt happier. Another spring—I would see Ernest whom I had launched, Gerald + Sarah who through my agency had been able to try the movies. At least life would be less drab; there would be parties with people who offered something, conversations with people with something to say. Later swimming and getting tanned and young and being near the sea.

It worked out beautifully didn't it. Gerald and Sarah didn't see us. Ernest and I met but it was a more irritable Ernest, apprehensively telling me his whereabouts lest I come in on them tight and endanger his lease. The discovery that half a dozen people were familiars there didn't help my self esteem. By the time we reached the beautiful Rivierra I had developed such an inferiority complex that I couldn't fase anyone unless I was tight. I worked there too, though, and the unusual combination exploded my lungs.

You were gone now—I scarcely remember you that summer. You were simply one of all the people who disliked me or were indifferent to me. I didn't like to think of you—You didn't need me and it was easier to talk to or rather at Madame Bellois and keep full of wine. I was grateful when you came with me to the Doctors one afternoon but after we'd been a week in Paris and I didn't try any more about living or dieing. Things were always the same. The appartments that were rotten, the maids that stank—the ballet before my eyes, spoiling a story to take the Troubetskoys to dinner, poisening a trip to Africa. You were going crazy and calling it genius—I was going to ruin and calling it anything that came to hand. And I think everyone far enough away to see us outside of our glib presentation of ourselves guessed at your almost meglomaniacal selfishness and my insane indulgence in drink. Toward the end nothing much mattered. The nearest I ever came to leaving you was when you told me you thot I was a fairy in the Rue Palatine but now whatever you said aroused a sort of detached pity for you. For all your superior observation and your harder intelligence I have a faculty of guessing right without evidence even with a certain wonder as to why and whence that mental short cut came. I wish the Beautiful and Damned had been a maturely written book because it was all true. We ruined ourselves—I have never honestly thought that we ruined each other.[5]

At about the same time, Zelda reviewed the deterioration of the marriage in a forty-two-page letter written to Fitzgerald from Prangins sanitarium in 1930. Describing the wretched Paris summers of 1928 and 1929, she blamed Fitzgerald's alcoholism and indicated her resentment of Hemingway's influence:

> We lived in the rue Vaugirard. You were constantly drunk. You didn't work and were dragged home at night by taxi-drivers when you came home at all. You said it was my fault for dancing all day. What was I to do? You got up for lunch. You made no advances toward me and complained that I was un-responsive. You were literally eternally drunk the whole summer. . . . You were angry when I wouldn't go with you to Mont Matre. You brought drunken under-graduates in to meals when you came home for them, and it made you angry that I didn't care any more. . . . We came back to rue Palantine and you, in a drunken stupor told me a lot of things that I only half understood: but I understood the dinner we had at Ernests'. Only I didn't understand that it mattered. You left me more and more alone, and though you complained that it was the apartment or the servants or me, you know the real reason you couldn't work was because you were always out half the night and you were sick and you drank constantly.[6]

In 1929, as in 1926, Fitzgerald was eager to preview Hemingway's novel in typescript; but Hemingway was reluctant to have him see it. Fitzgerald was allowed to read *A Farewell to Arms*—probably in June 1929—only after serialization had begun in the May issue of *Scribner's Magazine.* Fitzgerald again responded with a long document, which was stronger than the one he had prepared for *The Sun Also Rises.*

> 114–121 is slow + needs cutting*—it hasn't the incisiveness of other short portraits in this book or in yr. other books. The characters too numerous + too much nailed down by gags. <u>Please</u> cut! There's absolutely no psychological justification in introducing those singers—its not even

*Chapter 19 of *A Farewell to Arms:* The meeting with Meyers and his wife through the conversation with the opera singers and Ettore Moretti. This material is crossed out in Hemingway's typescript, perhaps indicating that he considered cutting it. These notes draw heavily upon Charles Mann's "F. Scott Fitzgerald's Critique of *A Farewell to Arms*," *Fitzgerald/Hemingway Annual 1976.* M.J.B.

bizarre—if he got stewed with them + in consequence thrown from hospital it would be O.K. At least reduce it to a sharp + self sufficient vignette. It's just rather gassy as it is, I think.

For example—your Englishman on the fishing trip in T.S.A.R. contributes to the tautness of waiting for Brett. You seem to have written this to try to "round out the picture of Milan during the war" during a less inspired moment.

(Arn't the Croats Orthodox Greeks?* or some Byzantine Christian Sect—Surely they're not predominantly Mohamedens + you can't say their not Christians.

122 ect. †

In "Cat in the rain" + in the story about "That's all we do isn't it, go + try new drinks ect," you were really listening to women—here youre only listening to youself, to your own mind beating our facily a sort of sense that isn't really interesting, Ernest, nor really much except a sort of literary exercise—it seems to me that this ought to be thoroughly cut, even re-written.

(Our poor old friendship probably won't survive this but there you are—better me than some nobody in the Literary Review that doesn't care about you + your future.)

P. 124 et sequitur§

This is definately dull—it's all right to say it was meant all the time + that a novel can't have the finesse of a short story but this has got to. This scene as it is seems to me a shame.

Later I was astonished to find it was only about 750 wds. which only goes to show the pace you set yourself up to that point. Its dull because the war goes further +

*Chapter 26: possibly a reference to the priest's statement, "The Austrians are Christians—except for the Bosnians." M.J.B.

†Chapter 19, pp. 134–135: Frederic and Catherine's conversation about the rain: "I'm afraid of the rain because sometimes I see me dead in it." The stories referred to the "Cat in the Rain" and "Hills Like White Elephants." Page references to *A Farewell to Arms* are keyed to the first edition (New York: Scribners, 1929). M.J.B.

§Chapter 20, pp. 136 ff.: the account of Frederic and Catherine's day at the races. M.J.B.

further out of sight every minute. "That's the way it was" is no answer—this triumphant proof that races were fixed!

—I should put it as 400 word beginning to Chap XXI

Still later Read by itself it has points, but coming on it in the novel I still believe its dull + slow

---

Seems to me a last echo of the war very faint when Catherine is dying and he's drinking beer in the Café.

Look over Switzerland and stuff for cutting

(i.e. 2nd page numbered 129)

129 (NW) Now here's a great scene*—your comedy used as part of you + not as mere roll-up-my-sleeves-+ pull-off a-tour-de-force as on pages 114–121

P. 130 †—

This is a comedy scene that really becomes offensive for you've trained everyone to read every word—now you make them read the word cooked (+ fucked would be as bad) one dozen times. It has ceased to become amusing by the 5th, for they're too packed, + yet the scene has possibilities. Reduced to five or six cooked it might have rhythm like the word "wops" in one of your early sketches. You're a little hypnotized by yourself here.

133–138§

This could stand a good cutting. Sometimes these conversations with her take on a naive quality that wouldn't please you in anyone else's work. Have you read Noel Coward?

Some of its wonderful—about brave man 1000 deaths ect. Couldn't you cut a little?

134‡

Remember the brave expectant illegitimate mother is an

*Chapter 22, pp. 152–155: Miss Van Campen's discovery of the empty bottles in Frederic Henry's hospital room. M.J.B.

†Chapter 21, pp. 142–143: Henry's report of the British major's analysis of the war. "Wops" refers to the "Chapter VIII" vignette of *In Our Time*. M.J.B.

§Chapter 21, pp. 146–151: The scene in which Catherine announces she is pregnant. M.J.B.

‡Chapter 21, p. 147: "I'm going to have a baby, darling." M.J.B.

old situation + has been exploited by all sorts of people you won't lower yourself to read—so be sure every line rings new + has some claim to being incarnated + inspired truth or you'll have the boys apon you with scorn.

By the way—that buying the pistol is a wonderful scene.*

Catherine is too glib, talks too much physically. In cutting their conversations cut some of her speeches rather than his. She is too glib—

I mean—you're seeing him in a sophisticated way as now you see yourself then—but you're still seeing her as you did in 1917 thru nineteen yr. old eyes. In consequence unless you make her a bit fatuous occasionally the contrast jars—either the writer is a simple fellow or she's Eleanora Duse disguised as a Red Cross nurse. In one moment you expect her to prophecy the 2nd battle of the Marne—as you probably did then. Where's that desperate, half-childish don't-make-me–think V.A.D. feeling you spoke to me about? It's there—here—but cut to it! Don't try to make her make sense—She probably didn't!

The book, by the way is between 80,000 + 100,000 wds—not 160,000 as you thought

P. 241† is one of the best pages you've ever written, I think

P 209— + 219§ I think if you use word cocksuckers here the book will be suppressed + confiscated within two days of publication.

All this retreat is marvellous the confusion ect.

The scene from 218‡ on is the best in recent fiction

*Chapter 23, pp. 158–159. M.J.B.

†Chapter 34, pp. 266–267: Frederic Henry's night soliloquy after his reunion with Catherine at Stresa—"If people bring so much courage to this world the world has to kill them to break them, so of course it kills them." Fitzgerald wrote in the margin of the typescript, "This is one of the most beautiful pages in all English literature." The note was erased, but is still readable. M.J.B.

§Chapter 30, pp. 228, 238. The word was replaced with dashes in print, M.J.B.

‡Chapter 30, pp. 237–241: Frederic Henry's arrest by the carabiniere and his escape. M.J.B.

I think 293–294* need cutting but perhaps not to be cut altogether.

Why not end the book with that wonderful paragraph on P. 241.† It is the most eloquent in the book + could end it rather gently + well.

A beautiful book it is![7]

Hemingway's annotation—"Kiss my ass EH"—indicates that he was less than pleased by Fitzgerald's critique, which came down hard on Catherine Barkley's glibness and criticized her "brave, expectant, illegitimate mother role" as stale. Hemingway subsequently became convinced that Fitzgerald's advice had been worthless. Writing to Arthur Mizener, Fitzgerald's first biographer, in 1951, Hemingway stated: "I have a letter in which he told me how to make A Farewell To Arms a successful book which included some fifty suggestions including eliminating the officer shooting the sergeant, and bringing in, actually and honestly to God, the U.S. Marines (Lt. Henry reads of their success at Belleau Woods while in the Cafe when Catherine is dying) at the end."[8] In 1953 Hemingway sent a report of Fitzgerald's memo to Charles Poore, who was editing *The Hemingway Reader,* stating that Fitzgerald wanted him to incorporate the news of the marines at Château-Thierry.[9] Fitzgerald may have made a suggestion about the marines in conversation; but it is not in his memo. Perkins also felt that Hemingway should reintroduce the war at the end of the novel to combine the themes of love and war. He wrote on 24 May: "Still, I can't shake off the feeling that war, which has deeply conditioned this love story—and does so still passively—should still do so actively and decisively."

Although Hemingway later insisted that he had rejected Fitzgerald's advice on *A Farewell to Arms,* he acted on the recommendation to cut Frederic Henry's cosmic ruminations at the opening of Chapter 40 (typescript pages 293–294):

We had a fine life; all the things we did were of no importance and the things we said were foolish and seem even more idiotic to write down but we were happy and I suppose wisdom and happiness do not go together, although

‡Opening of Chapter 40. This passage was cut by Hemingway. M.J.B.
§Chapter 34. M.J.B.

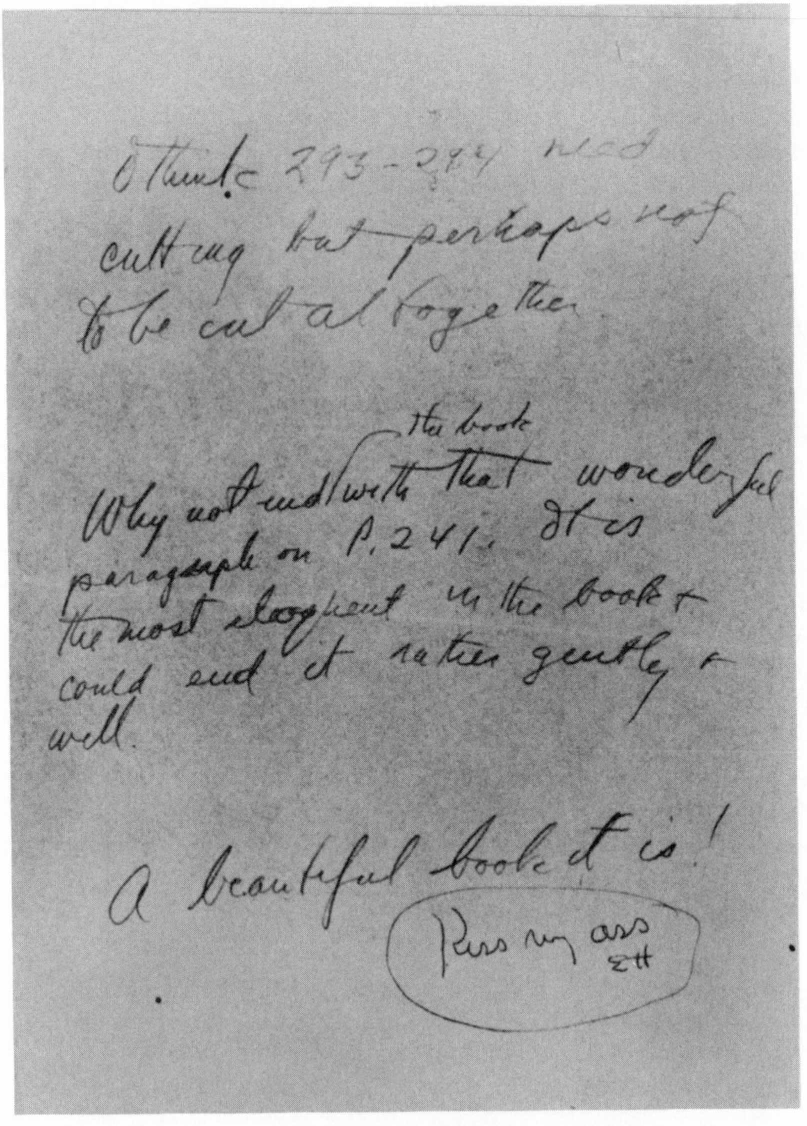

I think 293-294 need cutting but perhaps not to be cut altogether.

Why not end the book with that wonderful paragraph on P. 241. It is the most eloquent in the book & could end it rather gently & well.

A beautiful book it is!

Kiss my ass
EH

Hemingway's response to Fitzgerald's advice on A Farewell to Arms.
(*JOHN F. KENNEDY LIBRARY*)

⑥

FINCA VIGIA, SAN FRANCISCO DE PAULA, CUBA

in Chateau Thierry. This, Scott said, would make the American public understand the book better. He also did not like the scene in the old Hotel Cavour in Milano and wanted changes to be made in many other places "to make it more acceptable." Not one suggestion made sense or was useful (He never saw the Mss until it was completed as published) (this comes under being lonely when you have the point) I had learned not to show them to him a long time before. Will tell you about that some day; too long to write now when am trying to give you the gen you said you needed.

For Whom The Bell Tolls was written here and in Sun Valley Idaho then here. Scribner's files will show the dates.

As you know I was out of business as a writer except for 6 earlier pieces and the poems (where I tried to distill what I never knew if I would get to write) from early 1942 through 1945.

Letter to Charles Poore. (UNIVERSITY OF MARYLAND LIBRARY)

there is a wisdom in being a fool that we do not know much about and if happiness is an end sought by the wise it is no less an end if it comes without wisdom. It is as well to seize it as to seek it because you are liable to wear out the capacity for it in the seeking. To seek it through the kingdom of Heaven is a fine thing but you must give up this life first and if this life is all you have you might have remorse after giving it up and the kingdom of heaven might be a cold place in which to live with remorse. They say the only way you can keep a thing is to lose it and this may be true but I do not admire it. The only thing I know is that if you love anything enough they take it away from you. This may all be done in infinite wisdom but whoever does it is not my friend. I am afraid of God at night but I would have admired him more if he would have stopped the war or never let it start. Maybe he did stop it but whoever stopped it did not do it prettily. And if it is the Lord that giveth and the Lord that taketh away I do not admire him for taking Catherine away. He may have given me Catherine but who gave Rinaldi the syphillis at about the same time? The one thing I know is that I don't know anything about it. I see the wisdom of the priest at our mess who has always loved God and so is happy and I am sure that nothing will ever take God away from him. But how much is wisdom and how much is luck to be born that way? And what if you are not built that way? What if the things you love are perishable? All you know then is that they will perish. You will perish too and perhaps that is the answer; that those who love things that are immortal and believe in them are immortal themselves and live on with them while those that love things that die and believe in them die and are as dead as the things they love. If that were true it would be a fine gift and would even things up. But it probably is not true. All that we can be sure of is that we are born and that we will die and that everything we love will die too. The more things with life that we love the more things there are to die. So if we want to buy winning tickets we can go over on the side of immortality; and finally most of them do. But if you were born loving nothing and the warm milk of your mother's breast was never heaven and the first thing you loved was the side of a hill and the last thing was a woman and they took her away and you did not want another but only to have her; and she was gone; then you are not so well placed and it would have been better to have loved God from the start. But you did not love God. And it doesn't do any good to talk about it either. Nor to think about it.[10]

This windy passage weakens the conclusion of the novel by announcing Catherine's impending death and was omitted.

Fitzgerald was also unhappy with the original ending:

> There are a great many more details, starting with my first meeting with an undertaker, and all the business of burial in a foreign country and going on with the rest of my life—which has gone on and seems likely to go on for a long time.
>
> I could tell how Rinaldi was cured of the syphilis and lived to find that the technic learned in wartime surgery is not of much practical use in peace. I could tell how the priest in our mess lived to be a priest in Italy under Fascism. I could tell how Ettore became a Fascist and the part he took in that organization. I could tell how Piani got to

be a taxi-driver in New York and what sort of a singer Simmons became. Many things have happened. Everything blunts and the world keeps on. It never stops. It only stops for you. Some of it stops while you are still alive. The rest goes on and you go with it.

I could tell you what I have done since March, nineteen hundred and eighteen, when I walked that night in the rain back to the hotel where Catherine and I had lived and went

> upstairs to our room and undressed and slept finally, because I was so tired—to wake in the morning with the sun shining in the window; then suddenly to realize what had happened. I could tell you what has happened since then, but that is the end of the story.[11]

Hemingway tried out Fitzgerald's advice to replace this groping material with Frederic Henry's soliloquy from Chapter 34: "If people bring so much courage to this world the world has to kill them to break them, so of course it kills them. The world breaks every one and afterward many are strong at the broken places. But those that will not break it kills. It kills the very good and the very gentle and the very brave impartially. If you are none of these you can be sure it will kill you too but there will be no special hurry." Hemingway renumbered this page and inserted it in the typescript as the conclusion, but then restored it to its original position. Fitzgerald's admiration for this passage is attested by Morley Callaghan. When Callaghan expressed the reservation that it was perhaps " 'too deliberate,' " Fitzgerald was offended and began needling him about what it took to impress him. Finally he tried to stand on his head, asking if that would impress Callaghan.[12] After thirty-nine drafts, according to Hemingway, he wrote the much-admired understated ending: "After a while I went out and left the hospital and walked back to the hotel in the rain."

Callaghan's memoir reports Fitzgerald's analysis of Hemingway's marriages: " 'I have a theory that Ernest needs a new woman for each big book. There was one for the stories and *The Sun Also Rises.* Now there's Pauline. *A Farewell to Arms* is a big book. If there's another big book I think we'll find Ernest has another wife.' "[13]

June 1929 brought another strain on the vulnerable friendship between Fitzgerald and Hemingway, but the consequences were delayed. Hemingway had been boxing in Paris with Callaghan, whom he had known on the *Toronto Star.* Although Callaghan was four inches shorter than Hemingway, he had quick hands and was more than able to hold his own. Callaghan is one of the experienced boxers who have testified that Hemingway was clumsy in the ring. Fitzgerald knew about these boxing bouts and was eager to see them. Hemingway finally invited him to come along as timekeeper. Callaghan's account was published thirty-four years later in *That Summer in Paris:*

April 20, 1929 1883

From a photograph by Helen Breaker

The eagerly awaited New Novel by

ERNEST HEMINGWAY

"A FAREWELL TO ARMS"

begins in the

May SCRIBNER'S Magazine

A vivid love story woven into the texture of the debacle of Italian retreat. The sharp, direct, Hemingway style which distinguishes "The Sun Also Rises" and his stories in "Men Without Women," with an added power.

THREE GREAT STORIES NOW RUNNING IN SCRIBNER'S

An African Savage's Own Story — Mad Anthony Wayne — A Farewell to Arms

100,000 HOMES WILL "DOG-EAR" THIS MAY NUMBER OF THE NEW SCRIBNER'S MAGAZINE

(PUBLISHERS' WEEKLY)

On the way to the American Club in the taxi, it seemed to me that Scott and Ernest were at ease with each other. . . . Then Ernest had him take out his watch and gave him his instructions. A round was to be three minutes, then a minute for rest. As he took these instructions, listening carefully, Scott had none of Miró's air of high professionalism.* He was too enchanted at being there with us. Moving off the bench, he squatted down, a little smile on his face. "Time," he called.

Our first round was like most of the rounds we had fought that summer, with me shuffling around, and Ernest, familiar with my style, leading and chasing after me. No longer did he rush in with his old brisk confidence. Now he kept an eye on my left and he was harder to hit. . . .

"Time," Scott called promptly. When we sat down beside him, he was rather quiet, meditative, and I could tell by the expression on his face that he was mystified. He must have come there with some kind of picture of Ernest, the fighter, in his head. For Ernest and me it was just like any other day. We chatted and laughed. And it didn't seem to be important to us that Scott was there. He had made no comment that could bother us. He seemed to be content that he was there concentrating on the minute hand of his watch. "Time," he called.

Right at the beginning of that round Ernest got careless; he came in too fast, his left down, and he got smacked on the mouth. His lip began to bleed. It had often happened. It should have meant nothing to him. Hadn't he joked with Jimmy, the bartender, about always having me for a friend while I could make his lip bleed? Out of the corner of his eye he may have seen the shocked expression on Scott's face. Or the taste of blood in his mouth may have made him want to fight more savagely. He came lunging in, swinging more recklessly. As I circled around him, I kept jabbing at his bleeding mouth. I had to forget all about Scott, for Ernest had become rougher, his punching a little wilder than usual. His heavy punches, if they had landed, would have stunned me. I had to punch faster and harder myself to keep away from him. It bothered me that he was taking the punches on the face like a man telling himself he only needed to land one big punch himself.

*Spanish painter Joan Miró had served as timekeeper at a previous sparring session. M.J.B.

. . . I was wondering why I was tiring, for I hadn't been hit solidly. Then Ernest, wiping the blood from his mouth with his glove, and probably made careless with exasperation and embarrassment from having Scott there, came leaping in at me. Stepping in, I beat him to the punch. The timing must have been just right. I caught him on the jaw; spinning around he went down, sprawled out on his back.

If Ernest and I had been there alone I would have laughed. I was sure of my boxing friendship with him; in a sense I was sure of him, too. Ridiculous things had happened in that room. Hadn't he spat in my face?* And I felt no surprise seeing him flat on his back. Shaking his head a little to clear it, he rested a moment on his back. As he rose slowly, I expected him to curse, then laugh.

"Oh, my God!" Scott cried suddenly. When I looked at him, alarmed, he was shaking his head helplessly. "I let the round go four minutes," he said.

"Christ!" Ernest yelled. He got up. He was silent for a few seconds. Scott, staring at his watch, was mute and wondering. I wished I were miles away. "All right, Scott," Ernest said savagely, "If you want to see me getting the shit knocked out of me, just say so. Only don't say you made a mistake," and he stomped off to the shower room to wipe the blood from his mouth.

As I tried to grasp the meaning behind his fierce words I felt helpless with wonder, and nervous too; I seemed to be on the edge of some dark pit, and I could only stare blankly at Scott, who, as his eyes met mine, looked sick. Ernest had told me he had been avoiding Scott because Scott was a drunk and a nuisance and he didn't want to be bothered with him. It was plain now it wasn't the whole story. Lashing out with those bitter angry words, Ernest had practically shouted that he was aware Scott had some deep hidden animosity toward him. Shaken as I was, it flashed through my mind, Is the animosity in Scott, or is it really in Ernest? And why should it be in Ernest? Did Scott do something for him once? Is it that Scott helped him along and for months he's wanted to be free of him? Or does he think he knows something—knows Scott has to resent him? What is it? Not just that Scott's a drunk. I knew there was something else.

*Callaghan reports that when, on an earlier occasion, he cut Hemingway's mouth in boxing, Hemingway spat the blood at him, claiming that bullfighters did it to indicate their indifference to injury. M.J.B.

Then Scott came over to me, his face ashen, and he whispered, "Don't you see I got fascinated watching? I forgot all about the watch. My God, he thinks I did it on purpose. Why would I do it on purpose?"

"You wouldn't," I said, deeply moved, for he looked so stricken. For weeks he had been heaping his admiration of Ernest on me, his hero worship, and I knew of his eagerness for the companionship. Anyone who could say that he was under some secret and malevolent compulsion to let the round go on would have to say, too, that all men are twisted and no man knows what is in his heart. All I knew was that for weeks he had wanted to be here with us, and now that he was here it had brought him this.

"Look, Scott," I whispered. "If you did it on purpose you wouldn't have suddenly cried out that you had let the round go on. You didn't need to. You would have kept quiet. Ernest will see it himself." But Scott didn't answer. . . . The anguish in his face was the anguish of a man who felt that everything he had stood for when he had been at his best, had been belittled.

"Come on, Scott," I whispered. "Ernest didn't mean it. It's a thing I might have said myself. A guy gets sore and blurts out the first crazy thing that comes into his head."

"No, you heard him. He believes I did it on purpose," he whispered bitterly. "What can I do, Morley?"

"Don't do anything," I whispered. "Forget the whole thing. He'll want to forget it himself. You'll see."

He moved away from me as Ernest returned from the shower room. With his face washed, Ernest looked much calmer. He had probably done a lot of thinking, too. Yet he offered no retraction. For my part, I tried to ignore the whole incident. Since we had a good two or three minutes' rest to make up for the long round, why couldn't we go on now? I asked. It gave us something to do. Ernest and I squared off.

Scott, appearing alert and efficient, and hiding his terrible sense of insult and bitterness, called "Time." As I look back now I wonder why it didn't occur to me, as we began the round, that Ernest might try to kill me. But between us there was no hostility. The fact that I had been popping him, and then had clipped him and knocked him down, was part of our boxing. We went a good brisk round, both keeping out of trouble. When we clinched, my eye would wander to Scott, sitting there so white-faced. Poor Scott.

Morley Callaghan

> Then suddenly he made it worse. The corner of a wrestling mat stuck out from under the parallel bars, and when I half tripped on it and went down on one knee, Scott, to mollify Ernest, called out foolishly, but eagerly, "One knockdown to Ernest, one to Morley," and if I had been Ernest I think I would have snarled at him, no matter how good his intentions were.

The mood of the afternoon was changed when a stranger who had been watching the boxing offered Hemingway some advice and made himself foolish.

> The student's absurd intervention, adding to the general sense of humiliation, must have put Scott more on edge. He must have felt bewildered. Yet now my two friends began to behave splendidly. Not a word was said about the student. We were all suddenly polite, agreeable, friendly and talkative. I knew how Scott felt; he had told me. He felt bitter, insulted, disillusioned in the sense that he had been aware of an antagonism in Ernest. Only one thing could have saved him for Ernest. An apology. A restoration of respect, a lifting of the accusation. But Ernest had no

intention of apologizing. He obviously saw no reason why he should. So we all behaved splendidly. We struck up graceful camaraderie. Ernest was jovial with Scott. We were all jovial. We went out and walked up to the Falstaff. And no one watching us sitting at the bar could have imagined that Scott's pride had been shattered.[14]

On August 28, 1929, Hemingway sent Perkins a report of the bout, which differs from Callaghan's 1963 recollection.

> Did I ever write you about seeing Morley Callaghan in Paris—several times—he was working hard. You would not believe it to look at him but he is a *very* good boxer. I boxed with him 3 or 4 times. One time I had a date to box with him at 5 pm—lunched with Scott and John Bishop at Pruniers—ate Homard thermidor—all sorts of stuff—drank several bottles of white burgundy. Knew I would be asleep by 5—so went around with Scott to get Morley to box right away. I couldn't see him hardly—had a couple of whiskeys enroute. Scott was to keep time and we were to box 1 minute rounds with 2 minute rests on acct. of my condition. I knew I could go a minute at a time and went fast and used all my wind—then Morley commenced to pop me and cut my mouth, mushed up my face in general. I was pooped as could be and thought I had never known such a long round but couldn't ask about it or Morley would think I was quitting. Finally Scott called time. Said he was very sorry and ashamed and would I forgive him. He had let the round go three minutes and 45 seconds—so interested to see if I was going to hit the floor! We boxed 5 more rounds and I finally fought myself out of the alcohol and went all right. Can still feel with my tongue the big scar on my lower lip. He is fast, knows a lot and is a pleasure to box with. He can't hit hard—if he could he would have killed me. I slipped and went down once and lit on my arm and put my left shoulder out in that first round and it pulled a tendon so that it was pretty sore afterwards and did not get a chance to box again before we left. Morley had been boxing nearly every day in Toronto for a year. He is fat and looks in bad shape but is really darned good.
>
> What reminded me of this was how you could get rid of alcohol by exercise—after 5 rounds—during which I took a bad beating in the first. I was going well—judgment

> of distance good—in really good shape and out-pointing (or holding my own) with someone who had been beating me all over the place to sweat it out of me.

This letter does not express anger at Fitzgerald; the remark that he was "so interested to see if I was going to hit the floor" does not necessarily indicate that Fitzgerald deliberately prolonged the beating.

In 1951 Hemingway sent Mizener a detailed account claiming that Fitzgerald let the round go thirteen minutes—an eternity in the ring. Rounds in professional bouts are three minutes long.

> For your information the Callaghan thing was pretty bad. Scott, John Bishop and I had lunched at Pruniers and drunk a great deal of Sancerre. At the end of the lunch I remembered that I had promised to work out with Callaghan who was a good amateur boxer and promising writer but who could not hit a lick. I thought I could chance it anyway though ordinarily you do not box on a full stomach etc. John had an appointment and Scott went with me to our flat and then to the gym. We agreed on two minute rounds and at the end of the two minutes I was o.k. I figured on a minute's rest. Scott let the first round go *thirteen* minutes and Callaghan after about the fifth minute was hitting me freely and well for a period of some eight minutes. But he did me no harm and could not knock me down nor put me away. Scott liked the spectacle and was fascinated by it and I don't know why he ever called time at all. I was cut badly in the mouth and swallowed the blood.
>
> At the end of the round, which he had let go thirteen minutes, I said to Scott, "You son of a bitch."
>
> He said "What do you mean? I'm your greatest friend."
>
> I said "Did you like what you let happen to your best friend for eight full minutes when all you had to do was be honest and call time?"
>
> Callaghan had punched himself out on me and I did not have any difficulties with him in the other rounds. I am pretty sure I could have knocked him out. All of the Prunier lunch had been punched out of me and I felt good. Also I knew, *truly,* he couldn't hit. But I did not want to knock him out. He boxed well. He was a promiseing writer; and I liked him. Also no part of it was his fault. It meant a lot to him to knock me out and the only trouble was he could

not hit. I just was thankful to him for the regular exercise and I truly wished him well.[15]

For the time being the matter of the long round was dropped. Hemingway went to Spain for the bullfights; Fitzgerald went to the Riviera to work on his novel, now in its fourth year. Hemingway's torn July letter from Valencia does not refer to any of the strains of their Paris encounters.

We had a fin
down here v
Tarrogona. Am trying to write today and cant
this letter on the Pyramids.

Had a letter from Max dated June 20 enclosing a clipping about seizing the June issue of Scribenoff's Family Monthly in Boston—The Herald Tribune protested editorially against it saying they could find nothing obscene or lascivious and thanking the Police for calling their attention to it. Max sounded scared. If they get scared now and instead of using that publicity try and lay off the book I'll be out of luck. Haven't asked for an advance so far. I know I should because in the end it is more difficult to lay off a book if they have money tied up in it already. Max is such a damned fine fellow that I hate to act as I know I should act. Not that I think that they would lay off but there is always a

100 to 1

awfully hot here and am at
read all the papers) no news; except claims that I don't understand what I did.

Lost your address. So will send this
ough the bank. 11 bull fights start day after
tomorrow.

If you see Benchley's Parker—or Murphys give
them our love—

Have heard nothing from anybody—Everybody well
—wish the hell I could work—will try again now—

Best to Zelda—
Your affct. friend—
E. Cantwork Hemingstein.

This couldnt be a duller letter
but want to hear how you are and

hope your work and everything goes
well—
Address Hotel Regina
Valencia—
Spain
until Aug 3—Then Hotel Suizo
Santiago de Compostella
Spain[16]

Fitzgerald replied reassuringly about the threatened suppression of *A Farewell to Arms:*

12 Blvd. Eugene Gazagnaire
Cannes,
Aug 23d 1929

Dear Ernest:

I've been working like hell, better than for four years, + now am confident of getting old faithful off before the all-American teams are picked—hence the delay.

I wrote Max (not mentioning your letter) one of these don't-lose-your-head notes, though I, like you, never thot there was more than outside chance of his being forced to let you down. I felt sure that if it came to a crisis he'd threaten to resign + force their hand.

The book sticks with me, by the way; I'm sure it's all I thought at first + can't wait to read it in printing letters.

Its been gay here but we are, thank God, desperately unpopular + not invited anywhere. See the Murphys once a week or so—Gerald is older, less gay, more social, but not so changed as many people in five years. D. Parker is on the crest—tho I didn't see her as much as I'd liked.

Now—Ruth Goldbeck Voallammbbrrossa* not only had no intention of throwing you out in any case, but has even promised <u>on her own initiative</u> to speak to whoever it is—she knows her—has the place. She is a fine woman, I think one of the most attractive in evidence at this moment, in every sense, + is not deserving of that nervous bitterness.

Not knowing whether you've left Spain I'm sending this to Paris. Hoping you'll be here in Sept for a week or so.

*The Hemingways were subletting an apartment from Ruth Obre-Goldbeck-de Vallombrosa. M.J.B.

Bunny Wilson's book† has a fascinating portrait of Dos in it, + is full of good things, + to me interesting throughout. Oddly enough what it lacks is his old bogey form. It is shapeless as Wells at his wildest, or almost.

Have read nothing good recently save a book on the Leopold Loeb case + Harold Nicolson's Tennyson, neither recent.

This is a dull letter but it's late + what's left of the mind is tired.

Always Afftly Yrs

Scott

Best to Pauline.[17]

During the summer of 1929 Fitzgerald wrote "The Swimmers," a *Saturday Evening Post* story in which he obliquely commented on the term "lost generation" that had been given currency by *The Sun Also Rises.* Hemingway's novel had two epigraphs: one from *Ecclesiastes* describing the order of nature ("the earth abideth forever"); and one from Gertrude Stein ("You are all a lost generation"). Stein had reported to Hemingway this comment by a French garage owner about his young mechanic. The Stein statement was picked up by most readers as the key to *The Sun Also Rises.* It was generally assumed that the novel proclaimed the existence of a lost generation of war casualties—and that, moreover, Hemingway identified with them. Years later he corrected this impression, explaining that the Stein epigraph was intended by him ironically or sarcastically.[18] In *A Moveable Feast* he wrote, "But the hell with her lost-generation talk and all the dirty, easy labels."[19]

"The Swimmers" was an attempt to express Fitzgerald's feelings about the moral values of France and America, and it became a patriotic hymn. At the end of this story an American who is returning to France broods about the promises of America: "There is a lost generation in the saddle at the moment, but it seemed to him that the men coming on, the men of the war, were better; and all his old feeling that America was a bizarre accident, a sort of historical sport, had gone forever. The best of America was the best of the world."[20] Here Fitzgerald identifies as a lost generation those men who had been too old for the war, placing his hope in the idealistic younger men who had fought in the Great War.

Hemingway wrote from Madrid on September 4 urging Fitzgerald

†*I Thought of Daisy.* M.J.B.

to stick with his novel, repeating the charge that Fitzgerald had been constipated by Gilbert Seldes's review of *Gatsby:*

Madrid-Sept. 4
1929

Dear Scott—About that "nervous bitterness" You remember my blowing up about the people coming in to look at the Apt while I was working (I paid 3000 dollars on a promise to have it permanently and considered it our home) but you seem to have damned well forgot my coming around the next day to tell you that I thought Ruth Goldbeck Vallambrosa was a fine girl, had always admired her and told you for gods sake never to let her know that I had cursed about the apt. She did not know I was sore and the only way she would ever find out would be through you.

You said you understood perfectly and for me not to worry You would never mention it to her.

I'm damned glad you are going well. There is very small chance of our coming to the Riveria. There was some talk of Gerald and Sara coming here and we going back with them but a wire from Gerald yesterday says Sara has had to go to the mountains with Patrick and a letter following. Havent got the letter yet but believe their Spanish trip off. Would have been damned glad to see them. Havent spoken English to anyone since left Pamplona the 12th July except with Pauline. Havent even heard it. If they arent coming we will probably go north and see Bumby and Pat Bumby having good fishing in Brittany he writes.

I can't tell you how glad I am you are getting the book done. Fashionable thing is to deprecate all work and think the only thing is to go to pot gracefully and expensively but the poor bastards doing this giving up their writing etc. to compete with people who can do nothing and do nothing but go to pot.

Cant finish that Jeremiad without mentioning great friends and contemporaries—It sounds pretty bad anyway—Cant write that sort of tripe without a typewriter!

Of course all this may be premature and you may not be finishing your book but only putting me on the list of friends who receive the more glowing reports—

But I hope to God it's true. As far as I read it was better

than any thing I ever read except the best of Gatsby.* You know what part that is.

The good parts of a book may be only something a writer is lucky enough to overhear or it may be the wereck of his whole damn life—And one is as good as the other.

You could write such a damn fine book—What held you up and constipated you more than anything was that review of Seldes in the Dial—After that you became self conscious about it and knew you must write a Masterpiece. Nobody but Fairies ever writes Maspertieces or Masterpieces consciously—Anybody else can only write as well as they can going on the system that if this one when it's done isn't a Masterpiece maybe the next one will be. You'd have written two damned good books by now if it hadn't been for that Seldes review.

Of course there are other complications God knows but they are self made. They're not something that's done to you. Like using the juice to write for the Post and trying to write masterpieces with the dregs. But now if your using the juice and are desperate enough so you know you have to write one Seldes or No Seldes you will will write a damned fine book.

This should be enough from Jeremiah Hemingstein the great Jewish Prophet

If you want some news Dos is married And if you write a good and unsuperior letter with nothing about my nervous bitterness I'll write and tell you who he's married and all the dope.

On re-reading your letter I find it <u>Is not Snooty at all.</u> And old Hem wrong again.

Evidently a prey to his nervous bitterness! (This not sarcastic) But if I dont send this will never send any so throw out the N.B. in it (Son of a bitch if I have that!) and write care the Guaranty when your not too tired from work. I know how damned pooping it is and I'm gladder than I can ever let you know that it is going finely— Yours always affectionly

Ernest

Best to Zelda and Scotty from us.

Are you going to stay down in Cannes? How long. Might come down later when you get the book done.

*This sentence is the only evidence that Hemingway read the work in progress for Fitzgerald's novel. M.J.B.

Max is fine. He'd never let any body down and I never <worry about him>[21]

Hemingway's letter elicited Fitzgerald's September 9 reply, which is a mixture of the self-defense and the self-abnegation that would characterize much of his subsequent correspondence with Hemingway.

Villa Fleur des Bois
Cannes. Sept 9th 1929

Dear Ernest:

I'm glad you decided my letter wasn't snooty—it was merely hurried (incidently I thought you wanted a word said to Ruth G. if it came about naturally—I merely remarked that you'd be disappointed if you lost your apartment—never a word that you'd been exasperated.) But enough of pretty dismal matters—let us proceed to the really dismal ones. First tho let me say that from Perkins last your book like Pickwick has become a classic while still in serial form. Everything looks bright as day for it and I envy you like hell but would rather have it happen to you than to anyone else.

Just taken another chapter to typists + its left me in a terrible mood of depression as to whether its any good or not. In 2 ½ mos. I've been here I've written 20,000 words on it + one short story, which is suberb for me of late years. I've paid for it with the usual nervous depressions and such drinking manners as the lowest bistrop (bistrot?) boy would scorn. My latest tendency is to collapse about 11.00 and with the tears flowing from my eyes or the gin rising to their level and leaking over, + tell interested friends or aquaintances that I havn't a friend in the world and likewise care for nobody, generally including Zelda and often implying current company—after which the current company tend to become less current and I wake up in strange rooms in strange palaces. The rest of the time I stay alone working or trying to work or brooding or reading detective stories—and realizing that anyone in my state of mind who has in addition never been able to hold his tongue is pretty poor company. But when drunk I make them all pay and pay and pay.

Among them has been Dotty Parker. Naturally she having been in an equivalent state lacks patience—(this isn't

> snooty—no one likes to see people in moods of despair they themselves have survived. Incidently the Murphys have given their whole performance for her this summer and I think, tho she would be the last to admit it, she's had the time of her life.
>
> We're coming to Paris for 2 mos the 1st of October.
>
> Your analysis of my inability to get my serious work done is too kind in that it leaves out dissipation, but among acts of God it is possible that the 5 yrs between my leaving the army + finishing Gatsby 1919–1924 which included 3 novels, about 50 popular stories + a play + numerous articles + movies may have taken all I had to say too early, adding that all the time we were living at top speed in the gayest worlds we could find. This au fond is what really worries me—tho the trouble may be my inability to leave anything once started—I have worked for 2 months over a popular short story that was foredoomed to being torn up when completed. Perhaps the house will burn down with this ms + preferably me in it
>
> Always Your Stinking Old Friend
>
> Scott
>
> I have no possible right to send you this gloomy letter. Really if I didn't feel rather better with one thing or another I couldn't have written it. Here's a last flicker of the old cheap pride:—the Post now pay the old whore $4000. a screw. But now its because she's mastered the 40 positions—in her youth one was enough.[22]

Even though Fitzgerald had been unable to complete his novel, he was a productive writer. In his first decade as a professional (1919–1928) he published three novels, three volumes of stories, and a play. His short-story and article output in this period topped one hundred. That he squandered his talent on commercial short stories to make the money that he squandered is undeniable. Nonetheless, the stereotypical view of Fitzgerald as a writer who did not write is false. He was at least as productive as Hemingway. In his first decade as a nonjournalistic professional (1923–1932) Hemingway published two pamphlets, two novels, one book-length parody, two volumes of stories, and a nonfiction study of the bullfight; his total of published stories in this ten-year period was fourteen. The crucial difference was in the public images Fitzgerald and Hemingway projected. Hemingway radiated confidence and dedication. Everything he did seemed related to his work. Fitzgerald, who had an abysmal sense of literary public relations, became identified with dissipation and irresponsibility. As Hemingway recognized, at some point in the late 1920s, Fitzgerald seemed to relish failure. Perhaps it was a function of what Fitzgerald called his Puritan conscience developed in Minnesota to punish him for his failure to fulfill his ambitions. He knew how good he was: geniuses always know.

Hemingway replied in September with a warm and encouraging letter in which he assumes the role of the old pro:

> Dear Scott— Sept 13
>
> That terrible mood of depression of whether it's any good or not is what is known as The Artists Reward.
>
> I'll bet it's damned good—and when you get these crying drunks and start to tell them you have no friends for Christ's sake amend it—it'll be sad enough if you say no friends but Ernest the stinking serial king. You're not burned out and you know plenty to use— if you think your running out of dope Count on old Hem—I'll tell you all I know—whom slept with who and whom before or after whom was married—Anything you need to know—
>
> Summer's a discouraging time to work—you dont feel death coming on as the way it does in the fall when the boys really put pen to paper.
>
> Everybody loses all the bloom—we're not peaches—that doesnt mean you get rotten—a gun is better worn and with blue off—So is a saddle—People too by God. You lose everything that is fresh and everything that is easy and it always seems as though you could Never write—But you have more metier and you know more and when you get flashes of the old juice you get more results with them—
>
> Look how it is at the start—All juice and kick to the writer and cant convey anything to the reader—You use up the juice and the kick goes but you learn how to do it and the stuff when you are no longer young is better than the young stuff—
>
> You just have to go on when it is worst and most hopeless—There is only one thing to do with a novel and that is go straight on through to the end of the damn thing. I wish there was some way that your economic existence would depend on this novel or on novels rather than the damned stories Because that is one thing that drives you and gives you an outlet and excuse too—The damned stories—

Ah Hell. You have more stuff than anyone and you care more about it and for Christ sake just keep on and go through with it now and dont please write anything else until it's finished. It will be damned good—

(They never raise an old whore's price—She may know 850 positions—They cut her price all the same—So either you arent old or not a whore or both) The stories arent whoreing They're just bad judgement— You could have and can make enough to live on writing novels.

You damned fool. Go on and write the novel—

We drove here from Madrid in a day—Hendaye-Plage—Saw our noted contemporary L Bromfield. Going up to Paris—Have you heard from Max if the Farewell is out? Got a bunch of literary periodicals from Brommy—All full of Great German War Books—It was funny how I couldnt get into All Quiet etc but once in it it was damned good—Not so great as they think—But awfully good—L.Bromfield is writing a war book. It's bad luck may be that mine comes out now and after all that have not had opportunity to profit by them in writing it—In about 2-3 years a man should be able to write a pretty good war book.

Old Dos married Kate Smith—she went to school (college) (not convent) with Pauline—He met her down at Key West last winter—She's a damned nice girl—

We've had letters from Gerald and Sara. It's a damned shame about their Patrick being sick—I think he'll be all right.

Good day today—water nice to swim and the sun the last of summer—

If this is a dull shitty letter it is only because I felt so bad that you were feeling low—am so damned fond of you and whenever you try to tell anybody anything about working or "life" it is always bloody platitudes—

Pauline sends her love to you, Zelda and Scotty—

Yours always—
Ernest—[23]

Hemingway's statement that "You could have and can make enough to live on writing novels" does not recognize the circumstance that Fitzgerald's novels were not big sellers; *This Side of Paradise* sold 41,075 copies in 1920; *The Beautiful and Damned* sold 50,350 copies in 1922; *The Great Gatsby* sold some 23,000 copies in 1925. The total earnings from book sales for his three novels during 1920–1926 was $37,000—an average of $5,300 a year.

(3)

end of the damn thing. I wish there was some way that your economic existence would depend on this novel or on novels rather than the damned stories because that is one thing that drives you and gives you an outlet and an excuse too— The damned stories—

Oh Hell. You have more stuff than anyone and you care more about it and for Christ sake just keep on and go through with it now and dont please write anything else until its finished. It will be damned good—

(They never raise an old whore's price— She may know 850 positions— They cut her price all the same— So either you aren't old or not a whore or both) The stories aren't whoring. They're just bad judgement— you could have and can make enough to live on writing novels.

You damned fool. Go on and write the novel.

We drove here from Madrid in a day— Hendaye-Plage— Saw our noted contemporary L. Bromfield. Going up to Paris— Have you heard from Max if the Farewell is out?

The Fitzgeralds were spending $30,000 a year. Moreover, the eight-year interval between *Gatsby* and *Tender Is the Night* was not extraordinary; eight years elapsed between *A Farewell to Arms* and *To Have and Have Not,* but Hemingway's two nonfiction books intervened.

After serialization in *Scribner's Magazine, A Farewell to Arms* was published on September 27, 1929, and was an immediate success with readers and critics. In *The Nation* Clifton Fadiman hailed it as "a real occasion for patriotic rejoicing."[24] The first printing of 31,050 copies sold out promptly; two more printings were required in September, one in October, and three in November. By February 1930 more than 79,000 copies were in print—earning the author more than $30,000 in royalties. Fitzgerald's total income for 1929 was $32,448.18—of which $27,000 came from eight *Post* stories, and $31.71 from all his book sales.

In October Fitzgerald passed on to Hemingway a letter from Harold Ober, who had left the Reynolds agency to set up his own literary agency—taking Fitzgerald with him—explaining to Fitzgerald that Reynolds had tried to place Hemingway's stories without Ober's knowledge. Fitzgerald added a marginal note:

> As you'll see from this, while Ober was simply wondering if you wanted to use him Reynolds went ahead + constituted himself your agent, though as his only approach to you was through me, he was stepping forth. Of course this letter is nothing but Ober being sore and your work is financially safe with Reynolds as long as he doesn't go senile. I simply pass this on to show how the battle over your work increases in speed now that you don't need any help. In any case I shall step out here, not even answering this letter except in the vaguest terms I liked Cowly's review in Sun. Tribune. First intelligent one I've seen
>
> Scott[25]

Hemingway and Fitzgerald were both in Paris during the fall of 1929. Hemingway was no longer avoiding Fitzgerald, as shown by an undated torn note:

> Dear Scott—
>
> Sorry to miss you a<nd> not to have been home when you came around.
>
> When's the best time to get hold of you and have you a telephone?—

Have various things to ask you about but want to see you anyway—To hell with business. Hope everything is going well—

Yrs always—
Ernest—[26]

An undated Fitzgerald note survives from this time:

Dear Ernest:

Callaghan told me you had a Ford. Am anxious to know what you paid for it here with duty, transportation ect + amount of delay. Can you come in?

Scott Fitz

How about All Quiet on West Front
Have promised it.[27]

In October Hemingway relayed an invitation:

Dear Scott:—

Saw Gertrude Stein the other evening and she asked about you. She claims you are the one of all us guys with the most talent etc. and wants to see you again. Anyway she has written me a note asking me to ask you or youse if you would come around Wed. Eve. to her place—after 8.30 or so I fancy—Tate or Tates too—

A merchant named Bernard Fay or Benard Fairy to be there too.

Am going—Tate too—would you or youse like to call by here before 8.30 or then—if not Gertrude's address is

---

27 rue du Fleurus—But if you care we might go together—

By the way

Gallipoli Memories by Compton MacKenzie (yr. old school fellow) is damned good and the most amusing war book I've read since Repington—woudnt wonder if it wd go down with G. Moore's Hails and Farewells—

I'll be glad to buy it for you— There are to be 4 more volumes which is best news I've had in a long time——

Yrs always affect—
Ernest

No new news from Max What about yr. suit* against McCalls?[28]

On this occasion Stein generated a small crisis by declaring that Fitzgerald had stronger "flame" than Hemingway. It is not clear why Fitzgerald was troubled by Stein's praise, but he seems to have felt that she didn't mean it and was somehow belittling him or Hemingway or both. Hemingway sent Fitzgerald a four-page letter patiently explaining that Stein's compliment was sincere.

Friday morning

Dear Scott

Your note just came and am utilizing a good hangover to answer it.

I was not annoyed at anything you said (You surely know by now, I've written it often enough, how much I admire your work.) I was only annoyed at your refusal to accept the sincere compliment G. Stein was making to you and instead try and twist it into a slighting remark. She was praising her head off about you to me when you came up she started to repeat it and then at the end of the praise to spare you blushes and not be rude to me she said that our flames (sic) were maybe not the same—Then you brood on that—

It is O.K. to not accept the compliments if you dont wish (most compliments are horseshit) but there is no need for me to have to re-iterate that they were compliments not slights. I cross myself and swear to God that Gertrude Stein has never last night or any other time said anything to me about you but the highest praise. That is absolutely true. The fact that you do not value or accept it does not make it any less sincere.

As for comparison of our writings she was doing nothing of the kind—only saying that you had a hell of a roaring furnace of talent and I had a small one—implying I had to work a damn sight harder for results obtained—Then to avoid praising you to your face and pooping on me she said she wasnt saying the flame was of the same quality. If you would have pressed her she would have told you to

*Fitzgerald considered suing *McCall's* over a story commissioned by the magazine but then rejected. M.J.B.

a direct question that she believes yours a better quality than mine.

Naturally I do not agree with that—anymore than you would—any comparison of such a nonexistant thing as hypothetical "flames" being pure horseshit—and any comparison between you and me being tripe too—we started along entirely separate lines—would never have met except by accident and as writers have nothing in common except the desire to write well. So why make comparisons and talk about superiority—If you have to have feelings of superiority to me well and good as long as I do not have to have feelings of either superiority or inferiority to you.—There can be no such thing between serious writers—They are all in the same boat Competition within that boat—which is headed toward death—is as silly as deck sports are—The only competition is the original one of making the boat and that all takes place inside yourself—You're on the boat but you're getting touchy because you havent finished your novel—that's all—I understand it and you could be a hell of a lot more touchy and I wouldnt mind

This is all bloody rot to write in bed with a bad stomach and if you succeed in finding any slurs slights depreceations or insults in it the morning has been wasted (its wasted anyway) Gertrude wanted to organize a hare and tortoise race and picked me to tortoise and you to hare and naturally, like a modest man and a classicist, you wanted to be the tortoise—all right Tortoise all you want—It's all tripe any way—

I like to have Gertrude bawl me out because it keeps one opinion of oneself down—way down—She liked the book very much, she said—But what I wanted to hear about was what she didnt like and why—She thinks the parts that fail are where I remember visually rather than make up—That was nothing very new—I expected to hear it was all tripe—Would prefer to hear that because it is such a swell spur to work.

Anyway here is page 4—will enclose Max's letter—

I'm damn sorry Bromfield started that rumor but it cant hurt Scribners when I nail it by staying with them—I'd be glad to write him a letter he could publish if he wanted—

Look what tripe everything is—In plain Talk I learned to write from you—In Town and Country from Joyce—in Chic Trib from Gertrude—not yet reported the authorities on Dos Passos, Pound, Homer, McAlmon Aldous Huxley and E.E. Cummings—Then you think I shouldnt worry when some one says I've no vitality—I dont worry—who has vitality in Paris?—People dont write with vitality—they write with their heads—when I'm in perfect shape don't feel like writing feel too good! G.S. never went with us to Schruns or Key West or Wyoming or any place where you get in shape—If she's never seen me in shape Why worry? When they bawl you out ride with the punches

Any way will write no more of this—I'm sorry you worried—You weren't unpleasant— Yours always affectionatly

Ernest[29]

The delayed reactions to the June Hemingway-Callaghan bout commenced in November 1929 when reports appeared in American newspapers. On the 24th Isabel M. Paterson's "Turns With a Bookworm" column in the *New York Herald Tribune* printed this incorrect, trouble-making item:

> In "The Denver Post" Caroline Bancroft tells an amusing story of a singular encounter between Ernest Hemingway and Morley Callaghan.*
>
> "One night at the Dome Callaghan's name was mentioned and Hemingway said: 'Oh, you can easily see he hasn't any practical background for his fight stories—shouldn't think he knew anything about boxing.'. . . Callaghan, hearing of it, challenged Hemingway. . . . After arranging for rounds and a considerable audience, they entered the arena. Not many seconds afterward Callaghan knocked Hemingway out cold. The amateur timekeeper was so excited he forgot to count and the deflated critic had to stagger up and finish the round. When last seen Callaghan was demanding a bout with Jim Tully, saying that he wants to take on all the rough boys of literature."[30]

Callaghan saw the article in Toronto and, hoping to undo the mischief before Hemingway heard about it, sent a correction to Paterson on the 26th of November. His letter was published in the *Trib* on the 8th of December.

*On December 9, 1929, Caroline Bancroft informed Callaghan that her source for the boxing story was Virginia Hersch, who heard it in Paris. M.J.B.

> Last Saturday I saw the story of the "singular encounter" between Ernest Hemingway and me, taken from the "Denver Post." It is a fine story, and you can imagine how much I regret not deserving such a reputation, but this ought to be said:
>
> Hemingway, as far as I know, never sat at the Dome last summer.
>
> Certainly he never sat there panning my fight stories and whatever background I might have for them.
>
> I have only written one fight story anyway. I'll have to do some more at once.
>
> Nor did I ever challenge Hemingway.
>
> Eight or nine times we went boxing last summer trying to work up a sweat, and an increased eagerness for an extra glass of beer afterwards. We never had an audience.
>
> Nor did I ever knock out Hemingway. Once we had a timekeeper. If there was any kind of a remarkable performance that afternoon the time keeper deserves the applause.
>
> Being of a peaceful and shy disposition I have only envy for strong men who challenge each other and then knock each other out. But I do wish you'd correct that story or I'll never be able to go to New York again for fear of getting knocked about.[31]

Callaghan had a clear understanding of how Hemingway would react to any public disparagement of his boxing reputation. He observed in *That Summer in Paris:*

> I had discovered that Ernest's attitude to his boxing was related to the source of his power as an imaginative writer. His imaginative work had such a literal touch that a whole generation came to believe he was only telling what he, himself, had seen happen, or what had actually happened to him. His readers made him his own hero.[32]

Apart from Hemingway's concern for maintaining his heroic status, he reacted so strongly to the ridicule of his fighting prowess because *craft*—the ability to do things properly in order to derive maximum meaning from them—was integral to his work. If his physical skills were maligned, his creative powers could be damaged. For Hemingway there was a necessary connection between personal conduct and literary work.

Callaghan tried to control the damage by sending a copy of his *Trib* letter to Perkins on December 6, explaining that he hadn't sent it to Perkins before because he knew Perkins would see it when the *Trib* printed it. But now Callaghan was angry because he had just received a cable from Fitzgerald that placed the onus of the story on him. Callaghan said the story had been current in New York before he left Paris and that he told only three people in Paris about boxing with Hemingway.* He never spoke to anyone from the *Denver Post.* Callaghan asked Perkins to tell Hemingway that the story did not come from him. Callaghan did not write directly to Hemingway. Perkins replied on December 9: "I won't write to Ernest unless he sometime raises the point, because I think that would be a mistake;—but I shall write Scott and through him it will get to Ernest."[33]

Before his letter was printed in the *Trib,* Callaghan received a collect cable from Paris: HAVE SEEN STORY IN HERALD TRIBUNE. ERNEST AND I AWAIT YOUR CORRECTION. SCOTT FITZGERALD.[34] Callaghan did not know that Hemingway had pressured Fitzgerald to send the cable, and he reacted with an angry letter to Fitzgerald: "I told him it had been unnecessary for him to rush in to defend Ernest. For him to hurry out and send that cable to me collect without waiting to see what I would do was the act of a son of a bitch and I could only assume that he was drunk as usual when he sent it."[35]

This matter might have been defused if the parties had not been communicating by transatlantic ship mail. The bad feeling was aggravated by Hemingway's anger at Callaghan for repeating Robert McAlmon's gossip about the putative homosexuality of Fitzgerald and Hemingway. McAlmon was bisexual and had a malicious mouth. In October 1929 Perkins had informed Fitzgerald that McAlmon was in New York slandering Hemingway "both as a man and as a writer." Fitzgerald explained to Perkins on November 15: "Part of his quarrel with Ernest some years ago was because he assured Ernest that I was a fairy—God knows he shows more creative imagination

*Allen Tate was in Paris at the time; his later recollection of the events surrounding the Callaghan-Hemingway bout demonstrates how difficult it is to establish the truth about virtually everything involving Hemingway and Fitzgerald: "In a few seconds Ernest was lying flat on his back. Callaghan had knocked him out. Callaghan rushed straight to the shower, put on his clothes, and rushed to the nearest poste et telegraphe and sent a cable to his publisher: 'Just knocked out Ernest Hemingway.' Well, Ernest made Scott cable Max Perkins at Scribners denying the whole thing. Scott went on a drunk that lasted three weeks. He'd come around and say, 'What a son of a bitch I was to tell that lie' " ("Interview With Allen Tate," *Fitzgerald/Hemingway Annual 1974*). No such cables from Callaghan or Fitzgerald to Perkins exist.

in his malice than in his work. Next he told Callaghan that Ernest was a fairy.'' On December 10 Hemingway wrote to Perkins:

> Scott came to dinner last night and while drunk told me he had heard from you that McAlmon had told you various stories about me. He also told me a particularly filthy story Morley Callaghan had told him about me. Morley had gotten it from McAlmon.
>
> So I write to ask if McAlmon has any new stories— His stories that I am familiar with are (1) That Pauline is a lesbian (2) That I am a homosexual (3) That I used to beat Hadley and as a result of one of these beatings Bumby was born prematurely.
>
> Did he tell you these or did he have new ones? I'd appreciate not a general but a particular answer.
>
> Morley, it seems, asked Scott on meeting him if he knew it were true that I was a homo-sexual. He had just gotten the news from McAlmon! He may therefore be counted on to have spread it fairly thoroughly. He seems also to be having a great deal of success with a story about how I sneered at his boxing ability, he challenged me and knocked me cold.
>
> I sent McAlmon with a letter to you because I have tried to help materially everyone I know who is writing whether a friend or an enemy. Have tried especially to help people I did not like since my judgment might be warped in favor of my friends and hate to see people bitter about never having had a chance even though I may feel sure personally there is good and abundant cause for their failure. I do not try to get them published That's your business not mine. But to obtain them an extra-fair presentation to the publisher.
>
> But this has gone a little too far. There should be a limit to what lies people are allowed to tell under jealousies.
>
> I did not know until last night that Callaghan was definitely in that class. It is all pretty disgusting. Pauline says it is my own fault for having had anything to do with such swine. She is right enough. There will be a certain satisfaction in beating up Callaghan because of his boasting and because he is a good enough boxer. There is none in beating up McAlmon. I would have done it years ago if he wasnt so pitiful. But I will go through with it as I should have long ago because the only thing such people fear is physical correction. They have no moral feelings to hurt.

> I have, as far as I know, only one other—perhaps two other "enemies," that is people willfully seeking to do you harm through malice. One in a very minor way would seem to be Isabel Patterson whom I've never even seen and the other is a Russian Jew with a name like Lipschitzky who calls himself Pierre Loving and lies about everyone. He is a disappointed writer.
>
> Scott is the soul of honor when sober and completely irresponsible when drunk. If it's all the same I would rather you wrote me when you hear stories about me—not Scott. Please do not reproach Scott with a breach of confidence as he is absolutely incapable of such a thing sober and drunk he is no more responsible than an insane man. He did not say you had written him any definite stories—but told me stories he had heard from Callaghan as a type of thing McAlmon had probably told you.
>
> I had to sit, drinking Vichy, cold sober, and listen to an hour or more of that sort of thing last night. When McAlmon told one of those stories in the presence of Evan Shipman—Evan called him a liar and hit him. When McAlmon called Scott a homosexual to me (It is one of his manias) I told him he was a liar and a damn fool. It was not until after he had left for N.Y. that I heard the story he was telling about Pauline. Frankly I think he is crazy. Callaghan has no such excuse. He is a cheap, small town gossip anxious to believe and retail any filth no matter how improbable.
>
> ....
>
> This is nothing—I was starting to make a reflexion about people waiting 6 mo. to tell you when drunk some filthy story about you which they apparently never challenged physically or in any way but realized that since last night I have reflected entirely too damned much—

Fitzgerald came to think that McAlmon's gossip about him and Hemingway contributed to the destruction of their friendship. He observed in his *Notebooks:* "I really loved him, but of course it wore out like a love affair. The fairies have spoiled all that" (Appendix #62). Hemingway is not mentioned, but the reference is clear.

McAlmon's gossip led to punitive action by Hemingway, as recorded in a letter by James Charters (Jimmy the Barman), a popular Paris figure:

As I got within a few steps of the entrance to the bar I recognized Ernest Hemingway from behind. Hemingway didn't see or hear me behind him. He was also with another gentleman, whose face I didn't see. Well now only about three feet away and on a line with Hemingway and his friend was Bob McAlmon. All three making for my bar. Suddenly before I could do anything, Hemingway sent across a lightning right swing to Bob McAlmons chin saying at the same time. *Now tell that to your God-damn friends!* which I distinctly heard. Though Bob didn't fall with the blow for the wall of the bar in the street protected him he began bleeding from a cut from the lower part of his mouth and chin. Then as Hemingway and his friend moved into the bar I at the same time rushed over to Bob to help him into the bar where I got the proprietors wife to wash and bathe the wound and give him a clean handkerchief to hold to his face until the cut dried. Well it was a most embarrassing situation I'd been in for some time. Bob McAlmon as he received the unexpected blow, and without saying anything, looked straight at me very appealingly. At the same time Hemingway not expecting me to have shown up and saw what happened gazed at me rather surprised and somewhat embarrassed. He didn't speak either. Though I got both his and Bob McAlmons message from the expressions on each of their faces. Silence appeared to be the general key-note. I myself couldn't possibly take sides as they were both very good clients, and friends of mine. I really had to be at my most tactful best right to the end of that unfortunate affaire. Inside as Bob stood by the bar holding the new handkerchief to his face, everyone there appeared on edge. First all eyes where on Bob McAlmon, then onto Hemingway, and his friend, who were sitting at a small round table by the entrance. I'd already served them a scotch each with Ernest whispered to me to bring along. However after getting Bob to drink a good shot of brandy he seemed to feel, and looked much better I then asked him if he would like to go home to his hotel for the night and should I get him a taxi. He said yes. So when the taxi arrived Bob gave me his address to give the driver. At the same time I mentioned here to the driver that his passenger had just had an accident, and so would he please see him safely home. With that I bid both Bob and the driver good night, and returned to the bar. Just then Hemingway made a sign in mime for two more Scotchs. Well now I recognized

Hemingway's friend but pretended not to have done. For as we hadn't seen each other since the early 20s at the Dingo both he and Hemingway were hoping I didn't recognize him. It was Scott Fitzgerald. Fitzgerald kept silent all the way through at least within my close hearing or anyone elses in the bar who might understand what was said I also was waiting for Hemingway to tell me who his friend was, but this happened never. Ernest ordered the drinks and paid for them, so I had no reason to go to Scott, except to serve him his drinks. I gathered that Hemingway by keeping down to a minimum what might become a barroom scandal involving several famous people if the news leaked out. Scott Fitzgerald was completely protected by remaining quiet, not getting involved, or taking sides. Hemingway began talking to me as I stood by his side. Never once did he bring up the trouble between him and Bob McAlmon, but switched to asking me if I liked and was satisfied with the introduction he wrote for the Paris memoires. (*This Must Be the Place*)[36]

Charters's letter—written in 1973—places this scene in a bar off the Boulevard du Montparnasse "around 1932-33." If so, Fitzgerald could not have been present because the Fitzgeralds left Europe permanently in September 1931; moreover, Jimmy's identification of Fitzgerald seems shaky. If it happened in 1933 (Hemingway's introduction to *This Must Be the Place* was sent from Africa in 1933), then Fitzgerald was not there. If Fitzgerald was there, then it happened before September 1931.

About the 11th of December 1929—before copies of the December 8 *Trib* reached France—Hemingway wrote Fitzgerald a five-page letter absolving him of all blame for his timekeeping blunder. This letter shows Hemingway in a favorable light, trying to save a friendship by admitting his own character flaws.

Thursday—

Dear Scott—Your letter didnt come until last night—They'd held it at the bank.

I know you are the soul of honor. I mean that.

If you remember I made no cracks about your time keeping until after you had told me over my objections for about the fourth time that you were going to deliberately quarrel with me. The first time I thought I had convinced you. You came back to it and I, and Pauline, thought we had convinced you again. On the 4th time after I had also heard how McAlmon, whom I'd given a letter of introduction to Perkins had lied about me, how Callaghan whom I'd always tried to aid had come to you with preposterous stories   I was getting sore.

You'll remember though that I did not, sore as I was about everything in general, accuse you of any such time juggling. I only asked you if you had let the round go on to see what would happen. I was so appalled at the idea of you saying that you were going to deliberately quarrel with me that I didnt know (and just having heard this vile stuff from McA and C. which I thought I should have heard a long time sooner, if I was to hear it, and it was to go so long unresented) where the hell I stood on anything.

Besides if you had let the round go on deliberately—which I know you did not—I would not have been sore. I knew when it had gone by the time agreed. It is something that is done habitually at amateur bouts often. When two boys are really socking each other around the time keeper gives them an extra ten, fifteen or thirty seconds—sometimes even a minute to see how things come out. You seemed so upset that I thought you had done this and regretted it—But the minute you said you had not I believed you implicitly.

You as I say are a man of the greatest honor. I am not, in boxing at least. When I boxed Jean Prevost here in Paris I proposed Bill Smith as time keeper   I was in bad shape and told Bill to call time (we were supposed to box 2 minute rounds) anytime he saw me in trouble. One of the rounds was barely 40 seconds long! Prevost just thought the time went awfully quickly. When I had him going Bill let the rounds go 2 minutes and over.

Having done such things myself you cannot expect me to control my reflexes about what is happening to me. But you can believe me when I say that I at once threw out any such idea and coming home told Pauline you had been interested and forgotten all about time.

You may remember too that I put no importance on the incident afterwards and was more pleased then anything. I remember telling it with pleasure at the Deux Magot, praising Morley and giving him all credit for knocking me around. I thought, then, he was a friend of mine. It was only when I read his lying boast that I became angry. Then, being sore, I was sore at your carelessness which had given him the opportunity to make such a boast.

I would never have asked you such a thing if you hadnt gotten me nearly cuckoo with this talk about deliberately quarreling with me.

Let me repeat again—I have not the slightest suspicion of you having been disingeinous—I believe you implicitly and did at the time.

I know how valuable your sense of honor is to you, as it is to any man, and I would not wound you in it for anything in the world. So please believe me.

As an alternating circumstance though, please look at the different way we each look at sport—you look on it as a gentleman and that is the way it should be. But look how it has been with me—

One of the first times I ever boxed—A fellow named Morty Hellnick—after the bell for the end of the round I dropped my hands. The minute I dropped my hands he hit me with a right swing full to the pit of the stomach. After the fight I was sick for nearly a week. The 2nd time I boxed him I was winning easily—he had lost the fight anyway. So he fouled me—deliberately—have never had such pain in my life—one ball swelled up nearly as big as a fist—That is the way boxing is—Look—in so called Friendly bouts—You are never trying to knock them out—yet you never know but that they will try to knock you out—You get the complete habit of suspicion—Boxing in the gym with a fellow he let his thumbs stick out beyond his gloves in the infighting—the thumb caught me in the left eye and I was blinded by it—He blinded, in his life, at least 4 other men. Never intentionally—just the by-product of a dirty trick—I mention this only to excuse my reflex of suspicion which I never carried over for a minute.

It was only when you were telling me, against all my arguments and telling you how fond I am of you, that you were going to break etc and that you had a need to smash me as a man, etc that I relapsed into the damn old animal suspecion.

But I apologize to you again, I believe you implicitly and I have always, and I only wish to God you didnt feel so bum when you drink. I know it's no damn fun

> but I know too everything will be fine when your book is done.
>
> Callaghan and McAlmon are a couple of shits and as Pauline says our mistake was in having anything to do with such people.
>
> Anyway every kind of luck to you—Did you know Harry Crosby who shot himself yest? He told me about the girl before he went to N Y. McLeishes introduced her to him. He was a hell of a good boy and I feel awfully bad today about him. One of my best friends died two weeks ago and I'll be damned if I'm going to lose you as a friend through some bloody squabble.
>
> Best to you always—
> yr affectionate friend
> Ernest.[37]

Perkins tried to restore peace among his three authors; in a letter to Fitzgerald that was not mailed until December 17, 1929:

> I am enclosing a letter I got from Callaghan, and a note which he sent to the Herald Tribune, and which was printed there. They will show you how things stand. The girl who started the story is one Caroline Bancroft. She wanders around Europe every year and picks up what she can in the way of gossip, and prints it in the Denver paper, and it spreads from there. Callaghan told me the whole story about boxing with Ernest, and the point he put the most emphasis on was your time-keeping. That impressed him a great deal. He did say that he knew he was more adept in boxing than Ernest, and that he had been practising for several years with fighters. He was all right about the whole matter. He is much better than he looks.

On January 1, 1930, Fitzgerald, having seen Callaghan's correction in the *Trib,* wrote to him in Toronto:

> I apologize unreservedly for having sent you that stupid and hasty telegram, and believe that you took pains to deny the story immediately. . . . As to your starting the rumour I never had the ghost of ANY suspicion. . . . I am sorry that the wording was, evidently, ambiguous, which was entirely unintentional. . . . I have suffered enough myself from these devastating personal scandals to know that the stories stick

> forever unless they are expunged from the record. . . . I have never suggested to anyone including Ernest that you possibly had anything to do directly or indirectly as to the rumour. . . . But I have done you a serious injustice in my impatience and will gladly make amends to anyone concerned, or to you in person on my return in February. . . .*

On the 4th of January 1930 Hemingway responded to the letter Callaghan had sent Fitzgerald early in December:

> *January 4 1929*
>
> Dear Morley—
>
> I traced the story and found that Pierre Loveing was responsible for putting it out both in Paris and N Y—found out where he lived and sent him this wire to his address, Waverley Place N Y C.—"Understand you saw Morley Callaghan knock me cold answer Guaranty Trust Paris—' I received no answer.
>
> Scott wired you that he was waiting amiably to read your correction of the story (telling you where the story appeared) *at my request and against his own good judgment.* I did not know whether you had ever seen the story and since over 3 weeks had elapsed since it was first published in N Y Post it was up to him to correct it as a witness if you had not seen it and already done so. He, Scott, assured me you would have seen it and did not want to send the wire, (which contained no insinuations against you. Since I had not seen the story in 3 weeks I had no way of being sure you had seen it.
>
> It is, however *entirely my fault* that the wire calling your attention to the story was sent, and since some pretty tough words have been passed around apropos of who sent the wire I want you to know that it was in no way an idea of Scotts It was *entirely* my fault.
>
> If you wish to transfer to me the epithets you applied to Scott I will be in the States in a few weeks and and at your disposal any place where there is no publicity attached
>
> Yours always—
>
> Ernest Hemingway[38]

Callaghan replied that he couldn't transfer his remarks about Fitz-

*Excerpts from this letter were printed in David Mason's catalogue "*The Fight,*" Catalogue 63. The Callaghan correspondence was stolen from Mason's shop before he sold it.

gerald to Hemingway; since Hemingway had forced Fitzgerald to send the cable, Callaghan would require a new set of epithets for Hemingway.[39] Perkins, still acting as peacemaker, wrote Callaghan that Fitzgerald had tried to persuade Hemingway that the cable to Callaghan was unnecessary because Callaghan would promptly deny the false report. Perkins assured Callaghan that he had behaved like a gentleman. On the 17th of January Callaghan asked Perkins to send Caroline Bancroft's letter to either Fitzgerald or Hemingway. Fitzgerald's final communication about this vexed subject came on the twenty-first, when he wrote Perkins: "Thank you for the documents in the Callaghan case. I'd rather not discuss it except to say that I don't like him and that I wrote him a formal letter of apology. I never thought he started the rumor + never said nor implied such a thing to Ernest."

Hemingway wrote to Callaghan on February 21, 1930, from Key West admitting that he had overreacted and explaining that he had not intended to mail his January 4 letter—Pauline found it and mailed it while he was away. (This statement is supported by Hemingway's January 10 letter to Perkins, asking him to intercept a letter to Callaghan sent c/o Scribners.) Hemingway insisted that he could knock out Callaghan with small gloves, but suggested they call a truce.[40] Callaghan replied that he didn't think Hemingway could knock him out but that it was okay with him if Ernest believed it. He agreed to the armistice.[41] Callaghan never heard from Fitzgerald or Hemingway again. When in 1947 Samuel Putnam's *Paris Was Our Mistress* included an anecdote about how Hemingway beat up Callaghan for defeating him at tennis,[42] they both ignored it.

Around this time Hemingway provided advice for a trip to Spain Fitzgerald was considering as a respite for Zelda from the strain of her ballet training.

Friday

Dear Scott:

Your note just came. It's tough luck but there are no bullfights in Spain after end of November.

Climate in San Sebastian now on cloudy damp and drisly. Town deserted. Best medium luxe hotel damned good Hotel Biarritz—ARANA—More Moderate.

Pamplona, now cold, may be raining: rain comes from the sea:—or melting snow—nothing to do—

Hotels (1) Grand Deluxe deserted

(2) Quintana (The Montoya of Sun also pretty simple for your tastes perhaps.)

(3) La Perla—1/2 way between the two.

In winter Madrid is clear and cold—cold as hell—Hotel Savoy.

Where people go in Spain in winter for good climate is Tarrogona—Seville on the coast from Barcelona—Hotel de Paris—Lovely old Town on a hill above sea—

Malaga—further south—good climate—Hotel Regina—and Ronda—beautiful situation up on the RR from Gibraltar—lovely place—nothing much to do but beautiful and romantic where I would go for a honeymoon

for instance if had lots of money—Hotel
Maria Christina (maybe called Regina
Chiristina) Its neither its Reina Victoria—!
and the Hotel Royal.

P.S. I forgot to tell you to charge the wire to my account

Please forgive me. Glad you liked the book. Hope it (Graves) makes you glad.

If I can give you any dope let me know—But San Sebastian and Pamplona would be a hell of a disappointment to you in winter!

Ernest

PS

—continued from page 3

—You missed the war! It gives me a hell of a <   > for poor Siegfried Sassoon—Graves too!

Have read Lady Chatt—It didnt <   > me—[43]

The Fitzgeralds went to North Africa instead of Spain.

Chapter 6

1. 3 April 1929.
2. ALS, 2 pp. John Fitzgerald Kennedy Library.
3. Nancy Milford, *Zelda* (New York: Harper & Row, 1970), p. 153. Milford provides no source.
4. *That Summer in Paris* (New York: Coward-McCann, 1963), p. 207.
5. *A Life in Letters*, pp. 187–189.

6. *A Life in Letters*, pp. 189–195.
7. ALS, 10 pp. *A Life in Letters*, pp. 164–167.
8. 2 January 1951. University of Maryland Library.
9. 23 January 1953. University of Maryland Library.
10. Sheldon Norman Grebstein, *Hemingway's Craft* (Carbondale: Southern Illinios University Press, 1973), pp. 214–215.
11. *Ernest Hemingway: Critiques of Four Major Novels*, edited by Carlos Baker (New York: Scribners, 1962), p. 75.
12. *That Summer in Paris*, pp. 151–152.
13. *Ibid.*, p. 161.
14. *Ibid.*, pp. 212–219.
15. 4 January 1951. University of Maryland Library. *Selected Letters*, pp. 716–717.
16. ALS, 2 pp. Princeton University Library.
17. ALS, 2 pp. John Fitzgerald Kennedy Library.
18. Carlos Baker, *Hemingway: The Writer as Artist*, fourth edition (Princeton: Princeton University Press, 1972), p. 80.
19. Pp. 30–31.
20. *The Saturday Evening Post*, 202 (19 October 1929), 12–13, 150, 152, 154. *The Short Stories of F. Scott Fitzgerald*, edited by Bruccoli (NY: Scribners, 1989).
21. ALS, 6 pp. *Selected Letters*, pp. 304–306.
22. ALS, 2 pp. *A Life in Letters*, pp. 168–169.
23. ALS, 4 pp. *Selected Letters*, pp. 306–307.
24. "A Fine American Novel." *The Nation*, 129 (30 October 1929), 498.
25. ALS, 1 p. *Correspondence of F. Scott Fitzgerald*, pp. 230–231.
26. ALS, 1 p. Princeton University Library.
27. ALS, 1 p. John Fitzgerald Kennedy Library.
28. ALS, 3 pp. *Selected Letters*, pp. 308–309.
29. ALS, 4 pp. *Selected Letters*, pp. 309–311.
30. *New York Herald Tribune Books* (24 November 1929), 27.
31. P. 29.
32. P. 123.
33. The Callaghan-Perkins correspondence is in the Charles Scribner's Sons Archives, Princeton University Library.
34. *That Summer in Paris*, p. 243.
35. *Ibid.*, p. 244.
36. Jimmy Charters to MJB, 5 August 1973.
37. ALS, 5 pp. *Selected Letters*, pp. 312–314.

38. Princeton University Library. *Selected Letters*, pp. 318–319.
39. *That Summer in Paris*, p. 246.
40. *Ibid.*, pp. 248–250.
41. *Ibid.*, pp. 250–251.
42. (New York: Viking, 1947), pp. 130–131.
43. ALS, 4 pp. *Selected Letters*, pp. 319–320.

VII

In April 1930 Zelda Fitzgerald suffered a mental breakdown in Paris and was hospitalized in Switzerland until the fall of 1931, when the Fitzgeralds returned to America. There are no extant letters between Hemingway and Fitzgerald about Zelda's collapse. During his wife's hospitalization Fitzgerald's novel was again interrupted, as he wrote short stories to pay the substantial medical bills. Hemingway divided his time between Key West and Wyoming in the hot months, with trips to Spain to gather material for *Death in the Afternoon*. The first located letter in which Hemingway mentions Zelda's illness was written a year after her breakdown:

April 12—1931
Box 404
Key West—Fla.

Dear Scott:—

We're both terribly sorry that Zelda had such a rotten time and I would have written long ago. I hope to God she's getting along well now. And that you are too. I know you had hell. You have our deepest sympathy—

Outside of the arm* have been having a damned fine time and was going well on book until accident on Nov 1—Didnt write a line after that until this week—Feel in damned good shape now to go well—Nerve in arm has regenerated and paralysis all finished—

We come abroad in May—I'll be working all summer

*Hemingway's arm was broken in a car accident. M.J.B.

in Spain finishing book and will look forward like hell to seeing you—If youre still in Switzerland will come down there to see you in the fall—or we might take one of those topless motor trips—I havent kept up with Arland or any other of the boys and you could give me cultural synopsise of what the lads have be doing. My operatives in N.Y report you have become a grave, courageous and serious citizen—This all sounds like horseshit to me and have cut my operatives wage scale accordingly—Give my best to John Bishop when you see him or write him,—I would write him but can only write about 400 or so words still before arm poops out and am putting those 400 or so into reducing our national debt to Max—Will write him anyway—arm getting well fast—

Have you become a Communist like Bunny Wilson? In 1919 20-21 when we were all paid up Communists Bunny and all those guys thot it was all tripe—as indeed it proved to be—but suppose everybody has to go through some political or religious faith sooner or later—Personally would rather go through things sooner and get your disillusions behind you instead of ahead of you—

Ah Fitz but we are profound chaps—we word lads—

Enclose latest passport picture showing new alterations in pan caused by last summers defective horsemanship—

Best always to Zelda—tell her not to feel any worse than she can feel about dancing—She started it too late anyway—

You start it at 6 as in bull fighting to get well up in it—She wouldnt have wanted to start late and be the Sydney Franklin of the Ballet would she? You know us word merchants Fitz—always ready to give comforting advice to others while pewking with the other hand about our own troubles—

By Christ my only trouble now is to have pen and ink (pencil OK.) and paper and 3 mos. clear to write in—But imagine troubles will be furnished—

So long Scott and our best love to you both—

Ernest—(The Man who discovered
Curro Carillo)

How does your Ex-Marine write?

I'm sorry you had a trip to U.S. on such sad business—Hope to read your acct. of it between board covers—rather than in Post—Remember us writers have only one father

(BRUCCOLI COLLECTION)

and one mother to die— [*one and one-half lines deleted by EH*] But don't poop away such fine material—[1]

The photo Hemingway sent is probably the one inscribed "To Scott from his old bedfellow Richard Halliburton. Princeton 1931." Halliburton was a Princetonian whose travel-adventure books were very popular; he was also homosexual. The photo shows the well-dressed Hemingway in a double-breasted suit and striped tie—but not a Guards tie. There is no photo of Fitzgerald and Hemingway together.

Fitzgerald and Hemingway met in October 1931. Although the circumstances of the encounter are not known, it is stipulated on the chart of their meetings that Fitzgerald later prepared. At this time Fitzgerald and Hemingway began utilizing Perkins as a courier, relaying messages through him. Perkins tried to maintain the pretense that his two authors were still close friends, and his letters to each of them frequently included news about the other. The Fitzgeralds rented a house in Montgomery, Alabama, in the fall of 1931. In November-December Fitzgerald went alone to Hollywood to work on the screenplay for *Red-Headed Woman* at Metro-Goldwyn-Mayer. His screenplay was rejected; but he was paid $6,000, which he hoped would see him through his novel. On December 9 Hemingway wrote Perkins that he had not heard from Fitzgerald, except for a telegram from Hollywood recommending an agent to handle Hemingway's movie rights. Beginning in 1932, Fitzgerald's comments about Hemingway to Perkins manifested increasing guilt about his own work. In January 1932 he sent Perkins an optimistic progress report on his novel, adding: "Don't tell Ernest or anyone—let them think what they want—you're the only one whose ever consistently felt faith in me anyhow."

Fitzgerald's work plans were again changed when Zelda suffered a relapse in February 1932. She was placed at the Phipps Clinic of Johns Hopkins Hospital, and Fitzgerald rented La Paix outside Baltimore to be near her. At Phipps, Zelda Fitzgerald wrote her novel *Save Me the Waltz,* which Scribners published in 1932. In May Fitzgerald warned Perkins about Hemingway's possible resentment of Zelda's novel as competing with *Death in the Afternoon:*

> Now a second thing, more important than you think. You havn't been in the publishing business over twenty years without noticing the streaks of smallness in very large personalities. Ernest told me once he would "never publish a book in the same season with me", meaning it would lead to ill-feeling. I advise you, if he is in New York, (and always granting you like Zelda's book) *do not praise it, or even talk about it to him!* The finer the thing he has written, the more he'll expect your entire allegiance to it as this is

> one of the few pleasures, rich + full + new, he'll get out of it. I know this, + I think you do too + probably there's no use warning you. There is no possible conflict between the books but there has always been a subtle struggle between Ernest + Zelda, + any apposition might have curiously grave consequences-curious, that is, to un-jealous men like you and me.

In the summer of 1932 Perkins expressed to Hemingway the hope that Zelda could become a popular writer and take the financial pressure off Fitzgerald. Perkins and Fitzgerald had planned a tour of the Virginia Civil War battlefields and wanted Hemingway to come along. Fitzgerald hoped to join Perkins's next Key West fishing trip.[2] Hemingway did not come to Virginia, and Fitzgerald never got to Key West. On the 27th of July Hemingway wrote Perkins: "Poor old Scott. He should have swapped Zelda when she was at her craziest but still saleable back 5 or 6 years ago before she was diagnosed as nutty. He is the great tragedy of talent in our bloody generation." Later the same day Hemingway sent Perkins a note apologizing for his brutality about "poor Scott," explaining that the Fitzgerald marriage always made him bitter.

Death in the Afternoon, Hemingway's anatomy of tauromachy, was published on September 23, 1932. Hemingway sent Fitzgerald a copy inscribed: "To Scott with much affection Ernest."[3] The 10,300-copy first printing sold slowly. The Depression was blamed for the disappointing reception of this $3.50 volume, but it was not a book with much general appeal at the time. Bullfighting did not yet have an American following—although Hemingway would be largely responsible for subsequent American interest in the spectacle. Zelda Fitzgerald's novel *Save Me the Waltz* appeared on October 7 and fared less well. The 3,000-copy first printing did not sell out. Reviewers and readers were put off by her extravagant style, and the Fitzgeralds were no longer newsworthy enough to generate interest in a roman à clef about their marriage. Perkins sent Hemingway a copy of *Save Me the Waltz,* which he acknowledged on November 15, saying it was "completely and absolutely unreadable." He offered to give it to anyone Perkins thought "might be able to read it."

Fitzgerald worked effectively on his novel at La Paix in 1932 and 1933. After replacing the matricide plot with the story of Dick Diver, he had material that was close to him and made steady progress. The deterioration of the brilliant psychiatrist drew upon Fitzgerald's guilt

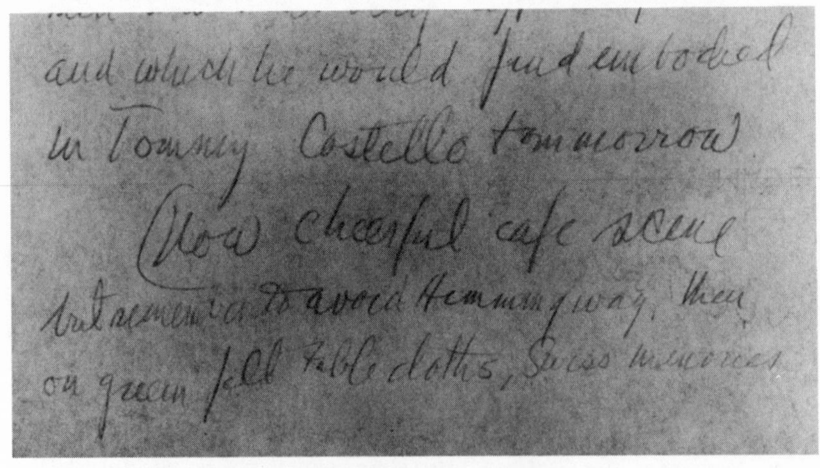
and which he would find embodied
in Tommy Costello tomorrow
(Now cheerful cafe scene
but remember to avoid Hemmingway, then
on green felt table cloths, Swiss memories

Fitzgerald's note to "avoid Hemingway" in Tender is the Night.
(PRINCETON UNIVERSITY LIBRARY)

about his own betrayal of his talent. While he was writing *Tender Is the Night,* Fitzgerald was keenly aware of Hemingway's techniques and made warning notes to himself in the manuscript: "Beware Ernest in this scene" and "Now a cheerful scene but remember to avoid Hemingway"[4]—referring to scenes that could have been written in clipped Hemingway dialogue.

The New York meeting between Fitzgerald and Hemingway in January 1933 was spoiled because Fitzgerald was on a bender. The occasion was a dinner with Edmund Wilson, at which Fitzgerald quarreled with both of them. Wilson recorded his memory of the evening:

> Scott with his head down on the table between us like the dormouse at the Mad Tea Party—lay down on floor, went to can and puked—alternately made us hold his hand and asked us whether we liked him and insulted us—told him he was a good writer—complimented him on story in *Mercury*, "Absolution," and asked him whether it was part of a novel, and he answered, None of your business. —Said at first he was looking for a woman—Hemingway said he was in no condition for a woman—then that he was done with men—perhaps he was really a fairy—Hemingway said they used to kid like that but not to overdo it. —Hemingway said, We'll have to be careful because some of the

best kids are so darn close to insults!—but he lectured him on his overhead—had to cut it down now, but he could have cut it down in Paris and had been so proud of his overhead! —Scott would say to me of Hemingway, Don't you think he's a strong personality? —At the Plaza, I stayed behind after Hemingway left, thinking Scott might open up, but he simply took off his coat, vest, pants, and shoes and put himself to bed and lay looking at me with his expressionless birdlike eyes. —I had asked him what he did in Baltimore—he replied truculently, The usual things! —I said I'd heard the theory advanced (by Dos Passos) that he was never really drunk but used the pretense of drunkenness as a screen to retire behind—this only made him worse if anything in order to prove that he was really drunk—though his answers to questions and remarks suggested he was in pretty good possession of his faculties. —Hemingway told him he oughtn't to let Zelda's psychoanalysis ball him up about himself—he was yellow if he didn't write. It was a good thing to publish a lousy book once in a while. —Hemingway sang a little Italian song about General Cadorna to the waiter. —Next morning Scott called me up and apologized for things he had said which might have wounded me and called Hemingway up and asked him to repeat something he'd said. —I remarked on the cold eye Scott had fixed me with when I'd first come in—he said, No confidence, eh? Well, you'll have to learn to take it? —He'd also said apropos of nothing, Shall I hit him?

When Scott was lying in the corner on the floor, Hemingway said, Scott thinks that his penis is too small. (John Bishop had told me this and said that Scott was in the habit of making this assertion to anybody he met—to the lady who sat next to him at dinner and who might be meeting him for the first time.) I explained to him, Hemingway continued, that it only seemed to him small because he looked at it from above. You have to look at it in a mirror. (I did not understand this.)[5]

Fitzgerald's *Notebook* includes his analysis of this reunion: "Very strong personalities must confine themselves in mutual conversation to very gentle subjects. Everything eventually transpired—but if they start at a high pitch as at the last meeting of Ernest, Bunny and me their meeting is spoiled. It does not matter who sets the theme or

The Fitzgeralds at the time Tender Is the Night *was published.*

what it is'' (see Appendix, 1277). Fitzgerald dutifully reported to Perkins on January 19:

> I was in New York for three days last week on a terrible bat. I was about to call you up when I completely collapsed and laid in bed for twenty-four hours groaning. Without a doubt the boy is getting too old for such tricks.* Ernest told me he concealed from you the fact that I was in such rotten shape. . . . Am going on the water-wagon from the first of February to the first of April but don't tell Ernest because he has long convinced himself that I am an incur-

*Fitzgerald had phoned Perkins. M.J.B.

> able alcoholic, due to the fact that we almost always meet on parties. I am *his* alcoholic just like Ring is mine and do not want to disillusion him, tho even Post stories must be done in a state of sobriety.

This 1933 meeting may have prompted Fitzgerald's *Notebook* entry: "I talk with the authority of failure—Ernest with the authority of success. We could never sit across the table again" (see Appendix, #1915). Hemingway's reaction to the reunion, expressed in January and February letters to Perkins, was that Fitzgerald could be saved only by the death of Zelda or an ailment that made it impossible for him to drink: "He's gone into that cheap irish love of defeat, betrayal of himself *etc.*" and "I dont know, frankly, whether Scott will ever come out of this thing or not. He seems so damned perverse about wanting to fail—it's that damned, bloody romanticism."[6]

Fitzgerald appears in Hemingway's "Homage to Switzerland," a minor story published by *Scribner's Magazine* in April 1933. An American tourist is teasing a waitress in a railroad station café:

> "Where did you learn your English?"
>
> "At the Berlitz school, sir."
>
> "Tell me about it," Johnson said. "Were the Berlitz undergraduates a wild lot? What about all this necking and petting? Were there many smoothies? Did you ever run into Scott Fitzgerald?"
>
> "Please?"
>
> "I mean were your college days the happiest days of your life? What sort of team did Berlitz have last fall?"[7]

The point of this Fitzgerald reference is to trivialize *This Side of Paradise* as well as Fitzgerald's devotion to Princeton. Hemingway resented the privileged educations of his Princeton-Yale-Harvard friends.

Fitzgerald remained loyal to, even protective of, Hemingway. When Gertrude Stein's *The Autobiography of Alice B. Toklas* was published in 1933 with belittling comments on Hemingway and praise of Fitzgerald, he was concerned and phoned Perkins to find out if Hemingway was upset.

From December 1933 to February 1934 Hemingway was on safari in Africa. *Tender Is the Night* was completed in the late fall of 1933 and began appearing serially in *Scribner's Magazine* with the January 1934 issue. In February Perkins predicted to Hemingway that Fitzgerald would be "completely reinstated" by *Tender;* after revision it would be "a masterpiece of its kind." Writing to Perkins about his novel, Fitzgerald observed in March:

> One time I had a talk with Ernest Hemingway, and I told him, against all the logic that was then current, that I was the tortoise and he was the hare, and that's the truth of the matter, that everything that I have ever attained has been through long and persistent struggle while it is Ernest who has a touch of genius which enables him to bring off extraordinary things with facility.

Tender Is the Night was published on April 12, 1934, in a first printing of 7,600 copies; it required two more small printings in 1934 and was dead on the shelves after 15,000 copies. It did not recover the money Fitzgerald had borrowed against it from Scribners. The critical reception was disappointing, and it has become a cliché that the socially conscious critics of the Thirties dismissed the novel because it dealt with wealthy American expatriates in the Twenties. Examination of the reviews does not support this interpretation. The reviewers were more troubled by the structure of the novel than by the material, finding the flashback plan distracting.[8]

Although their friendship had cooled, Fitzgerald would come up fighting for Hemingway. One night in April 1934 James Thurber was with Fitzgerald in a saloon on 52nd Street in New York, when Fitzgerald overheard two men "not unlike the Killers in Hemingway's story" disparaging Hemingway. He stood up and said to them, " 'I am Scott Fitzgerald.' " Before he could demand an apology, the men walked away. Fitzgerald was presumably sober at the time. In his account of that long drinking night, Thurber is alone in claiming that Fitzgerald held his liquor well.[9]

Hemingway wrote to Perkins on April 30 complaining that *Tender Is the Night* was emotionally unsound:

> Now about Scott's book. I finished it and it has all the brilliance and most of the defects he always has. In spite of marvellous places there is something wrong with it and, as a writer, this is what I believe is wrong. He starts with two people Gerald and Sara Murphy. He has the accent of their voices, their home, their looks marvellously. But he knows nothing about them. Sara Murphy is a lovely and a marvellously strong woman. Gerald is a man of great charm

but very complicated emotionally and Scott depicts his charm very well at various times. He knows *nothing* about him emotionally.

But he takes these people who are formed by certain things, suffer from certain faults, which he knows nothing of because when he was with them he was busy making them into romantic figures instead of knowing what they were about (you do not learn about people by asking them questions), creating these romantic figures and then asking them concrete questions such as 'did you sleep with your wife before you married her?' in order to obtain ''facts'' to insert in the plasticine of his figures to try to make them seem true—it's awfully silly.

But anyway he takes a strong woman like Sara, a regular pioneer mother, and first arbitrarily makes her into a psychopathic case then makes her into Zelda, then back into Sara, finally into nothing. It's bloody hopeless.

Gerald is Gerald for a while, then made-up, the made-up part is good, then becomes Scott and has things happen to him that could never happen to Gerald. The beating up by the carabiniere in Rome etc. So you are never convinced about him going to pieces.

He has taken a series of incidents, good incidents from his life and used them quite arbitrarily, made the story conform to the few wows he had saved up out of his life.

It isn't the way prose is written when the prose is any damned good—but then by Jesus he has so lousy much talent and he has suffered so without knowing why, has destroyed himself so and destroyed Zelda, though never as much as she has tried to destroy him, that out of this little children's, immature, misunderstood, whining for lost youth death-dance that they have been dragging into and out of insanity to the tune of, the guy all but makes a fine book, all but makes a splendid book.

But the hell of it is that you can't write Prose after you are thirty five unless you can think straight. And it is the flashes where he *does* think straight that carry this book in spite of all the worn christmas tree ornaments that are Scott's idea of literature.

The trouble is that he wouldn't learn his trade and he won't be honest. He is always the brilliant young gentleman writer, fallen gentleman writer, gent in the gutter, gent ruined, but never a man. If he is writing about a woman going crazy he has to take a woman who has gone crazy.

> He can't take one woman who would never go crazy and and make her go. [*marginal note*: In life she wouldnt go crazy. That's what makes it false] If he is writing about himself going to hell as a man and a writer he has to accept that and write about that. He can make it all up and imagine it all but he must imagine it truly. That is If he wants it to be literature. You can make up every word, thought, and action. But you must make them up truly. Not fake them to suit your convenience or to fit some remembered action. And you must know what things are about. He misunderstands everything. But he has this marvellous talent, this readability, and if he would write a good one now, making it all up, he could do it. But using actual stuff is the most difficult writing in the world to have good. Making it all up is the easiest and the best. But you have to know what things are about before you start and you have to have confidence. It is like navigating once you have dropped the shore out of sight astern. If you have confidence you are all right.
>
> But to have confidence you have to know your stuff.
>
> . . . .
>
> Dont show any of this above to Scott or tell him I said anything. I'll write him but have been too busy so far. . . .

Perkins replied on May 3 admitting that much of what Hemingway said about *Tender* was true but noted that "a great deal of the good writing he has done has come from that very fact of a sort of adolescent romanticism" and that all of Fitzgerald's troubles were based on his inner confusion and unreal ideas about fundamentals. Perkins didn't think that Fitzgerald's hopelessness was justified, but it was useless to try to talk to him about it. In an undated letter Hemingway admitted to Perkins that *Tender* was "*much* better" than he had said in his April 30 letter: "I was only seeking for the bad—The essential weakness that made you feel there was something wrong. I didnt give proper credit to the good part however, you knew its value as well as I did." Perkins replied in May that *Tender* had too much extraneous material Fitzgerald couldn't bear to cut. "I know of course, that there is that conflict in Scott's character and a kind of basic illusion which causes a defect in the book and did not cause one in 'The Great Gatsby' which was completely fitted to the illusion and the conflict," the editor observed.[10]

Fitzgerald was anxiously awaiting Hemingway's response to

Tender. A month after publication he sent Hemingway the first surviving letter between them since April 1931.

1307 Park Avenue,
Baltimore, Maryland,
May 10, 1934.

Dear Ernest:

Did you like the book? For God's sake drop me a line and tell me one way or another. You can't hurt my feelings. I just want to get a few intelligent slants at it to get some of the reviewers jargon out of my head.

Mr. Ernest Hemingway — Ever Your Friend
Key West Florida — Scott

All I meant about the editing was that if I'd been in Max's place I'd have urged you to hold the book for more material. It had neither the surprise of I.O.T (nessessessarily) nor its unity. And it did not have as large a proportion of 1st flight stories as M.W.W. I think in a "general presentation" way this could have been attoned for by sheer bulk. Take that opinion for what it's worth.

On the other hand: you can thank God you missed this publishing season! I am 5th best seller in the country + havn't broken 12,000[11]

Winner Take Nothing, Hemingway's third short-story collection, had been published in October 1933. Fitzgerald's previous comment on it has not been found. *Winner* was the least impressive of Hemingway's three story volumes, with only one major story—"A Clean, Well-Lighted Place." It included "The Gambler, the Nun, & the Radio" and weak stories like "The Mother of a Queen," "One Reader Writes," "Homage to Switzerland," and "A Day's Wait." Nonetheless, it had a first printing of 20,300 copies and outsold *Tender Is the Night.*

Hemingway sent Fitzgerald a harsh assessment of *Tender Is the Night* from Key West on May 29, 1934:

Box 406
Key West
May 28

Dear Scott:

I liked it and I didn't like it. It started off with that marvelous description of Sara and Gerald (goddamn it Dos took it with him so I can't refer to it. So if I make any mistakes–) Then you started fooling with them, making them comes from things they didn't come from, changing them into other people and you can't do that Scott. If you take real people and write about them you cannot give them other parents than they have (they are made by their parents and what happens to them) you cannot make them do anything they would not do. You can take you or me or Zelda or Pauline or Hadley or Sara or Gerald but you have to keep them the same and you can only make them do what they would do. You cant make one be another. Invention is the finest thing but you cannot invent anything that would not actually happen.

That is what we are supposed to do when we are at our

best—make it all up—but make it up so truly that later it will happen that way.

Goddamn it you took liberties with peoples pasts and futures that produced not people but damned marvellously faked case histories. You, who can write better than anybody can, who are so lousy with talent that you have to—the hell with it. Scott for gods sake write and write truly no matter who or what it hurts but do not make these silly compromises. You could write a fine book about Gerald and Sara for instance if you knew enough about them and they would not have any feeling, except passing, if it were true.

There were wonderful places and nobody else nor none of the boys can write a good one half as good reading as one that doesn't come out by you, but you cheated too damned much in this one. And you don't need to.

In the first place I've always claimed that you can't think. All right we'll admit you can think. But say you couldn't think; then you ought to write, invent, out of what you know and keep the people's antecedants straight. Second place a long time ago you stopped listening except to the answers to your own questions. That's what dries a writer up (we all dry up. That's no insult to you in person.) not listening. And we sprout again as grass does after rain when we listen. That is where it all comes from. Seeing, listening. You see well enough. But you stop listening.

[*written in left margin:* It's a lot better than I say But its not as good as you can do]

[*written in right margin:* You had good stuff in two that it didnt need]

You can't study Clausewitz in the field and economics and psychology and nothing else will do you any bloody good once you are writing. We are like lousy damned acrobats but we make some might fine jumps, bo, and they have all these other acrobats that won't jump.

For Christ sake write and don't worry about what the boys will say nor whether it will be a masterpiece nor what. I write one page of masterpiece to ninety one pages of shit. I try to put the shit in the wastebasket. You feel you have to publish crap to make money to live and let live. All write but if you write enough and as well as you can there will be the same amount of masterpiece material (as we say at Yale) You can't think well enough to sit down and write a deliberate masterpiece and if you could get rid of

Seldes and those guys that nearly ruined you and turn them out as well as you can and let the spectators yell when it is good and hoot when it is not you would be all right.

Forget your personal tragedy. We are all bitched from the start and you especially have to be hurt like hell before you can write seriously. But when you get the damned hurt use it—don't cheat with it. Be as faithful to it as a scientist—but don't think anything is of any importance because it happens to you or anyone belonging to you.

About this time I wouldn't blame you if you gave me a burst. Jesus its's marvellous to tell other people how to write, live, die etc.

I'd like to see you and talk about things with you sober. You were so damned stinking in N.Y. we didn't get anywhere. You see, Bo, you're not a tragic character. Neither am I. All we are is writers and what we should do is write. Of all people on earth you needed discipline in your work and instead you marry someone who is jealous of your work, wants to compete with you and ruins you. It's not as simple as that and I thought Zelda was crazy the first time I met her and you complicated it even more by being in love with her and, of course you're a rummy. But you're no more a rummy than Joyce is and most good writers are. But Scott good writers always come back. Always. You are twice as good now as you were at the time you think you were so marvellous. You know I never thought so much of Gatsby at the time. You can write twice as well now as you ever could. All you need to do is write truly and not care about what the fate of it is.

Go on and write.

[following paragraph written at bottom right margin and top of page three]

Anyway I'm damned fond of you and I'd like to have a chance to talk sometime. We had good times talking. Remember that Guy we went out to see dying in Neuilly? He was down here this winter. Damned nice guy Canby Chambers Saw a lot of Dos. He's in good shape now. And he was plenty sick this time last year. How is Scotty and Zelda? Pauline sends her love. We're all fine. Shes going up to Piggott for a couple of weeks with Patrick. Then bring Bumby back. We have a fine boat. Am going good on a very long story. Hard one to write

Always Your Friend

Ernest/

[*on back of envelope*] I didnt put in about the good parts. You know how good they are.
Youre write about the book of stories. I wanted to hold it for more. That last one I had in Cosmopolitan* would have made it.[12]

Though clearly hurt, Fitzgerald sent a calm reply.

1307 Park Avenue,
Baltimore, Maryland,
June 1, 1934.

Dear Ernest:

Your letter crossed, or almost crossed, one of mine which I am glad now I didn't send, because the old charming frankness of your letter cleared up the foggy atmosphere through which I felt it was difficult for us to talk any more.

Because I'm going egoist on you in a moment, I want to say that just exactly what you suggested, that the edition of that Chinamen-running story in the Cosmopolitan would have given Winner Take Nothing the weight that it needed was in my head too. Allow me one more criticism, that while I admire your use of purely abstract titles I do not think that one was a particularly fortunate choice.

Next to go to the mat with you on a couple of technical points. The reason I had written you a letter was that Dos dropped in in passing through and said you had brought up about my book what we talked about once in a cafe on the Avenue de Neuilly about composite characters. Now, I don't entirely dissent from the theory but I don't believe you can try to prove your point on such a case as Bunny using his own father as the sire of John Dos Passos, or in the case of this book that covers ground that you personally paced off about the same time I was doing it. In either of those cases how could you trust your own detachment? If you had never met any of the originals then your opinion would be more convincing.

Following this out a little farther, when does the proper and logical combination of events, cause and effect, etc, end and the field of imagination begin? Again you may be entirely right because I suppose you were applying the idea particularly to the handling of the creative faculty in one's mind rather than to the effect upon the stranger reading it.

*"One Trip Across," *Cosmopolitan* (April 1934). M.J.B.

Nevertheless, I am not sold on the subject, and especially to account for the big flaws of Tender on that ground doesn't convince me. Think of the case of the Renaissance artists, and of the Elizabethan dramatists, the first having to superimpose a medieval conception of science and archeology, etc. upon the bible story; and in the second, of Shakespeare's trying to interpret the results of his own observation of the life around him on the basis of Plutarch's Lives and Hollinshed's Chronicles. There you must admit that the feat of building a monument out of three kinds of marble was brought off. You can accuse me justly of not having the power to bring it off, but a theory that it can't be done is highly questionable. I make this point with such persistence because such a conception, if you stick to it, might limit your own choice of materials. The idea can be reduced simply to: You can't say accurately that composite characterization hurt my book, but that it only hurt it for you.

To take a case specifically, that of Gerald and Sara. I don't know how much you think you know about my relations with them over a long time, but from certain remarks that you let drop, such as one "Gerald threw you over," I guess that you didn't even know the beginning of our relations. In that case you hit on the exact opposite of the truth.

I think it is obvious that my respect for your artistic life is absolutely unqualified, that save for a few of the dead or dying old men you are the only man writing fiction in America that I look up to very much. There are pieces and paragraphs of your work that I read over and over—in fact, I stopped myself doing it for a year and a half because I was afraid that your particular rhythms were going to creep in on mine by process of infiltration. Perhaps you will recognize some of your remarks in Tender, but I did every damn thing I could to avoid that. (By the way, I didn't read the Wescott story of Villefranche sailors till I'd done my own version. Think that was the wisest course, for me anyhow, and got a pleasant letter from him in regard to the matter.)

To go back to my theme song, the second technical point that might be of interest to you concerns direct steals from an idea of yours, an idea of Conrad's and a few lines out of David-into-Fox-Garnett. The theory back of it I got from Conrad's preface to The Nigger, that the purpose of a work of fiction is to appeal to the lingering after-effects in the reader's mind as differing from, say, the purpose of oratory or philosophy which leave respectively leave people in a fighting or thoughtful mood. The second contribution to the burglary was your trying to work out some such theory in your troubles with the very end of A Farewell to Arms. I remember that your first draft—or at least the first one I saw—gave a sort of old-fashioned Alger book summary of the future lives of the characters: "The priest became a priest under Fascism," etc., and you may remember my suggestion to take a burst of eloquence from anywhere in the book that you could find it and tag off with that; you were against this idea because you felt that the true line of a work of fiction was to take a reader up to a high emotional pitch but then let him down or ease him off. You gave no aesthetic reason for this—nevertheless, you convinced me. The third piece of burglary contributing to the symposing was my admiration of the dying fall in the aforesaid Garnett's book and I imitated it as accurately as it is humanly decent in my own ending of Tender, telling the reader in the last pages that, after all, this is just a casual event, and trying to let him come to bat for me rather than going out to shake his nerves, whoop him up, then leaving him rather in a condition of a frustrated woman in bed. (Did that ever happen to you in your days with MacCallagan or McKisco,* Sweetie?)

Thanks again for your letter which was damned nice, and my absolute best wishes to all of you (by the way, where did you ever get the idea that I didn't like Pauline, or that I didn't like her as much as I should? Of all that time of life the only temperamental coolness that I ever felt toward any of the people we ran around with was toward Ada MacLeish, and even in that case it was never any more than that. I have honestly never gone in for hating. My temporary bitternesses toward people have all been ended by what Freud called an inferiority complex and Christ called "let him without sin—" I remember the day he said it. We were justlikethat then; we tossed up for who was going to go through with it—and he lost.

I am now asking only $5,000 for letters. Make out the check to Malcolm Republic, c/o The New Cowlick.†

Ever your friend,

Scott

*"MacCallagan" is a composite name for McAlmon and Callaghan. Albert McKisco's name in *Tender Is the Night* was a play on "McAlmon." M.J.B.

†Malcolm Cowley was an editor of *The New Republic*. M.J.B.

P.S. Did you ever see my piece about Ring in the New Cowlick*—I think you'd have liked it.
P.S.S. This letter and questions require no answers. You are "write" that I no longer listen, but my case histories seem to go in largely for the same magazines, and with simple people I get polite. But I listen to you and would like damn well to hear your voice again.[13]

This letter raises the question of possible cross-pollination between Fitzgerald and Hemingway. The places in their work that may indicate such an influence are rare. The series of "Yes" answers by Anson Hunter in "The Rich Boy," when he visits Paula and her husband, resemble Hemingway's dialogue; but the evidence is slender. Fitzgerald and Hemingway had developed their styles before they met; they were beyond imitation in 1925. Nevertheless, other forms of influence were possible. The specific aesthetic influence of Hemingway on *Tender* that Fitzgerald acknowledged in his letter was the theory about the function of the ending of a novel. Fitzgerald and Hemingway had concluded that a novel should not end on an emotional peak—a principle Fitzgerald found substantiated in the work of Joseph Conrad and David Garnett. Soon after *Tender* was published, Fitzgerald commented to H. L. Mencken about the reviewers' failure to understand the intention of the novel: ". . . the motif of the 'dying fall' was absolutely deliberate and did not come from any diminuition of vitality, but from a definite plan. That particular trick is one that Ernest Hemmingway and I worked out—probably from Conrad's preface to 'The Nigger'—and it has been the greatest 'credo' in my life, ever since I decided that I would rather be an artist than a careerist."[14] In 1936 Fitzgerald explained to John O'Hara:

—the only effect I ever had on Ernest was to get him in a receptive mood and say let's cut everything that goes before this. The the pieces got mislaid and he caould never find the part that I said to cut out. And so he published it without that and later we agreed that it was a very wise cut. This is not literally true and I don't want it established as part of the Hemingway Legend, but it's just about as far as one writer can go in helping another. Years later when Ernest was writing *Farewell to Arms* he was in doubt about the ending and marketed around to half a dozen peo-

*"Ring," *New Republic* (October 11, 1933). M.J.B.

> ple for their advice. I worked like hell on the idea and succeeded in evolving a philosophy in his mind utterly contrary to everything that he thought an ending should be and later convinced me that he was right and made me end *Tender Is the Night* on a fade away instead of a staccato.[15]

When Edmund Wilson was editing *The Crack-Up,* he showed Fitzgerald's carbon copy of this letter to Hemingway, who annotated it: "This is all nonsense. EH He is referring to my cutting the first paragraphs of a story called Fifty grand. It is a funny story which I would be glad to give you if you like EH."[16]

A year after publication of *Tender* Fitzgerald admitted to Perkins that Part III of his novel was not tightly organized: "If I had one more crack at it cold sober I believe it might have made a great difference. Even Ernest commented on sections that were needlessly included and as an artist he is as near as I know for a final reference."[17]

Chapter 7

1. ALS, 2 pp. *Selected Letters*, pp. 339–340.
2. 22 July 1932.
3. Harry Ransom Humanities Research Center, University of Texas, Austin.
4. *F. Scott Fitzgerald Manuscripts*, introduced and arranged by Bruccoli (New York: Garland, 1991): *Tender Is the Night: The Diver Version, Part 1*, Volume IVb, pp. 117, 142.
5. *The Thirties: From Notebooks and Diaries of the Period*, edited by Leon Edel (New York: Farrar, Straus and Giroux, 1980), pp. 301–303.
6. 23 February 1933 and c. late January 1933.
7. *Scribner's Magazine*, 93 (April 1933), 204–208. *The Complete Short Stories of Ernest Hemingway: The Finca Vigía Edition* (New York: Scribners, 1987), p. 325.
8. See Bruccoli, *The Composition of Tender Is the Night* (Pittsburgh: University of Pittsburgh Press, 1963), pp. 1–16.
9. " 'Scott in Thorns,' " *Credos and Curios* (New York: Harper & Row, 1962), p. 158.
10. 23 May 1934.
11. TLS with holograph postscript, 1 p. *A Life in Letters*, p. 259.

12. TLS with holograph additions, 3 pp. *Selected Letters*, pp. 407–409.
13. TLS, 6 pp. *A Life in Letters*, p. 262–264.
14. *A Life in Letters*, pp. 255–256.
15. *A Life in Letters*, pp. 302–304.
16. Yale University Library.
17. 11 March 1935. *A Life in Letters*, pp. 277–278.

VIII

In 1933 Arnold Gingrich, editor of the new publication *Esquire,* made a deal with Hemingway to pay him the magazine's top price of $250 each for a series of monthly articles to be called letters, in which he discussed personal topics. A passionate admirer of both Hemingway's and Fitzgerald's writing, Gingrich was pleased to add Fitzgerald to his roster of authors at $250 per contribution the next year. Fitzgerald's first *Esquire* appearance was "Show Mr. and Mrs. F. to Number——," a two-part retrospective article by-lined F. Scott and Zelda Fitzgerald in the May and June 1934 issues. During 1934–1936 eleven issues of *Esquire* had appearances by both Fitzgerald and Hemingway. The contrast was striking. Fitzgerald's best *Esquire* contributions were the confessional pieces. Hemingway provided letters about his hunting and fishing experiences, as well as two major stories—"The Snows of Kilimanjaro" and "The Capital of the World."

During the summer of 1934 Max Perkins was trying to expedite publication of Fitzgerald's fourth story collection, *Taps at Reveille,* which Fitzgerald was holding in order to remove the story passages that he had used in *Tender.* Perkins assured him that such repetition was permissible: "Hem has done it."[1] Fitzgerald replied firmly on August 24: "The fact that Ernest has let himself repeat here and there a phrase would be no possible justification for my doing the same. Each of us has his virtues and one of mine happens to be a great sense of exactitude about my work. He might be able to afford a lapse in that line where I wouldn't be and after all I have got to be the final judge of what is appropriate in these cases." *Taps* was published on March 20, 1935, in a printing of 5,000 copies—which satisfied the demand. The stories were largely retrospective, with seven of the Basil and Josephine stories about teenage characters; the collection also included two of Fitzgerald's best stories—"The Last of the Belles" and "Babylon Revisited."

After *Tender Is the Night* Fitzgerald projected a novel set in ninth-century France, an account of the attempts by young Philippe, Count of Villefranche, to reclaim his father's territory. The characterization of Philippe was based on Ernest Hemingway. Fitzgerald made this *Notebook* entry: "Just as Stendahl's portrait of a Byronic man made *Le Rouge et Noir* so couldn't *my* portrait of Ernest as Phillipe make the real modern man" (see Appendix, #1034). It was clear that *Tender* was not going to solve Fitzgerald's money problems, and his ability to write stories for *The Saturday Evening Post* was fading. His plan was to develop the Philippe material as a series of stories in *Redbook* for ready cash and then to revise the stories into a novel. The first story, "In the Darkest Hour," was published in October 1934. Three more Philippe stories were written, which *Redbook* bought with mounting reluctance; and Fitzgerald abandoned the project in 1935—at least for the time being. While he was working on them, Fitzgerald had a scare when he learned that Hemingway had a new book ready. On November 20, 1934, Fitzgerald wrote to Perkins: "I hope to God it isn't the crusading story that he once had in mind, for I would hate like hell for my 9th century novel to have to compete with *that.*" Hemingway's new book was *Green Hills of Africa.*

The medieval stories—Fitzgerald's only extended attempt at historical fiction—were bad and have been ignored. Fitzgerald later wrote Perkins: "You will remember that the plan in the beginning was tremendously ambitious—there was to have been Philippe as a young man founding his fortunes—Philippe as a middle-aged man participating in the Captian founding of France as a nation—Philippe as an old man and the consolidation of the feudal system. It was to have covered a span of about sixty years from 880 A.D. to 950."[2] In the first four stories twenty-year-old Philippe enters the Loire Valley, organizes the peasants, defeats a band of marauding Vikings, builds a stronghold, treats with the powers of Church and State, and enters into a compact with a witchcraft cult. He is determined, resourceful, and unbelievable. The most obvious difficulty was linguistic, as Fitzgerald tried to convey the speech of medieval French peasants by making them talk like American sharecroppers. Philippe uses a kind of hard-boiled slang that seems to derive from the pulp detective magazines. The effect is incongruous and unintentionally funny: " 'Call me "Sire!" . . . And re*mem*ber; There's no bedroom talk floating around this precinct!' "[3] Anyone who did not know that Philippe was modeled on Hemingway would not have been likely to make the identification. There is nothing to indicate that Hemingway recognized himself—or that he read the stories. Fitzgerald never really gave up on the medieval material; in 1939 when he was planning *The Love of the Last Tycoon* he was still considering whether it would be better to return to Philippe instead.

In May 1934, after his return from Africa, Hemingway acquired the *Pilar,* a thirty-eight-foot Wheeler cruiser, and began inviting friends to Key West for fishing trips. Arnold Gingrich was invited for December and proposed bringing Fitzgerald along. Hemingway agreed, but on December 3 Fitzgerald wired:

> DEAR ERNEST SEEMS IMPOSSIBLE TO GET DOWN THIS WEEK AND I CERTAINLY REGRET IT AND I APPRECIATE YOUR INVITATION HAD SO MANY THINGS TO TALK TO YOU ABOUT WITH BEST WISHES ALWAYS TO YOU AND YOURS=SCOTT.

Gingrich and Fitzgerald cooked up the excuse that his mother's illness prevented him from leaving Baltimore, but Fitzgerald was intimidated by the prospect of being with Hemingway in his Florida principality. He explained to Perkins: "Your suggestion to go to Key West is tempting as hell but I don't know whether it would be advisable on either Ernest's account or mine." Perkins was scheduled to go to Key West in January 1935 to read the typescript of *Green Hills of Africa.* He, too, asked permission to bring Fitzgerald. Hemingway replied on December 28, 1934, that he would like to see Fitzgerald after the revision of *Green Hills:*

> I do *not* believe I could do revising and rewriting which is, with me, an un-alcoholic business requiring absolutely complete attention with Scott there but I would love to see him once that is over.
>
> He was to come down with Gingrich and I spent a week getting ready for him. But his mother was ill. I would like to see him very much but it would be better *not* when we are discussing, seriously, treatment of a book or when I am finishing a book. His judgement about a book—cutting re-writing etc. is deplorable. It is always to make it like the

Perkins and Hemingway in Key West

> last considerable success. I will show you some time as a curiosity his suggestions to me on how to improve the type script of A Farewell to Arms which included writing in a flash where the hero reads about the victory of the U. S. Marines. He got this idea quite legitimately from a story I told him about hearing about the U. S. Marines while I was in Italy and not believing it but it was un-necessary in the book since the book was a work of fiction designed to stand without last minute shots of sure fire journalism. He also made many other suggestions none of which I used. Some were funny, some were sad, all were well meant.

Perkins reported to Hemingway in February 1935 that Fitzgerald was on the wagon and suggested that Hemingway might be able to encourage him to stay sober. From March through June Perkins sent

Hemingway bulletins announcing that Fitzgerald was still dry. Whether he did quit drinking altogether is questionable. Like most alcoholics, he defined being on the wagon in special ways; at this time it probably meant drinking only beer. In 1935 Fitzgerald became anxious about a recurrence of tuberculosis and began making trips to the mountain area around Asheville, North Carolina. After Zelda suffered her third breakdown, Fitzgerald placed her in the Highland Hospital at Asheville in April 1936 and moved to the Grove Park Inn.

The 1935–1937 period in Fitzgerald's life has become known as "the crack-up," from the *Esquire* essay he wrote about it. No longer able to produce the short stories that had brought $4,000 each from *The Saturday Evening Post,* he sank into debt, despair, and illness. His income came from an occasional sale to the slick magazines (which had cut his price), $250 checks from *Esquire* (which would take virtually anything he submitted), and advances from agent Harold Ober (which were really loans).

Hemingway's judgment of his work continued to matter to Fitzgerald. Perkins relayed a message from Hemingway on April 8, 1935: "A strange thing is that in retrospect his Tender Is the Night gets better and better. I wish you would tell him I said so." Fitzgerald responded to Perkins, "Thanks for the message from Ernest. I'd like to see him too and I always think of my friendship with him as being one of the high spots of my life. But I still believe that such things have a mortality, perhaps in reaction to their very excessive life, and that we will never again see very much of each other. I appreciate what he said about 'Tender is the Night.' "[4]

On May 13, 1935, Fitzgerald tried to arrange a reunion with Hemingway, indicating that he would be sober:

> WANT TO SEE YOU AS AM GOING TO CAROLINA FOR SUMMER COULD MAKE THREE DAY STAY KEYWEST ARRIVING THIS THURSDAY BUT WANT TO INTERFERE YOUR PLANS STOP NOT UP TO ANYTHING STRENUOUS PROBABLY RESULT OF TEATOTALING SINCE JANUARY WIRE THIRTEEN NAUGHT SEVEN PARK AVENUE BALTIMORE=SCOTT.

Pauline wired that Ernest was in Bimini.

Green Hills of Africa, Hemingway's nonfiction account of his safari, was published October 25, 1935, after serialization in *Scribner's Magazine.* The first printing of 10,550 copies sold slowly. The reviews were mixed, with several critics objecting to the irrelevance of the material to contemporary problems. In the *New Masses* Granville Hicks urged Hemingway to write a novel about a strike. Hemingway anticipated the response from the Left and had eloquently answered it in the book: "A country, finally, erodes and the dust blows away, the people all die and none of them were of any importance permanently, except those who practised the arts, and these now wish to cease their work because it is too lonely, too hard to do, and is not fashionable. A thousand years makes economics silly and a work of art endures forever, but it is very difficult to do and now it is not fashionable."[5] *Green Hills of Africa* includes an oblique reference to Fitzgerald. Discoursing on the ways American writers are destroyed, Hemingway notes that at present there are "two good writers who cannot write because they have lost confidence through reading critics. If they wrote, sometimes it would be good and sometimes not so good and sometimes it would be quite bad, but the good would get out. But they have read the critics and they must write masterpieces. The masterpieces the critics said they wrote. They weren't masterpieces, of course. They were just quite good books. So now they cannot write at all. The critics have made them impotent."[6] Those writers are not identified, but one is clearly Fitzgerald. Here Hemingway again advances his pet theory that Fitzgerald was blocked by the Seldes review of *The Great Gatsby*. Fitzgerald's reaction to this passage is unknown.

Fitzgerald was analyzed in the *Green Hills of Africa* manuscript in a passage cut before publication: "The charming ones were cowards and so you were never really comfortable with them and they were never really comfortable with themselves. . . . Scott was a coward of great charm. I wondered why the cowards all had so much charm."[7]

Fitzgerald's letter to Hemingway responding to *Green Hills of Africa* is lost, but it expressed reservations. Hemingway replied:

Key West, December I6,1935.

Dear Scott,

It was good to hear from you but a shame you thought you had to write about the book. I only asked Max whether he'd heard if you ever got it because of you changing addresses and one thing and another. It didn't require any bread and ink letter.

How are you anyway? I hear that you're not drinking

and haven't been for months. Then that you're on it. That your insides are on the bum etc. etc. Let me know how you are and what you're doing will you? The line about the body was very good. But I'd rather know really what you have or haven't.

Was delighted from the letter to see you don't know any more about when a book is a good book or what makes a book bad than ever. That means, anyhow, that you're not haveing any sudden flashes of insight or intelligence that would mean The End. The other day going through some stuff found the fifteen some pages you wrote me about what would have to come out and what should go in Farewell To Arms and this letter you have written is just the same.

When did I erroneously think you didn't like Death In The Afternoon? And why? and what about it? You know you are like a brilliant mathematician who loves mathematics truly and always gets the wrong answers to the problems. Of course you're like a hell of a lot of other things too but what the hell. Also you are like nobody but yourself and in spite of the fact that you think when you meet an old friend that you have to get stinking drunk and do every possible thing to humiliate yourself and your friend your friends are still fond of you. I'm damned fond of you. Up in Saranac Sara talked for a whole afternoon about how much she cared about you. She said you wrote her a swell letter.

I started up to see you last September in Asheville. Then the infantile paralysis was so bad (in N. and S. Carolina (had Bumby and Pat with me) that left the car in Columbia S.C. and took them on a train to N.Y. I miss seeing you and haveing a chance to talk. In talk you can winnow out the bullshit which we put out so pontifically when we write literary letters and we get a good sound understanding. I got your wire about coming down two weeks after you sent it when we were cruising in the Bahamas. Tried to get Max and Gingrich both to bring you down.

The more I think back to it the better book Tender Is The Night is. This may irritate you but it's the truth. Why don't you come down here? Am going over to Havana to see the Louis-Gastanaga fight there on Dec. 29th. Come on down and we'll go together. I can get two press seats.

Write here will you—will be here all winter. Dont know whether Dos is coming down or not. Have a hell of a lot of things to tell you that dont go in letters. A couple you could get a good story out of.

Best Always. Ernest.[8]

On the 21st of December 1935 Hemingway replied to a gloomy letter from Fitzgerald—which has not been located—inviting Fitzgerald to Key West and lecturing him on his regret for lost youth:

Key West, Dec. 2I

Dear Scott-

Well Louis must have figured on your necesseties because the fight is put off until Feb 2. So come on down then if it's all right to leave Zelda. I'm terribly sorry she was so ill again. And you with a bad liver, lung and heart. That's damned awful. How are you doing now? We all get those livers. Mine was in a hell of a state about six or seven years ago but got it all cleared up. What is the matter with your heart? And your lung? I mean what does the Doctor say? Non sleeping is a hell of a damned thing too. Have been haveing a big dose of it now lately too. No matter what time I go to sleep wake and hear the clock strike either one or two then lie wide awake and hear three -four and five. But since I have stopped giving a good goddamn about anything in the past it doesn't bother much and I just lie there and keep perfectly still and rest through it and you seem to get almost as much repose as though you slept. This may be no use to you but it works with me.

If I get exercise and go out in the boat sleep like a log right through the night or if I wake on the boat can go right back to sleep. Or if I lay awake on the boat I'm all right. The trouble is that if you start thinking about anything in that wakeing time you go all through it and exhaust it and are pooped in the morning when you have to write. If you can lie still and take it easy and just consider your life and everything else as an outsider and <u>not give a damn</u>—it is a hell of a help.

You put so damned much value on youth it seemed to me that you confused growing up with growing old but you have taken so damned much punishment I have no business trying to tell you anything. Would like to see you though. There is a good chance the fight is off because the niggers that own Louis think he is too valuable a piece of property to risk so far away as Havana where there is shooting etc. The next revolution is being financed by

2

Lin es To Be Re d At the Casting of Scott FitzGerald's balls into the Sea from Eden Roc (A ntibes Alpes Maritimes)

Whence from these grey
Heights unjockstrapped wholly stewed he
Flung
Himself ?
No.
Some waiter ?
Yes.
Push tenderly oh green shoots of grass
Tickle not our Fitz's nostrils
Pass
The grey moving unbenfinneyed sea depths deeper than
our debt to Eliot
Fling flang them flung his own his two finally his one
Spherical, colloid , interstitial ,
uprising lost to sight
in fright
natural
not artificial
no ripple make as sinking sanking sonking sunk

As hell you'll have to get MacLeish to write the mystic poem . I'll just give a few personal reminiscences of his Paris Period . Get that insurance now ,pal . If they won't give you health or life insurance get accident insurance .

So long Scott —
Let me hear from you —
Merry Christmas! Pauline sends her love —
yours always affectionately —
Ernest

(PRINCETON UNIVERSITY LIBRARY)

money raised through kidnapping, bank robbery etc. It's damned strange the violence that is bred from violence and what a lot of those kids have turned into. Cuba is a hell of an interesting place now and has been for last five years. Probably before too you say. But only know what I've seen. Anyway am writing a story about this next revolution.

Come on down any time and I'll take you over there in the boat and you'll get a goodstory out of it anyway. If you really feel blue enough get yourself heavily insured and I'll see you can get killed. All you'll have to do is not put your hands up quick enough and some nigger son of a bitch will shoot you and your family will be provided for and you won't have to write anymore and I'll write you a fine obituary that Malcom Cowley will cut the best part out of for the new republic and we can take your liver out and give it to the Princeton Museum, your heart to the Plaza Hotel, one lung to Max Perkins and the other to George Horace Lorimer. If we can still find your balls I will take them via the Ile de France to Paris and down to Antibes and have them cast into the sea off Eden Roc and we will get MacLeish to write a Mystic Poem to be read at the Catholic School (Newsman?) you went to. Would you like me to write the mystic poem now. Let's see.

Lin es To Be Read At the Casting of Scott FitzGerald's balls into the Sea from Eden Roc (A ntibes Alpes Maritimes)

Whence from these gray
Heights unjockstrapped wholly stewed he
Flung
Himself?
No.
Some waiter?
Yes.
Push tenderly oh green shoots of grass
Tickle not our Fitz's nostrils
Pass
The gray moving unbenfinneyed sea depths deeper than
our debt to Eliot
Fling flang them flung his own two finally his one
Spherical, colloid, interstitial,
uprising lost to sight
in fright
natural
not artificial
no ripple make as sinking sanking sonking sunk

Aw hell you'll have to get MacLeish to write the mystic poem. I'll just give a few personal remeniscences of his

Paris Period. Get that insurance now, pal. If they won't give you health or life insurance get accident insurance.

So long Scott—

Let me hear from you—

Merry Christmas Pauline sends her love—

Yours always affectionately—

Ernest[9]

This is the last located letter from Hemingway to Fitzgerald.

By August 1936 thirteen Fitzgerald pieces had appeared in *Esquire,* most of which were retrospective essays. The contributions that attracted the most attention were the group of confessional articles—beginning with "The Crack-Up" in the February 1936 issue—in which Fitzgerald analyzed his "emotional bankruptcy." In "Pasting It Together" (March 1936) Fitzgerald stipulated his admiration for Hemingway: "That a third contemporary had been an artistic conscience to me—I had not imitated his infectious style, because my own style, such as it is, was formed before he published anything, but there was an awful pull toward him when I was on a spot."[10] Hemingway was not named, but the identification was obvious.

Perkins and Ober felt that these articles were seriously damaging Fitzgerald's reputation and urged him to stop writing them. Ernest felt more strongly about them, regarding such public confessions as shameless and contemptible. On February 7 Hemingway wrote to Perkins about Fitzgerald's perverse pride in defeat as revealed in the *Esquire* articles:

> Feel awfully about Scott. I tried to write him once (wrote him several times) to cheer him up but he seems to almost take a pride in his shamelessness of defeat. The Esquire pieces seem to me to be so miserable. There is another one comeing too. I always knew he couldn't think—he never could—but he had a marvellous talent and the thing is to use it—not whine in public. Good God, people go through that emptiness many times in life and come out and do work. I always thought from when I first met him, that if Scott had gone to that war that he always felt so bad about missing, he would have been shot for cowardice. But that has nothing to do with his writing, a writer can be a coward but at least he should be a writer. Hell I can't write about this and it is rotten to speak against Scott after all he had to go through. But I saw all the first part of it and it was

> so avoidable and self imposed and always from the one source—though the source spread into many channels and some of them you would never believe came from the same spring. Maybe the Church would help him. You can't tell. Work would help him; noncommercial, honest work—a paragraph at a time. But he judged a paragraph by how much money it made him and ditched his juice into that channel because he got an instant satisfaction. While if you don't make so much and somebody said it was no good he would be afraid. It was a terrible thing for him to love youth so much that he jumped straight from youth to senility without going through manhood. The minute he felt youth going he was frightened again and thought there was nothing between youth and age. But it is so damned easy to criticize our friends and I shouldn't write this. I wish we could help him.

During the Thirties Hemingway's letters to Gerald and Sara Murphy mentioned Fitzgerald infrequently and contemptuously. After publication of *The Crack-Up,* Hemingway compared the Murphys' anxieties about the illness of their son to Napoleon's retreat from Moscow—from which Scott would have deserted during the first week.[11] Describing how amberjacks chased a fish he had hooked, Hemingway commented that they chased the fish because it ran: "Make a note of that for Mr. FitzGerald."[12]

Hemingway's reaction to the "Crack-Up" articles was probably intensified by seeing them in the magazine where he was the star contributor. *Esquire* was Fitzgerald's only dependable market. The August 1936 issue published Fitzgerald's "Afternoon of an Author" and Hemingway's "The Snows of Kilimanjaro." "Afternoon of an Author" is a sketch about a weary writer who is unable to write: ". . . the same review had also spoken of him as being indefatigable. Something in the sound of the world in his mind broke him momentarily and feeling tears of weakness behind his eyes he turned away. It was like in the beginning fifteen years ago when they said he had 'fatal facility,' and he labored like a slave over every sentence so as not to be like that."[13] "The Snows of Kilimanjaro," a long story about a dying writer who has become corrupted by his marriage to a wealthy woman, includes the comment that "poor Scott Fitzgerald" was "wrecked" by his "romantic awe" of the rich. "Snows" quotes the observation that "The very rich are different from you and me," from Fitzgerald's story "The Rich Boy," followed by the

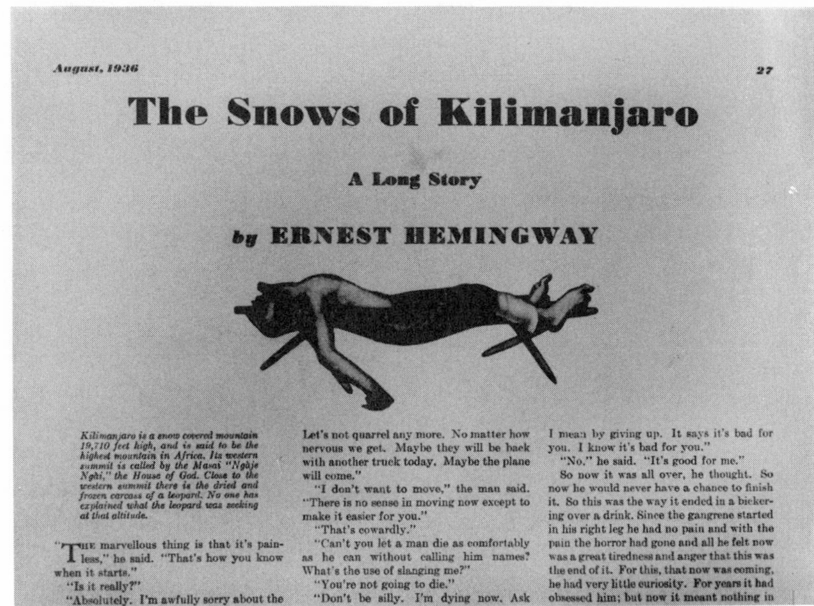
August, 1936 27

The Snows of Kilimanjaro

A Long Story

by ERNEST HEMINGWAY

Kilimanjaro is a snow covered mountain 19,710 feet high, and is said to be the highest mountain in Africa. Its western summit is called by the Masai "Ngàje Ngài," the House of God. Close to the western summit there is the dried and frozen carcass of a leopard. No one has explained what the leopard was seeking at that altitude.

"THE marvellous thing is that it's painless," he said. "That's how you know when it starts."

"Is it really?"

"Absolutely. I'm awfully sorry about the Let's not quarrel any more. No matter how nervous we get. Maybe they will be back with another truck today. Maybe the plane will come."

"I don't want to move," the man said. "There is no sense in moving now except to make it easier for you."

"That's cowardly."

"Can't you let a man die as comfortably as he can without calling him names? What's the use of slanging me?"

"You're not going to die."

"Don't be silly. I'm dying now. Ask I mean by giving up. It says it's bad for you. I know it's bad for you."

"No," he said. "It's good for me."

So now it was all over, he thought. So now he would never have a chance to finish it. So this was the way it ended in a bickering over a drink. Since the gangrene started in his right leg he had no pain and with the pain the horror had gone and all he felt now was a great tiredness and anger that this was the end of it. For this, that now was coming, he had very little curiosity. For years it had obsessed him; but now it meant nothing in

Hemingway's belittling reference to Fitzgerald in Esquire *permanently damaged their friendship.*

rejoinder, "Yes they have more money." Fitzgerald's July 16, 1936, response from Asheville was remarkably controlled:

> Dear Ernest:
>
> Please lay off me in print. If I choose to write de profundis sometimes it doesn't mean I want friends praying aloud over my corpse. No doubt you meant it kindly but it cost me a night's sleep. And when you incorporate it (the story) in a book would you mind cutting my name?
>
> It's a fine story—one of your best—even though the "Poor Scott Fitzgerald ect" rather spoiled it for me
>
> Ever Your Friend
>
> Scott
>
> Riches have never facinated me, unless combined with the greatest charm or distinction.[14]

In 1936 Perkins was with Hemingway and Mary Colum when Hemingway—who had been hobnobbing with the yachting and game-fishing set in Bimini—remarked, "I am getting to know the rich"; and Colum responded, "The only difference between the rich and other people is that the rich have more money.''[15] The mechanism of Hemingway's reaction seems clear: a standard way to purge an embarrassment is to assign it to someone else. In this case ''poor Scott Fitzgerald'' provided a target of opportunity. Perkins did not mention the ''poor Scott'' reference in his July 21 letter to Hemingway praising ''Snows.''

Hemingway wrote to Perkins on the 23rd of July, commenting on Fitzgerald's letter of protest:

> I got a letter from Scott who was sore because I used his name in that Snows of Kilimanjaro story. He had only been writing those awful things about himself since Feb. in Esquire but if I took issue with his analysis of his proclaimed break-up he gets sore. I told him that for five years I have not written a line about anybody I knew because I was so sorry for them all but that I felt time was getting short now and am going to cease being a gent and go back to being a novelist. Most of my friends were not of my own selection anyway.

Hemingway's letter to Fitzgerald does not survive: Arnold Gingrich read it and described it thirty years later in ''Scott, Ernest and Whoever'' as ''brutal,'' with language ''that you'd hesitate to use on a yellow dog.'' Gingrich never explained his decision to print the story with the ''poor Scott Fitzgerald'' passage in *Esquire,* but the explanation seems obvious. Gingrich was so proud to have Hemingway as a regular contributor in *Esquire* that he did not want to run the risk of alienating him. Gingrich's 1966 article reports that when he was fishing with Hemingway at Bimini in June 1936 he committed the blunder of praising Fitzgerald's style and was shushed by a member of Hemingway's entourage: '' 'We don't say things like that around here.' '' Gingrich was himself obeying the don't-upset-Ernest rule: ''Thinking back on it now, it occurs to me that at that very moment the presses were turning, back in Chicago, with the August '36 issue of Esquire containing the first printed appearance of *The Snows of Kilimanjaro* with its line, later changed, referring to 'poor Scott Fitzgerald,' but I'm sure I never gave that a thought at the time.''[16]

On the 15th of September 1936—two months after ''Snows'' appeared—Fitzgerald wrote to Beatrice Dance, with whom he had been involved in a brief affair in North Carolina, providing a report of his correspondence with Hemingway:

> As to Ernest, at first I resented his use of my name in the story and I wrote him a somewhat indignant letter, telling him it must not be republished in a book. He answered, agreeing, but rather resentfully and saying that he felt that since I had chosen to expose my private life so "shamelessly" in "*Esquire*", he felt that it was sort of an open season for me, and I wrote him a hell of a letter which would have been sudden death for somebody the next time we met, and decided, hell let it go. Too often literary men allow themselves to get into inter-necine quarrels and finish about as victoriously as most of the nations at the end of the World War. I consider it an example of approaching maturity on my part and am proud of my self control. He is quite as nervously broken down as I am but it manifests itself in different ways. His inclination is toward megalomania and mine toward melancholy.[17]

Four days later Fitzgerald wrote to Perkins:

> I feel that I must tell you something which at first seemed better to leave alone: I wrote Ernest about that story of his, asking him in the most measured terms not to use my name in future pieces of fiction. He wrote me back a crazy letter, telling me about what a great Writer he was and how much he loved his children, but yielding the point—"If I should out live him—" which he doubted. To have answered it would have been like fooling with a lit firecracker. Somehow I love that man, no matter what he says or does, but just one more crack and I think I would have to throw my weight with the gang and lay him. No one could ever hurt him in his first books but he has completely lost his head and the duller he gets about it, the more he is like a punch-drunk pug fighting himself in the movies.

Carlos Baker, Hemingway's biographer, has suggested that "Snows" reveals his morbid concern that he might die without having fulfilled his talent.[18] He had not, in fact, published a novel in seven years. Fitzgerald recognized that around 1936 Hemingway underwent a personality shift—as though he had come to believe the

Hemingway legends. Nonetheless, Fitzgerald was determined to avoid a final break with the living writer he most admired.

Perkins replied to Fitzgerald in September: "As for what Ernest did, I resented it, and when it comes to book publication, I shall have it out with him. It is odd about it too because I was present when that reference was made to the rich, and the retort given, and you were many miles away." Perkins did not tell Fitzgerald about the actual exchange between Hemingway and Mary Colum. Nor did he protest to Hemingway, although he wrote Elizabeth Lemmon, who was Fitzgerald's friend, that Hemingway had behaved contemptibly.[19]

On March 19, 1937, Perkins assured Fitzgerald that "poor Scott" would be deleted from "Snows": "As for Ernest, I know he will cut that piece out of his story. He spoke to me a while ago about it, and his feelings toward you are far different from what you seem to suspect. I think he had some queer notion that he would give you a 'jolt' and that it might be good for you, or something like that. Anyhow, he means to take it out."

Given the hurt generated by "The Snows of Kilimanjaro," it is significant that Fitzgerald turned to Hemingway for help in September 1936 when he was again publicly humiliated. On his fortieth birthday—September 24, 1936—Fitzgerald gave an interview in Asheville to Michel Mok, which appeared in the *New York Post* the next day headlined: "The Other Side of Paradise / Scott Fitzgerald, 40, / Engulfed in Despair / Broken in Health He Spends Birthday Re- / gretting That He Has Lost Faith in His Star." The article portrayed him as a defeated, crying drunk. When he saw it Fitzgerald attempted suicide by swallowing morphine, which he vomited up. Fitzgerald felt that Mok had ruined him, the more so since the interview was picked up in *Time*. Among the Fitzgerald papers there is a Western Union form dated September 28 for a wire to Hemingway at Cook City, Montana, written in an unidentified hand: "If you ever wanted to help me your chance is now Stop A man named Michael Moch has taken advantage of an interview to spread me all over the N.Y. Evening Post in an absurd position Stop It cuts in on me directly and indirectly—Scott." There is no evidence that this wire was sent or delivered, but Fitzgerald sent another wire to Hemingway c/o Scribners. Hemingway replied that he had not seen the Mok article but was ready to help.[20] Fitzgerald wired back:

> WIRED UNDER IMPRESSION YOU WERE IN NEW YORK NOTHING CAN BE DONE AT LONG RANGE AND ON COOLER CONSIDERATION

SEEMS NOTHING TO BE DONE ANYHOW THANKS BEST ALWAYS SCOTT.

On the first of October 1936 Perkins sent Hemingway a situation report on Fitzgerald. After repeating his congratulations on ''Snows,'' Perkins explained that he had opened the telegram Fitzgerald sent Hemingway:

> I don't know exactly what you could do for him, but the interview he gave the Post was frightful. It gave me a chill to read it. It seemed as if Scott were bent upon destroying himself. He was trusting the reporter, and so was his nurse—when a man gets himself a trained nurse, it's time to despair of him—and both of them said things which the reporter must have known were not meant to go into print,-the nurse said them when Scott was out of the room. It gave you the impression of a completely licked and very drunk person, bereft of hope, acquiesing in his ruin. Scott had just written me that his mother had died, and that he was to come into twenty thousand dollars. I had known that this was a probability, and I had thought that there was his chance. So I wrote him that he must take that opportunity to work two years on ten thousand a year, without anxiety or the necessity of potboiling. I told him this was the only way to answer what this reporter had done. I hope Scott will turn up here tomorrow. It may be that having hit bottom, and having the shock of this story, he might rebound with the help of the money. Fortunately, hardly anybody reads the New York Post.

The Spanish Civil War broke out in July 1936, but Hemingway did not go to report it until March 1937. He was committed to the Loyalists, who were backed by Russia, and for a time it appeared that Hemingway had entered a period of political activism. The Left assumed so and began to welcome him into the fold, interpreting his involvement with the Loyalists as evidence that he had outgrown his egotistical and irrelevant pursuits. The Leftists were naive, for Hemingway's anti-Fascism never made him a pro-Communist. He was always suspicious of organizations and movements, trusting only his own instincts and what he called the ''true gen.'' Above all, Hemingway was suspicious of any attempt to organize writers.

The hurt over ''Snows'' remained, but Fitzgerald maintained his interest in Hemingway's career and wrote Perkins, predicting that the Spanish War would provide Hemingway with new material:

> Ernest ought to write a swell book now about Spain—real Richard Harding Davis reporting or better. (I mean not the sad jocosity of P.O.M.* passages or the mere callender of slaughter). And speaking of Ernest, did I tell you that when I wrote asking him to cut me out of his story he answered, with ill grace, that he would—in fact he answered with such unpleasantness that it is hard to think he has any friendly feeling to me any more. Anyhow please remember that he agreed to do this if the story should come in with me still in it.[21]

In Spain Hemingway began his liaison with writer Martha Gellhorn, who became his third wife in 1940. During the spring of 1937 Hemingway wrote war dispatches for the North American Newspaper Alliance and worked on a propaganda movie, *The Spanish Earth.*

On June 4, 1937, Hemingway addressed the American Writers' Congress at Carnegie Hall in New York. The meeting was sponsored by the League of American Writers, whose president was Donald Ogden Stewart—Bill Gorton in *The Sun Also Rises*—now a screenwriter and political activist. Earl Browder, the secretary of the American Communist Party, was also on the program. Archibald MacLeish chaired the meeting. Hemingway's short speech was an attack on Fascism: "There is only one form of government that cannot produce good writers, and that system is fascism. For fascism is a lie told by bullies."[22] Although the speech was not eloquent, it received thunderous applause from the Leftist audience, who regarded it as a symbolic event. Hemingway was with them. The most famous living American writer had joined the cause.

The Carnegie Hall event provided the occasion for the penultimate meeting between Fitzgerald and Hemingway. At this time Fitzgerald was coming out of his "crack-up" and was seeking movie employment as the only way to pay off his debts—which may have amounted to $40,000. Hemingway's appearance in New York was well publicized in advance, and Fitzgerald made a trip from North Carolina to attend the event. The only evidence of this reunion is Fitzgerald's note mailed to Hemingway from the train at Washington on June 5:

*In *Green Hills of Africa* Pauline was referred to as P.O.M. (Poor Old Mama). M.J.B.

> It was fine to see you so well + full of life, Ernest. I hope you'll make your book fat—I know some of that *Esquire* work is too good to leave out. All best wishes to your Spanish trip—I wish we could meet more often. I don't feel I know you at all.
>
> Ever Yours
>
> Scott
>
> Going South always seems to me rather desolate + fatal and uneasy. This is no exception. Going North is a safe dull feeling[23]

Even at this stage Fitzgerald retained an almost proprietary interest in Hemingway's career. Hemingway was considering including stories with *To Have and Have Not,* and Fitzgerald's letter endorses that plan. (The published volume included only the novel.)

Harold Ober arranged a six-month contract for Fitzgerald at Metro-Goldwyn-Mayer for $1,000 a week, with a renewal option for a year at $1,250. Fitzgerald arrived in Hollywood the first week of July 1937. A few days later Hemingway came to show *The Spanish Earth* and raise money for the Loyalists. This occasion was the final meeting between Fitzgerald and Hemingway. In *An Unfinished Woman* (1969) Lillian Hellman published her fabricated recollections of this evening—which she misdated as occurring in 1938. According to this widely read account, Fitzgerald was present when Hemingway showed *The Spanish Earth* at the home of Fredric March. Afterward some of the guests were invited to Dorothy Parker's house for drinks. Fitzgerald offered to drive Hellman but said he didn't want to go in. On the wagon and nervous, he was intimidated by Hemingway. She coaxed Fitzgerald into the house. As they entered the living room, Hemingway—who had his back to the door—threw a glass into the fireplace. Fitzgerald wanted to leave but Hellman took him to the kitchen, where Dashiell Hammett was talking to Dorothy Parker.[24]

Martha Gellhorn published a correction under the title "On Apocryphism": "This apocryphism is a whopper. Hemingway and Ivens took *The Spanish Earth* to California on July 10, 1937. Since Miss H. writes truthfully . . . that she met Hemingway for the first time on 'those pre-Moscow Paris weeks,' *August or September, 1937*, she could not have been present at Hemingway's only showing of the film in Hollywood."[25] A researcher working on Fitzgerald and Hemingway is forced to conclude that there may not be such a thing as a reliable eyewitness for events involving them.

The morning after the movie showing, Fitzgerald wired Hemingway: THE PICTURE WAS BEYOND PRAISE AND SO WAS YOUR ATTITUDE-SCOTT. On July 15 Fitzgerald reported to Perkins: "I felt he was in a state of nervous tensity, that there was something almost religious about it."

At MGM Fitzgerald was put to work revising *A Yank at Oxford* and then was given the choice assignment to write the screenplay for Erich Maria Remarque's *Three Comrades*. He stayed on the wagon for the time being. Although he quarreled with producer Joseph Mankiewicz on *Three Comrades,* the movie was well received, and his option was picked up at the end of 1937. Fitzgerald's problem as a screenwriter was that he could not work well with collaborators, which was the way most screenplays were put together. Shortly after his arrival in Hollywood he met Sheilah Graham, an English movie columnist, who became his companion. They made a life together, and Fitzgerald found a measure of happiness and even peace in Hollywood. Zelda Fitzgerald remained at Highland Hospital; Fitzgerald's trips east to see her were usually disastrous.

With Fitzgerald in Hollywood and Hemingway in Spain or Cuba or Sun Valley, Perkins continued to keep them informed about each other. In August 1937 Hemingway and critic Max Eastman engaged in a well-publicized brawl in Perkins's office. Eastman had referred to Hemingway's false hair-on-the-chest manner in reviewing *Death in the Afternoon,* which Hemingway interpreted as impugning his masculinity. On September 3 Fitzgerald responded to Perkins's detailed account:

> I was thoroughly amused by your descriptions, but what transpires is that Ernest did exactly the same asinine thing that I knew he had it in him to do when he was out here. The fact that he lost his temper only for a minute does not minimize the fact that he picked the exact wrong minute to do it. His discretion must have been at low ebb or he would not have again trusted the reporters at the boat.
>
> He is living at the present in a world so entirely his own that it is impossible to help him, even if I felt close to him at the moment, which I don't. I like him so much, though, that I wince when anything happens to him, and I feel rather personally ashamed that it has been possible for imbeciles to dig at him and hurt him. After all, you would

think that a man who has arrived at the position of being practically his country's most imminent writer, could be spared that yelping.

Hemingway's third novel, *To Have and Have Not,* was published on October 15, 1937. It was a disappointing work for his first novel since 1929, but it sold 36,000 copies. *To Have and Have Not* did not represent eight years of work, and it wasn't really a novel. Occupied with Spain and Martha Gellhorn, Hemingway assembled a book from two previously published stories (''One Trip Across'' [1934] and ''The Tradesman's Return'' [1936]), adding a long third section. It looked patched together. The working draft of *To Have and Have Not* included unpublished comments on writers—including the diagnosis that Fitzgerald began writing too young and lacked the intelligence to develop his talent.[26]

On February 3, 1938, Perkins reported to Hemingway that Fitzgerald had been in New York and was in good shape. He had called Hemingway ''the most dynamic personality'' in the world. Hemingway replied that he would have liked to see ''old Scott,'' but stated that he never wanted to be dynamic; he just wanted to be a writer.

Fitzgerald continued to worry about ''The Snows of Kilimanjaro,'' and on March 4, 1938, he reminded Perkins to remove his name when the story was published in book form:

> The enclosed letter. . . . shows quite definitely how a whole lot of people interpreted Ernest's crack at me in ''Snows of K.'' When I called him on it, he promised in a letter that he would not reprint it in book form. Of course, since then, it has been in O'Brien's collection,* but I gather he can't help that. If, however, you are publishing a collection of his this fall, do keep in mind that he has promised to make an elision of my name. It was a damned rotten thing to do, and with anybody but Ernest my tendency would be to crack back. Why did he think it would add to the strength of his story if I had become such a negligible figure? This is quite indefensible on any grounds.

Perkins reassured Fitzgerald on March 9: ''You know my position about Ernest's story 'The Snows'.—Don't be concerned about it.''

**The Best Short Stories of 1937* (Boston: Houghton Mifflin, 1937). M.J.B.

During the summer of 1938 Perkins was working with Hemingway on his collected short stories to be published as *The Fifth Column and the First Forty-Nine Stories*. On the 9th of August Perkins reminded him about his promise to amend "Snows": "And by the way, you were going to take out F.S.F. weren't you, from 'The Snows of Kilimanjaro'?" Hemingway revised the passage but retained the name "Scott." Perkins responded on August 23 in his best diplomatic style:

> As to the Scott passage, you amended it very neatly.—But I greatly wish his name could come out altogether. If people reading the story do not identify "Scott" as F.S.F., it might as well be some other name (one realizes he is a writer in the very next sentence) and if they do identify him, it seems to me it takes them out of the story for a moment. It takes their attention to the question of what this means about Scott. You did take out the things that could hurt and I showed the amended passage to two people who had never read the story and they thought Scott might still feel badly, being very sensitive, but that they hardly thought there was much reason for it now. If his name could come out without hurting, it would be good.—But I'll bring up the matter when you are here.

After Hemingway came to New York, Perkins wrote to Fitzgerald on September 1 saying that he wished he could talk to him about Hemingway. Perkins was uncertain about his plan for a new work and wanted to have Fitzgerald's reaction. Scribners was going to publish Hemingway's collected stories: "One of the new stories is 'The Snows of Kilimanjaro' and you are not in it." The final decision was to change "poor Scott Fitzgerald" to "poor Julian," leaving the rest of the passage unrevised. All subsequent Scribners printings have retained "Julian."

In 1951 Hemingway informed Mizener that Fitzgerald should have known that Harry would have mentioned him in "Snows" the same way that Fitzgerald used real things in his own writing.[27] Hotchner reported that in 1955 Hemingway told him that it was time to put Scott back in the story.[28]

From Hollywood, Fitzgerald tried to supervise his daughter's reading at Vassar, and Hemingway was one of the authors he assigned her. On November 15, 1938, he reprimanded Scottie: "How you could possibly have missed the answer to my first question I don't know, unless you skipped pages 160 to 170 in *Farewell to Arms.** Try again!''[29]

When Thomas Wolfe's *The Web and the Rock* (1939) portrayed Perkins as Foxhall Edwards, Fitzgerald wrote to Perkins on February 25, 1939: "It is astonishing what people will do though. Earnest's sharp turn against me always seemed to have pointless childish quality—so much so that I really never felt any resentment about it."

There is a published report of a final Hollywood reunion between Fitzgerald and Hemingway; but it did not happen. Aaron Latham's *Crazy Sundays* (1971) includes Charles Marquis Warren's account of how Hemingway came to stay with Fitzgerald at Malibu Beach in the summer of 1938.[30] According to Warren—a young movie writer Fitzgerald had encouraged—Hemingway was broke and Fitzgerald gave him a $25-a-week allowance. Warren described how Hemingway wrote *For Whom the Bell Tolls* on the beach at night by lantern light and gave him one of the sleeping-bag scenes to read. One day, according to Warren, Fitzgerald took Hemingway to MGM. After calling producer Bernard Hyman a "Heeb," Hemingway insulted Louis B. Mayer, who had him thrown off the lot. It did not happen. None of it ever happened. Warren's account is not substantiated by anyone else, and Sheilah Graham—who was living with Fitzgerald—refuted it.[31] In the summer of 1938 Hemingway was in Key West and Wyoming; he did not start *For Whom the Bell Tolls* until 1939 in Cuba.

After Fitzgerald's MGM contract elapsed in January 1939, he freelanced at other studios while planning a Hollywood novel. On March 25, 1939, Hemingway wrote Perkins that he had just reread *Tender Is the Night:*

> It's amazing how excellent much of it is. If he had integrated it better it would have been a fine novel (as it is) much of it is better than anything else he ever wrote. How I wish he would have kept on writing. Is it really all over or will he write again? If you write him give him my great affection. (I always had a very stupid little boy feeling of superiority about Scott—like a tough little boy sneering at a delicate but talented little boy.) But reading that novel much of it was so good it was frightening.

*Chapters 23–24 in the first edition, Frederic Henry's parting from Catherine in Milan. M.J.B.

Fitzgerald pasted an excerpt from this letter in his scrapbook.[32]

Fitzgerald was not finished. By late summer 1939 he was writing *The Love of the Last Tycoon.* The work went slowly, but it went. With no salary and no savings, Fitzgerald was supporting himself and his family with short free-lance jobs and $250 checks from *Esquire* for the Pat Hobby stories about a broken-down Hollywood hack.

Through 1939 and 1940 Perkins kept Hemingway informed about the progress of Fitzgerald's novel—obeying Fitzgerald's instructions to keep the nature of the material a secret. Perkins told Hemingway that Fitzgerald expected Scribners to bankroll him with an advance but that Perkins could not justify it. In December 1939 Perkins wrote Hemingway that Fitzgerald was sick but that it was hard to tell what the situation really was because Scott always hired trained nurses: "I would feel as if it might as well be an undertaker, and even more embarrassing." After a few benders, Fitzgerald was again on the wagon. An indication of Fitzgerald's respect for Hemingway's authority, as well as Fitzgerald's sense of isolation from him, is provided by his June 6, 1940, letter to Perkins inquiring about Hemingway's sense of how World War II would go—asking for "at least a clue to Ernest's attitude."

While Fitzgerald was struggling against illness and debt to write *The Love of the Last Tycoon,* Hemingway enjoyed his greatest success when *For Whom the Bell Tolls* was published in October 1940. His first major work of fiction since 1929, the novel sold more than 270,000 copies in its first year. Hemingway sent his novel to Fitzgerald inscribed "To Scott with affection and esteem Ernest."[33] The ironic reversal of their fortunes since 1925 was painfully apparent to Fitzgerald. In his weekly letter to Zelda of October 26 he commented:

> Ernest sent me his book and I'm in the middle of it. It is not as good as the "Farewell to Arms". It doesn't seem to have the tensity or the freshness nor has it the inspired poetic moments. But I imagine it would please the average type of reader, the mind who used to enjoy Sinclair Lewis, more than anything he has written. It is full of a lot of rounded adventures on the Huckleberry Finn order and of course it is highly intelligent and literate like everything he does. I suppose life takes a good deal out of you and you never can quite repeat. But the point is he is making a fortune out of it—has sold it to the movies for over a hundred thousand dollars and as it's The Book-of-the-Month selection he will make $50,000 from it in that form.

Fitzgerald at the time he was writing The Love of the Last Tycoon.
(Photo by Belle O'Hara)

> Rather a long cry from his poor rooms over the saw mill in Paris.[34]

Fitzgerald acknowledged the inscribed copy with a warm letter of congratulation, obliquely referring to his efforts to complete his own novel:

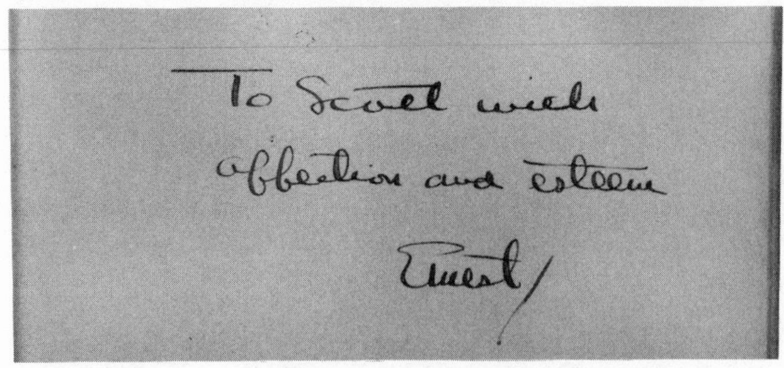

To Scott with
affection and esteem
Ernest

(BRUCCOLI COLLECTION)

November
8
1940

Dear Ernest:

It's a fine novel, better than anybody else writing could do. Thanks for thinking of me and for your dedication.* I read it with intense interest, participating in a lot of the writing problems as they came along and often quite unable to discover how you brought off some of the effects, but you always did. The massacre was magnificent and also the fight on the mountain and the actual dynamiting scene. Of the side shows I particularly liked the vignette of Karkov and Pilar's Sonata to death—and I had a personal interest in the Moseby guerilla stuff because of my own father. The scene in which the father says goodbye to his son is very powerful. I'm going to read the whole thing again.

I never got to tell you how I liked To Have and to Have Not either. There is observation and writing in that that the boys will be imitating with a vengeance—paragraphs and pages that are right up with Dostoiefski in their undeflected intensity.

Congratulations too on your new book's great success. I envy you like hell and there is no irony in this. I always liked Dostoiefski with his wide appeal more than any other

*Fitzgerald meant the inscription; the dedicatee was Martha Gellhorn. M.J.B.

European—and I envy you the time it will give you to do what you want.

With Old Affection,

P.S. I came across an old article by John Bishop about how you lay four days under dead bodies at Caporetto and how I flunked out of Princeton (I left on a stretcher in November—you can't flunk out in November) and how I am an awful suck about the rich and a social climber.* What I started to say was that I do know something about you on the Italian front, from a man who was in your unit—how you crawled some hellish distance pulling a wounded man with you and how the doctors stood over you wondering why you were alive with so many perforations. Don't worry—I won't tell anybody. Not even Allan Campbell who called me up and gave me news of you the other day. P.S. (2) I hear you are marrying one of the most beautiful people I have ever seen. Give her my best remembrance.[35]

This was the last letter from Fitzgerald to Hemingway.

Writing to Perkins on October 14, 1940, Fitzgerald had made an accurate prediction about Hemingway's third marriage: "It will be odd to think of Ernest married to a really attractive woman. I think the pattern will be somewhat different than with his Pygmalion-like creations."

Fitzgerald had strong reservations about *For Whom the Bell Tolls*. His *Notebook* entries read: "It is so to speak Ernest's 'Tale of Two Cities' though the comparison isn't apt. I mean it is a thoroughly superficial book which has all the profundity of Rebecca." And, comparing his work in progress on *The Love of the Last Tycoon* with Hemingway's novel: "I want to write scenes that are frightening and inimitable. I don't want to be as intelligible to my contemporaries as Ernest who as Gertrude Stein said, is bound for the Museums. I am sure I am far enough ahead to have some small immortality if I can keep well" (Appendix, #2066 and #2068.)

All of his life Fitzgerald had a list-making compulsion. Perhaps because his personal life had been so unstructured, he felt a compensatory need to keep records. The most elaborate attempt was his *Ledger,* which is virtually an autobiography. He would also make

* "The Missing All," *Virginia Quarterly Review* (Winter 1937). M.J.B.

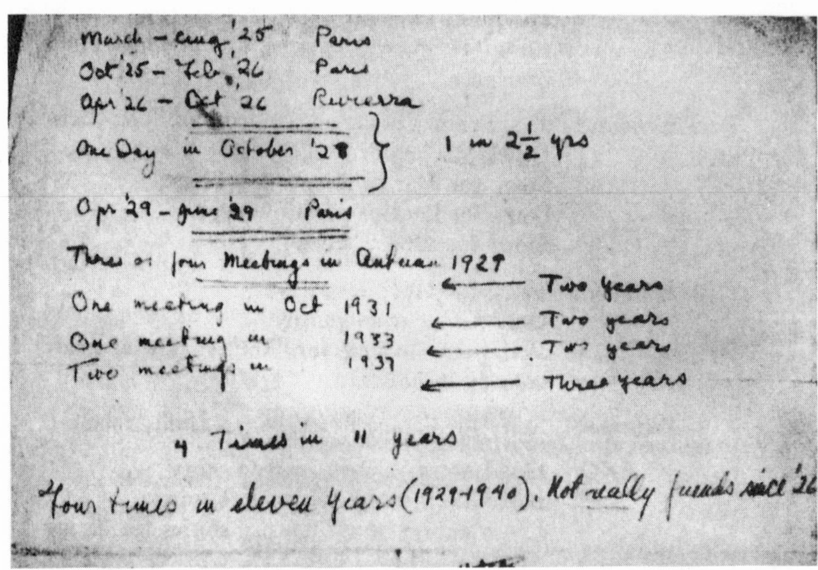
March – Aug '25 Paris
Oct '25 – Feb '26 Paris
Apr '26 – Oct '26 Riviera
One Day in October '28 } 1 in $2\frac{1}{2}$ yrs
Apr '29 – June '29 Paris
Three or four Meetings in Autumn 1929 ← Two years
One meeting in Oct 1931 ← Two years
One meeting in 1933 ← Two years
Two meetings in 1937 ← Three years
4 Times in 11 years
Four times in eleven years (1929-1940). Not really friends since '26

Fitzgerald's records of his meetings with Hemingway. (PRINCETON UNIVERSITY LIBRARY)

lists on single sheets of paper. One of these, dating from the year of his death, is a chronology of Fitzgerald's meetings with Hemingway from 1925 to 1937. At the end of it he noted: "Four times in eleven years (1929-1940). Not *really* friends since '26."

Chapter 8

1. 20 August 1934.
2. 4 January 1939
3. "The Count of Darkness," *Redbook*, 65 (June 1935), 21.
4. 15 April 1935.
5. P. 109.
6. Pp. 23–24.
7. Alderman Library, The University of Virginia.
8. TLS with holograph additions, 1 p. *Selected Letters*, pp. 424–425.
9. TLS, 2 pp. *Selected Letters*, pp. 427–429.
10. *Esquire*, 5 (March 1936), 183; collected in *The Crack-Up*.
11. To Sara Murphy, c. 27 February 1936. *Letters From the Lost Generation: Gerald and Sara Murphy and Friends*, edited Linda Patterson Miller (New Brunswick, N.J.: Rutgers University Press, 1991), pp. 157–159.

12. To Sara Murphy, 11 February 1936. *Letters From the Lost Generation*, pp. 155–156.
13. *Esquire*, 6 (August 1936), 35, 170. *The Short Stories of F. Scott Fitzgerald*, pp. 734–738.
14. ALS, 1 p. *A Life in Letters*, p. 302.
15. Maxwell Perkins to Elizabeth Lemmon, 15 August 1936. A. Scott Berg, *Max Perkins: Editor of Genius* (New York: Thomas Congdon/E. P. Dutton, 1978), p. 305.
16. *Esquire*, 66 (December 1966), 186–189, 322–325.
17. TL, 2 pp (incomplete). Princeton University Library.
18. *Ernest Hemingway: A Life Story* (New York: Scribners, 1969), p. 291.
19. 15 August 1936.
20. This wire has not been located. Baker refers to it in *Ernest Hemingway: A Life Story*, p. 295.
21. C. March 1937.
22. "Fascism Is a Lie," *New Masses*, 23 (22 June 1937), 4. *Conversations With Ernest Hemingway*, edited by Bruccoli (Jackson: University Press of Mississippi, 1986), pp. 193–195.
23. ALS, 1 p. *A Life in Letters*, p. 324.
24. Boston: Little, Brown, 1969; pp. 66–69.
25. *Paris Review*, 79 (Spring 1981), 280–301.
26. Robert E. Fleming, *The Face in the Mirror: Hemingway's Writers* (Tuscaloosa: University of Alabama Press, 1994), p. 75.
27. 4 January 1951. *Selected Letters*, p. 716.
28. A. E. Hotchner, *Papa Hemingway* (New York: Random House, 1966), p. 164.
29. *The Letters of F. Scott Fitzgerald*, edited by Andrew Turnbull (New York: Scribners, 1963), p. 64.
30. *Crazy Sundays: F. Scott Fitzgerald in Hollywood* (New York: Viking, 1971), pp. 177–179.
31. In conversation with M.J.B.
32. *The Romantic Egoists*, edited by Scottie Fitzgerald Smith, Bruccoli, and Joan P. Keer (New York: Scribners, 1974) p. 201.
33. Bruccoli Collection.
34. CC, 1 p. Princeton University Library.
35. CC, 1 p. *A Life in Letters*, pp. 469–470.

IX

F. Scott Fitzgerald died of a heart attack in Hollywood on December 21, 1940, leaving *The Love of the Last Tycoon* unfinished. On the day of his death he told Sheilah Graham that he hoped to write about the war in Europe: " 'Ernest won't have that field all to himself, then.' "[1] It is not known how or when in Cuba Hemingway learned of Fitzgerald's death. He did not attend the funeral in Rockville, Maryland, on December 27. Perkins sent Hemingway an account of Fitzgerald's funeral on the 28th: "I thought of telegraphing you about Scott but it didn't seem as if there were any use in it, and I shrank from doing it."

It has been incorrectly stated that F. Scott Fitzgerald died with his books out of print. At the time of his death all nine of his books were in stock—including copies of the 1925 second printing of *The Great Gatsby*. In 1940 all of Fitzgerald's books sold a total of seventy-two copies.

Ernest Hemingway outlived F. Scott Fitzgerald by twenty-one years.

Hemingway made no public statement on Fitzgerald after his death. He was not among the writers (Budd Schulberg, John O'Hara, Glenway Wescott, John Peale Bishop, Malcolm Cowley, and John Dos Passos) who contributed to the Fitzgerald reassessments and tributes assembled by Edmund Wilson in 1941 for *The New Republic*.[2] It is not known whether he was asked to participate.

Perkins kept Hemingway informed of his endeavors to salvage Fitzgerald's work in progress on *The Love of the Last Tycoon* and apparently considered asking Hemingway to complete the novel. If so, it was the worst idea the great editor ever had.[3] The idea was promptly abandoned, partly at Zelda Fitzgerald's insistence. Her response to Perkins conveyed her doubts about Hemingway's suitability without mentioning his name: "May I suggest that, rather than bringing into play another forceful talent of other inspiration it would be felicitous to enlist a pen such as that of Gilbert Seldes, whose poetry depends on concision of idea and and aptitude of word rather than on the spiritual or emotional transports of the author."[4] The final decision was that Edmund Wilson would edit the work in progress; it was published by Scribners in 1941 as *The Last Tycoon* in a volume that also reprinted *The Great Gatsby* and five stories.

The reviews were warmly receptive, and critics endorsed Wilson's statement that the novel would have been Fitzgerald's most mature work. Stephen Vincent Benét's assessment in the *Saturday Review of Literature* received considerable attention: "You can take off your hats now, gentlemen, and I think perhaps you had better. This is not a legend, this is a reputation—and seen in perspective, it may be one of the most secure reputations of our time."[5]

Hemingway was not impressed when he reported to Perkins on reading *The Last Tycoon* in November 1941:

> I read all of Scott's book and I don't know whether I ought to tell you what I truly think. There are very fine parts in it, but most of it has a deadness that is unbelievable from Scott. I think Bunnie Wilson did a very credible job in explaining, sorting, padding and arranging. But you know Scott would never have finished it with that gigantic, preposterous outline of how it was to be. I thought the part about Stahr was all very good. You can recognize Irving Thalberg, his charm and skill, and grasp of business, and the sentence of death over him. But the women were pretty preposterous. Scott had gotten so far away from any knowledge of people that they are very strange. He still had the technique and the romance of doing anything, but all the dust was off the butterfly's wing for a long time even though the wing would still move up until the butterfly was dead. The best book he ever wrote, I think, is still "Tender Is The Night" with all of its mix-up of who was Scott and Zelda and who was Sara and Gerald Murphy. I read it last year again and it has all the realization of tragedy that Scott ever found. Wonderful atmosphere and magical descrip-

tions and none of the impossible dramatic tricks that he had outlined for the final book.

Scott died inside himself at around the age of thirty to thirty-five and his creative powers died somewhat later. This last book was written long after his creative power was dead, and he was just beginning to find out what things were about.

I read over the stories and I think Bunnie Wilson made a very poor selection. "The Rich Boy" if you read it, is really profoundly silly. "The Diamond As Big As The Ritz" is simply trash. When you read in "The Rich Boy" about his gradual decay and suddenly see that Scott has given twenty-eight as the age for the oldness setting in, it is hardly credible that he could write that way.

I am happy the book had such a fine review by J. Donald Adams in the Sunday Times with such a good picture of Scott. I think that should please Scotty very much and be very good for her because she never really knew how good Scott was. But J. Donald Adams is not really a very intelligent man, and to someone who knew Scott truly well and is in the same trade, the book has that deadness, the one quality about which nothing can be done in writing, as though it were a slab of bacon on which mold had grown. You can scrape off the mold, but if it has gone deep into the meat, there is nothing that can keep it from tasting like moldy bacon.

When you wrote Martha, you said that Hollywood had not hurt Scott. I guess perhaps it had not because he was long past being hurt before he went there. His heart died in him in France, and soon after he came back, and the rest of him just went on dying progressively after that. Reading the book was like seeing an old baseball pitcher with nothing left in his arm coming out and working with his intelligence for a few innings before he is knocked out of the box.

I know you're impressed by all the stuff about riding in aeroplanes on account of you not doing that and Scott had done it so recently that it impressed him too and he got something of the old magic into it. But in the things between men and women, the old magic was gone and Scott never really understood life well enough to write a novel that did not need the magic to make it come alive.

This sounds gloomy and critical, but I know you would want me to write what I really thought about it. You've

> had three guys. Scott, Tom Wolfe and me. Two of them are already dead, and no one can say what will happen to the third one. But I think it is best to criticize strongly so when you get the new ones that will come along afterwards, you can talk to them truly.
>
> . . . .
>
> That's all I know about to write now. Please excuse the long letter, and if I sound deprecatory about Scott, remember I know how good he is and was only criticizing Wilson's selections and the posthumous work.[6]

This letter introduces Hemingway's conviction that Fitzgerald would not have been able to fulfill the outline for the novel—a charge that he repeated. Hemingway also employs the butterfly metaphor that he recycled in *A Moveable Feast*.

During World War II Hemingway enlarged his legend. After running a civilian Q-boat operation in Cuba, he went to Europe. Nominally a *Collier's* correspondent, he led irregular soldiers in France, personally liberating the Paris Ritz and Sylvia Beach. In 1944 he met correspondent Mary Welsh, who became his fourth wife in 1946.

On February 17, 1944, Perkins briefed Hemingway on Wilson's projected Fitzgerald miscellany. Perkins never liked the plan and had declined to publish the volume because he was embarrassed by Fitzgerald's articles in *Esquire*. The publication of *The Crack-Up* by New Directions in 1945 was catalytic in the Fitzgerald revival.

Hemingway replied to Perkins from Cuba on February 25, 1944, offering to write about Scott after the war:

> I wish you would keep all the Scott letters for a definitive book instead of letting Bunny Wilson pee them away in his usual malicious driblets. He never asked me for any letters from Scott and I have very many; unfortunately all packed in Key West but available anytime I have something to do besides this war. Have letters from Gatsby period all through the Paris time and all the rest. All of them about writing and showing Scott's great strength and most of his weaknesses. I should suggest you save all of your letters; don't give permission for any of them to be used; until we could get out a good book on Scott and his letters. I know him, through some periods, better than anyone and would be glad to write a long, true, just, detailed (all of those I mean in the measure that anyone can do any such thing)

account of the years I knew him. It might be better to wait and write it for my own memoirs but my memoir expectancy has been so slight these last years that might be good to write a good piece about Scott before I get too punchy to remember. Would suggest that John Peale Bishop who knew, loved, and understood Scott much better than Wilson ever did edit the letters. John is unfailably kind, impersonal and disinterested while Wilson is usually twisting the facts to cover some expressed error of critical judgment he has made in the past or some prejudice or lack of knowledge or scholarship. He is also extremely dishonest; both about money and about his friends and other writers. I know no one who works so hard at being honest and less true inner honesty within himself. His criticism is like reading second rate gospels written by some one who is out on parole. He reads most interestingly on all the things one does not know about. On the things one knows about truly he is stupid, inaccurate, uninformative and pretentious. But because he is so pretentious his inaccuracies are accepted by all those with less knowledge of what he is writing about than he has. He is the great false-honest, false-craftsman, falsegreat-critic of our exceedingly sorry times which, if every one was honest in himself and what he writes, have no need to be sorry in any way. You can trace the moral decay of his criticism on a parallel line with the decline in Dos Passos's writing through their increasing dishonesty about money and other things, mostly their being dominated by women. But let us not attack that theme with limited time available. Anyway above is my suggestion with regard to Scott's letters. When I am through with this war will have to get in training and shape again to write and would be glad to help on the Scott book to warm up and get going.

When *The Crack-Up* was published, Hemingway asked Perkins to send him a copy but withdrew his offer to write about Fitzgerald:

Will you have them send me Bunny's book on Scott? I feel badly not to write anything about Scott when I knew him, possibly, the best of any of them. But you cannot write anything true as long as Zelda is alive anymore than I can write with my bitch of a mother still able to read. When I was liveing with Georgie Wertenbaker's P47 group there was a man named Jonah something or other (a preposterous name) maybe not even Jonah; who gave me all the

> Gen on Scott's last time.* He was with him when he died etc. Also at the terrible thing with Sheilah. He never would have finished the book of course. It was more an outline to draw advances on; a mock-up of a project than a book.† That was why the wonderful grandiloquence of it so impresses those people who are not in the secret of how writers are. The Epic, as we know, is usually false. And he pitched that at an Epic note that would be impossible for anyone to sustain. It wasn't by accident that the Gettysburg address was so short. The laws of prose writing are as immutable as those of flight, of mathematics, of physics. Scott was almost completely uneducated. He knew none of the laws. He did everything wrong; and it came out right. But geometry always catches up with you. I always feel that you and I can talk truly about Scott because we both loved him and admired him and understood him. Where other people were dazzled by him we saw the good, the weakness and the great flaw that was always there. The cowardice, the dream world that was not a late symptom as (reading the reviews Bunny seems to feel). He always had the dream of football greatness, war (which he knew *nothing* of) (The Sour Science) and when he couldn't walk across Fifth Avenue in traffic he thought, 'With what I *know* now what a great broken field runner I would be.'
>
> Next time I'll write what was good in him. But we take it for granted people should be good. And in a horse, a regiment, a good writer I look for what is wrong. Take it for granted they are good or would not be looking at them.[7]

Hemingway's report on reading *The Crack-Up* has not been found; he is referred to fourteen times in the "Notebooks" section of the book (see Appendix).§

Maxwell Perkins died in June 1947.

Zelda Fitzgerald perished in a fire at Highland Hospital, Asheville, North Carolina, in March 1948.

*Jonah Ruddy, Sheilah Graham's leg-man in Hollywood, was not present at Fitzgerald's death. Ruddy never wrote about Fitzgerald and was not interviewed by any of Fitzgerald's biographers. M.J.B.

†Fitzgerald did not receive advances for *The Love of the Last Tycoon*. M.J.B.

§In an August 18, 1954, letter to Harvey Breit, Hemingway commented on one of the *Crack-Up* notes: "that thing about how he spoke with the authority of failure and I with the authority of etc. and so we would never be able to sit at table together again. A fairly smug version."

Hemingway's first published post-mortem mention of Fitzgerald appeared in his introduction to the 1948 Scribners illustrated edition of *A Farewell to Arms,* where "Scott FitzGerald" is included without comment in a list of friends who have died since the novel was published. When Arthur Mizener was working on the first biography of Fitzgerald in 1949 and 1950, Hemingway wrote him seven letters and granted permission to quote from his letters to Fitzgerald. In his July 6, 1949, letter Hemingway reports that his letters from Fitzgerald are stored in Key West and have probably been eaten by mice or roaches; advises Mizener to contact Jonah Ruddy "who could give you an enormous amount of really true gen"; and offers to talk with Mizener in Cuba:

> I loved Scott very much but he was extremely difficult with that situation he got himself into and Zelda constantly making him drink because she was jealous of his working well. There are lots of other aspects of it and if you are writing a really good biography of him I would be glad to tell you many things as truly as I can remember them from the first time I met him. Geismar's stuff on him made me sick.* John O'Hara's introduction to THE POTABLE FITZGERALD was wrapped in O'Hara's old coonskin coat that he never wore to Yale. Bunny Wilson and John Bishop were his pals but they never saw much of him when he was at his best, which was over a short time. He had a very steep trajectory and was almost like a guided missile with no one guiding him.[8]

Mizener's July 1949 inquiry appears to have started a flow of thoughts about Fitzgerald. Writing to Charles Scribner, president of the firm, in August 1949, Hemingway told him about Fitzgerald's penis anxiety and repeated the charge that the outline for *The Love of the Last Tycoon* was a con for borrowing money: "But what a lovely writer he was, within his ignorance and lack of education, and his adoration if the rich. He should have been a spanial. And I love my springer Black Dog very much. Actually he did not rate to be a Spaniel: neither cocker nor springer nor the other breeds."[9] Hem-

*Maxwell Geismar's *The Last of the Provincials* (Boston: Houghton Mifflin, 1947) includes a favorable chapter on Fitzgerald; it is not clear what Hemingway objected to. Geismar's *Writers in Crisis* (Boston: Houghton Mifflin, 1942) expresses reservations about Hemingway's works. M.J.B.

ingway subsequently wrote Scribner that "Scott was a rummy and a liar and dishonest about money with the in-bred talent of a dishonest and easily frightened angel."[10] There is no confirming evidence for Hemingway's charge of financial irregularity. Fitzgerald had paid off most of his debts with his Hollywood salary, but he still owed money to Scribners and to Perkins personally when he died.

Hemingway's April 1950 letter to Mizener provides material that was expanded in *A Moveable Feast,* including Zelda's complaint about Fitzgerald's penis—which Mizener did not use and almost certainly could not have used then.

> Poor Scott how he would have loved all this big thing about him now. I remember one time in N.Y. we were walking down Fifth Avenue and he said, "If only I could play foot-ball again with everything I know about it now."
>
> I suggested that we walk across Fifth through the traffic since he wanted to be a back-field man (It isn't difficult at all really for anyone who can do it). But he said I was crazy.
>
> Then there was always the war. He was lucky he never was in a war. It was almost like being broken hearted because you had missed the San Francisco earthquake (the fire).
>
> None of this is for quotation. Am only trying to give a brother writer something I know, or think I know, about another brother writer once he is dead. I never say or write anything about him I would not say to his face or write him. I never had any respect for him ever except for his lovely, golden, wasted talent.
>
> If he would have had fewer pompous museings and a little sounder education it would have been better maybe. But any time you got him at all straightened out and taking his work seriously Zelda would get jealous of him and knock him out of it.
>
> Also alcohol, that we use as the Giant Killer, and that I could not have lived without many times; or at least would not have cared to live without; was a straight poison to Scott instead of a food.
>
> Here's something you should know too; he never slept with another girl except Zelda until Zelda went officially crazy. She was crazy all the time I knew them but not yet net-able. I remember her at Antibes saying, "Don't you

think Al Jolson is greater than Jesus?'' I said, ''No,'' which was the only answer I knew at the moment.

. . . .

Did I write or tell you how Zelda really ruined Scott? Probably I did. Anyway, in case I didn't, she told him A: That he had never given her sexual satisfaction. B: That it was because his sexual organ was too small (am sending this through the mails so employ these high-flung terms).

He told me this at lunch and I told him to come to the lavoratory with me and would give him a reading on it. His sexual organs were perfectly normal. I told him this (the lunch was at Michauds on the rue Jacob). (He wanted to lunch there because Joyce and I used to eat there.) He wouldn't believe me and said that his organ did look small when he looked at it. I explained that that was because he observed it from above and thus he saw it fore-shortened. Nothing would convince him. So you can see he was not designed to take a punch.

He was romantic, ambitious, and Christ, Jesus, God knows how talented. He was also generous without being kind. He was un-educated and refused to educate himself in any way. He would make great studies about foot-ball say and war but it was all bull-shit. He was a charming cheerful companion when he was sober although a little embarrassing from his tendency always to hero-worship. His heros were Tommy Hitchcock, Gerald Murphy and me. He probably had others that I don't know about. But in those three he certainly played the field. Above all he was completely undisciplined and he would quit at the drop of a hat and borrow some-ones hat to drop. He was fragile Irish instead of tough Irish. I wish he were here and I could give him this letter to read so he would not ever think I would say things behind his back.[11]

Hemingway's May letter advises Mizener not to be influenced by Wilson and discusses his own literary metaphysics. He ends with an appraisal of Fitzgerald's fiction:

Scott took LITERATURE so solemnly. He never understood that it was just writing as well as you can and finishing what you start.

The Last Tycoon, after the part that is written, and was as far as he could write, is really only a scheme to borrow money on. For me the best of the books, in spite of any inconsistencies, is Tender Is The Night. He seemed more grown up in it in spite of the starting with Sara and Gerald and then shifting to Zelda. I thought Gatsby was ok with reservations. No one of the stories is a great story but the best are Babylon Revisited and The Rich Boy I guess. I am probably unjust but remember I am writing as a pro and someone who would like things to be perfect. I thought, when I read it at the time, haveing come home from Italy that This Side of Paradise was comic. Couldn't read The Beautiful and the Damned. I remember thinking who the hell said they were beautiful and what the hell were they damned by? I thought the people on the Grappa and Posubio and the Basso Piave were damned and it did not seem to me you were necessarily damned because you made a little money.[12]

Hemingway's fifth novel, *Across the River and Into the Trees,* was published in September 1950, while he was corresponding with Mizener. It includes a concealed acknowledgment to Fitzgerald: "They were coming up on Mestre fast, and already it was like going to New York the first time you were ever there in the old days when it was shining, white and beautiful. I stole that he thought."[13] Hemingway is referring to the last sentence of Fitzgerald's essay on New York, "My Lost City," published in *The Crack-Up*: "Come back, come back, O glittering and white!"[14]

Across the River and Into the Trees was a best seller when it was published in September 1950 but a critical disaster; the attention it received confirmed Hemingway's position as the most celebrated American author. John O'Hara's *New York Times* review began: "The most important author living today, the outstanding author since the death of Shakespeare, has brought out a new novel. . . . The author, of course is Ernest Hemingway, the most important, the outstanding author out of the millions of writers who have lived since 1616."[15] This declaration was entirely serious. (O'Hara's introduction to the 1945 *Portable F. Scott Fitzgerald* had identified him as "our best novelist, one of our best novella-ists, and one of our finest writers of short stories.")[16]

On the second of January 1951 Hemingway wrote Mizener about Fitzgerald's advice on rewriting the ending of *A Farewell to Arms*:

I'll give you the corrections when I finish my book. The long one. Have the first third (the sea part) whipped now.

I hope it will please you, eventually, more than details of my life which I do not give a shit about. Incidentally I never knew Scott was sore at me except in a drunken fashion. He would write angry letters sometimes and I would try to answer him as you would some one who was not responsable. I always thought he wrote beautifully when he wrote beautifully and stupidly when he wrote stupidly. Thought he was a rummy (for cause) as well as a straight alcoholic. I have a letter in which he told me how to make A Farewell To Arms a successful book which included some fifty suggestions including eliminateing the officer shooting the sergeant, and bringing in, actually and honest to God, the U.S. Marines (Lt. Henry reads of their success at Belleau Woods while in the Cafe when Catherine is dying) at the end. It is one of the worst damned documents I have ever read and I would give it to no one.[17]

The Far Side of Paradise was published on the 29th of January, but Mizener sent Hemingway an advance copy, which he acknowledged on the fourth. Although Hemingway was not enthusiastic about the biography, his letter is civil:

[See pp. 128–129 for Hemingway's account in the same letter of the Fitzgerald timekeeping crisis.]

You know it is a horrible thing to be somebody's hero and have them attribute all sort of qualities to you when you are only a man trying to work at it as well as you can. If this is megalomania make the most of it. But I was Scott's bloody hero for a while and Archie's* and it was only embarrassing to me. They both got cured of it. One by death and the other—.

The reason I criticized Scott's books, except for kidding, was because I wanted him to write perfectly and straighten up and fly right.

It embarrassed me when Scott wanted to make a hero out of me and I didn't like it when he would get sore, and finally I decided it was not important any more. We had the Spanish war and then China and then all the rest of it and I couldn't be interested when he was so rum-dumb. He always wanted to play foot-ball and wouldn't cross the street through traffic. He had a great fantasy about going to war and asked me how he would have been. I told him

*Archibald MacLeish. M.J.B.

that for his actions in civil life as a criterion he would probably have been re-classified or shot for cowardice.

This was too rough; but it was always trying to get him to work and tell the truth at least to himself.

Well the hell with all of it. He's dead and you've buried him for better or for worse and what he wrote that will stand up will stand up.

It was good of you to work so hard on the research. I like Budd Shulberg very much but I felt his book was grave robbing. Your's is good undertakeing. Almost as good as the job they did on my father's face when he shot himself. One remembers the face better as it actually was. But the undertaker pleases those who come to the funeral.

It is good to counter Geismar and such people though. But why shouldn't critics have to write a book sometime to become familiar with the process ie. move out of the discecting room into the operating room? Poor Bunny Wilson writes prose and many people like it. (Please excuse the typewriter which has become very sticky and must be sent in for complete cleaning. But hate to have it go out when I am working well)

The above is unjust about critics as many have written well; not many; but a few.

We, the writers, like them when we learn something from them. I have learned much from this book.

Best luck for what looks like as bad a year as we have seen.[18]

Before *The Far Side of Paradise* was published, Mizener's "F. Scott Fitzgerald's Tormented *Paradise*" appeared in the January 15, 1951, issue of *Life*. This article revealed nothing that was not in the biography—which was being serialized in *The Atlantic*—but Hemingway reacted with outrage.* On the 18th of January he wrote Mizener: "For your information I would gladly clean sewers for a living, every day, or bounce in a bad whore house or pimp for a living than to sign such an article."[19] The *Life* headnote connected Fitzgerald with the Jazz Age and identified him as "both its foremost literary spokesman and one of its most conspicuous examples of frenetic living." Hemingway's name does not appear, although John

*Malcolm Cowley subsequently informed Hemingway that *Life* editors revised Mizener's article "and wrote those horrible captions and headings" (June 8, 1951, Neville Collection). The subhead reads "The rediscovered novelist of the '20s was beset by drink, debt, a mad wife"; the photo captions are inoffensive. M.J.B.

LIFE
IN THIS ISSUE
YUGOSLAVIA TODAY
THE FABULOUS
SCOTT FITZGERALD
GRAND MARSHAL
OF ROSE PARADE
20 CENTS
JANUARY 15,
CIRCULATION
5,200,000
MRS S J LANAHAN
6711 BROOKVILLE RD
CHEVY CHASE MD

O'Hara, John Peale Bishop, Edmund Wilson, Dorothy Parker, Stephen Vincent Benét, and Malcolm Cowley are mentioned or quoted. Hemingway was not nurturing a grudge against *Life;* he had been well treated there in Cowley's "A Portrait of Mister Papa" (January 10, 1949). Concerned that his stature had been damaged by *Across the River and Into the Trees,* Hemingway may have been irritated by the attention being accorded the resurrected Fitzgerald. Writing to Harvey Breit of the *New York Times Book Review* in February, Hemingway expressed his incremental fury:

> The Mizener thing was shocking, truly (LIFE) and I can imagine how poor Scotty felt. Do you think Mizener and I might trade 6 starting at ten paces and walking forward? It seems the most indecent piece of body snatching I have ever known and I would like to kill him if it is o.k.
>
> Have never killed but three men I wished to kill in my life. All the others were forced on me by circumstance.
>
> It is a great sin but a very old one. Killing Mizener after I have seen the face (in yr. Book Review) and read the LIFE thing would be a healthy, sound thing to do. Would be sound for everyone I think. I was not a bit sore until the Life thing.[20]

Budd Schulberg's *The Disenchanted,* a novel based on Fitzgerald and published in November 1950, was dedicated to Mizener. In April 1951 Hemingway expressed his feelings about the "Schulberg-Mizener Axis" to Malcolm Cowley:

> It was good to hear from you. I had the same reaction you did about what a shame it was for Scott not to be around for his own revival. But to be revived by such strange people: First Schulberg, a very nice guy everybody says, and most pleasant when I met him once in Key West, writes something that really balls up everything about Scott and Zelda. I never saw Scott in that stage of his life. But the way Zelda is handled makes the whole thing sort of pointless.
>
> Mizener deceived me completely by his letters. I though he was a straight guy and then came that unspeakable piece of grave robbery he wrote for LIFE. When a man, and fellow writer, has a daughter, married and with children

liveing to hang a heritage of insanity onto them, for money, seems hardly a Christian act.

Poor Scott; what robes, or shroud, he had were torn and sold by very strange people. I hope to hell you will be able to set some things right. As you know only a few of the short stories are good. Gatsby is good and Tender Is The Night is mixed up but absolutely excellent. The Last Tycoon is very good. But it was more a beautifully organized scheme to borrow advances on than a completed novel. I am sure Scott would have fought to complete it. But from what I heard from the people who were with him at the end; especially one man I knew and who told me very detailed things, he was quite incapable of finishing it. But Scott tried hard and did not die from dear old Dartmouth nor on the playing fields of Princeton and I am afraid I think both Schulberg and Mizener are swine: not matter how plausible.

You are a decent man and whatever you do, according to Scott's wishes, about Tender Is The Night is ok. People have a choice of reading either version. But that Shulberg-Mizener Axis could well be hanged, head down, in front of any second rate garage.[21]

Hemingway's only public comment on Schulberg and Mizener appeared when the *New York Herald Tribune Book Review* asked him in 1951 for a list of books he liked; he provided six titles he would have liked to have read if they had been published—including ''*Longevity Pays: The Life of Arthur Mizener* by F. Scott FitzGerald and *The Schulberg Incident* by F. Scott FitzGerald.''[22]

Biographical interest in Fitzgerald generated a new readership for his fiction. In 1951 Cowley edited *The Stories of F. Scott Fitzgerald* and the so-called ''author's final version'' of *Tender Is the Night,* which restructures the novel in straight chronological order. Cowley sent Hemingway the introduction to his *Tender* edition before publication, and Hemingway provided an account of his first meeting with Fitzgerald that differs slightly from the report in *A Moveable Feast:*

Scott caught the surface and the people that he knew or met with a fine brightness. But he always used to interrogate everybody. ''Did you sleep with your wife before you were married?'' I've heard him ask that to someone the first time he met them. How could he expect to get the truth that way. His great hero Gerald was involved in certain relationships that would have shocked Scott. But Scott never knew about them.

There are writers to whom people come all their lives and tell things that writer would give anything not to know. But he hears them and never uses them except as the knowledge he invents from. But Scott would mix up (as in Tender I.T.N.) himself and Zelda with Gerald and Sara and they were very different. He got balled up inventing from mixtures of opposites in people instead of inventing from his knowledge of people themselves. How could he know people except on the surface when he never fucked anybody, nobody told him anything except as an answer to a question, and he was nearly always too drunk late at night to remember what anybody really said.

I think you gave too little importance to the alcoholic thing with Scott. The first time I ever met him he was with Dunc Chaplin, an old Princeton pitcher, and very good guy. Dunc came with him when he was trying to locate me in Montparnasse. Scott wanted to go to some boite and drink champagne. All this time he was talking about writing and makeing compliments to me and I was very embarrassed. I took him to the old Dingo that Wilson still ran in the rue Delambre. We hadn't finished a bottle of champagne (good) when his face started to change and be like a skull. I was worried and looked at Dunc and he just shook his head. By the end of the bottle Scott passed out with his face white and the skin drawn on it like a dead mans. Dunc said not to worry about him. That he always did that when he was excited and liquor was poison for him. Dunc took him home in a taxi.

That was the year Scott published The Great Gatsby. I think but would have to check. In that, and the next few years, I saw him drunk hundreds of times when I was sober and he was always drunk on very little to drink. Every time I would get him to stop drinking or drink only wine Zelda would get jealous and get him off of it. If he was not an alcoholic I never saw one nor met one, nor knew one well in my life.

Maybe the strain of trying to out-write himself ruined him, as you said. But he was a true rummy when I met him when I was married to Hadley and living in the Rue Notre Dame des Champs and he he was worse than a rummy when I went down to Elerslie (probably mis-spelled) to visit

> them and he was a last ditch rummy when I met him again in Paris when Zelda was in the sanitarium in Switzerland.
>
> I ought to write about him because I knew him better than you and his entombers Mizener and Shulberg did. We lived across the road from each other in Juan le Pins and I saw him every day there and in Paris and we made trips together. I don't mean write about him as a rummy. But that was one of his big problems, that and Zelda, and cowardice, and ambition and love of earning money which meant social, economic, and for a while, he figured, artistic success. But it is Mizener, who never met him, that writes about him.[23]

When Hemingway read Cowley's edition of *Tender* in November 1951, he responded with a defense of the first edition:

> Scribner's sent the new edition of Tender Is The Night yesterday and I have read it until page 206.
>
> Truly I did not want the reforms to turn out as I was afraid they might. But I am afraid the whole idea was just a bad idea of Scott's.
>
> In the straight chronological order the book loses the magic completely. Starting off with a case history there is no secret to discover and no mystery and all sense of a seemingly magical world (the world of Sara and Gerald Murphy) being destroyed by something that is unknown is lost.
>
> By the time the bath-room incident comes off the reader knows everything which was to come as a shock. In the form it is now it is simply a pathological and not a nice one at that. It has all the dullness of all stories of the insane and where it had the charm of the strange mixture that was Scott it is now about as much fun to read as The Snake Pit.
>
> I know you did it for Scott and it was what he wanted. But I think if he had been completely sane I could have argued him out of it.
>
> It is just like takeing the wings off a butterfly and arrangeing them so he can fly straight as a bee flies and loseing all the dust that makes the colors that makes the butterfly magical in the process.
>
> Errors: relizing for realizing on page 194.
> caviare for caviar (this first spelling is obsolete and is a bastard one at best. But it is used throughout.).

> Also you can't see a Valais night at a clinic described as a short way out of Zurich.
>
> There are other small things you will catch in any future editions and if you want to spell caviar as caviare that is a question of taste. It is legal.
>
> None of the above is important unless everything is important in writing. But truly I think the changeing about of the material is. Probably all critics will back you and Scott up. I didn't want to read it this way because I had a terrible hunch that this would be what would happen to it. And I read it hopeing I would be wrong.
>
> The insoluble problem (skip my mistakes in spelling because I am not writing for keeps and haven't read these letters in galley proof) Scott had in the story was makeing Sara into Zelda. The closer he faced this problem and the less of the apparatus of mystification he used the more insoluble the problem became and the less credible the book becomes. He started to write about Sara and Gerald and as they changed and as Zelda passed through her various pathological phases he had to keep changeing the book in his mind.
>
> Well it is over now and skinning dead race horses is not my trade. I thought I ought to tell you what I thought of it. But I can always avoid that by not sending this letter. If you're happy about it that is your good and bad luck.[24]

The Old Man and the Sea was published in 1952 to immense acclaim. The report that Ernest and Mary Hemingway were missing in an African plane crash in January 1954 made the front pages all over the world, and Hemingway was able to read his obituaries. In October 1954 Hemingway was awarded the Nobel Prize for Literature.

In 1957 Hemingway began work on a memoir of Fitzgerald for the one hundredth anniversary issue of *The Atlantic Monthly* but dropped it because, he told Breit, he didn't want to cash in on Fitzgerald: "I started to write about Scott and how I first met him and how he was; writing it all true and it was tough to write and easy to remember and I thought it was very interesting. But when I read it over I remembered that character writing about his friend Mr. Dylan Thomas and thought people would think I was doing that to Scott and him dead. So I had worked a month on it and finished it good and then put it away and wrote them a story."[25] This project almost certainly initiated work on a book of Paris reminiscences he had been considering for some time, posthumously published as *A Moveable Feast* in 1964.

Suffering from depression, hypertension, and diabetes, Ernest Hemingway shot himself at Ketchum, Idaho, July 2, 1961.

Chapter 9

1. Graham and Gerold Frank, *Beloved Infidel* (New York: Holt, 1958), p. 329.
2. 104 (3 March and 17 March 1941).
3. See "Introduction," *The Love of the Last Tycoon: A Western*, edited by Bruccoli (Cambridge: Cambridge University Press, 1993), p. lxviii.
4. C. 27 January 1941. Princeton University Library.
5. "Fitzgerald's Unfinished Symphony," *Saturday Review of Literature*, 24 (6 December 1941), 10.
6. *Selected Letters*, pp. 527–528.
7. *Selected Letters*, pp. 556–557.
8. 6 July 1949. *Selected Letters*, pp. 657–658.
9. 16 August 1949. Princeton University Library.
10. 18–19 May 1951. *Selected Letters*, pp. 725–728.
11. 22 April 1950. *Selected Letters*, pp. 689–691.
12. 12 May 1950. *Selected Letters*, 694–695.
13. P. 34.
14. P. 33.
15. "The Author's Name Is Hemingway." *New York Times Book Review* (10 September 1950), 1.
16. "Introduction," *The Portable Fitzgerald*, edited by Dorothy Parker (New York: Viking, 1945), pp. vii-xix.
17. University of Maryland Library.
18. *Selected Letters*, pp. 716–718.
19. Jacqueline Tavernier-Courbin, *Ernest Hemingway's A Moveable Feast: The Making of Myth* (Boston: Northeastern University Press, 1991), p. 12. No location provided.
20. 8 February 1951. Harvard University Library.
21. 19 April 1951. Neville Collection.
22. *New York Herald Tribune Book Review* (9 December 1951), 3.
23. 16 September 1951. Neville Collection.
24. 10 November 1951. Neville Collection.
25. 16 June 1957. Harvard University Library.

Appendix

Fitzgerald's *Notebooks* References to Hemingway Printed in *The Crack-Up**

62 I really loved him, but of course it wore out like a love affair.
The fairies have spoiled all that.

370 They have more money (Earnest's wisecrack)

612 Ernest—until we began trying to walk over each other with cleats.

1002 As to Ernest as a boy—reckless, adventurous, etc. Yet it is undeniable that the dark was peopled for him. His bravery and acquired characteristics.

1019 Nevertheless value of Ernest's feeling about the pure heart when writing—in other words the comparatively pure heart, the "house in order."

1021 T.S.P. A Romance and a Reading List
Sun also Rises. A Romance and a Guide Book

1031 That Willa Cather's poem shall stand at beginning of Mediaval and that it shall be the story of Ernest.

1034 Just as Stendahl's portrait of a Byronic man made *Le Rouge*

*These entries have been transcribed from *The Notebooks of F. Scott Fitzgerald,* ed. Matthew J. Bruccoli (New York: Harcourt Brace Jovanovich/Bruccoli Clark, 1978); the texts in *The Crack-Up* are inaccurate.

et Noir so couldn't *my* portrait of Ernest as Phillipe make the real modern man.

1035 But there was one consolation: They could never use any of Mr. Hemingway's four letter words, because that was for fourth class and fourth class has been abolished—

(The first class was allowed to cheat a little on on the matter.)

But on the other hand they could never use any two letter words like NO. They *had* to use three letter words like YES!

1045 Didn't Hemingway say this in effect:

If Tom Wolfe ever learns to separate what he gets from books from what he gets from life he will be an original. All you can get from books is rhythm and technique. He's half-grown artistically—this is truer than what Ernest said about him. But when I've criticized him (several times in talk) I've felt bad afterwards. Putting sharp weapons in the hands of his inferiors.

1177 Ernest Hemingway, while careful to avoid cliches in his work, fairly revels in them in his private life, his favorite being Parbleu ("So what?") French, and "Yes, We Have No Bananas." Contrary to popular opinion he is not as tall as Thomas Wolfe, standing only six feet five in his health belt. He is naturally clumsy with his body, but shooting from a blind or from adequate cover, makes a fine figure of a man. We are happy to announce that his work will appear in future exclusively on United States postage stamps.

1277 Very strong personalities must confine themselves in mutual conversation to very gentle subjects. Everything eventually transpired—but if they start at a high pitch as at the last meeting of Ernest, Bunny and me their meeting is spoiled. It does not matter who sets the theme or what it is.

1528 Most Pleasant Trips

. . . .

Auto Ernest and I North

. . . .

1915 I talk with the authority of failure—Ernest with the authority of success. We could never sit across the table again.

Fitzgerald's *Notebooks* References to Hemingway Not Printed in *The Crack-Up*

728 Snubs—. . . Ernest apartment.

757 Day with a busy man. Combine the day of Ernest's pictures, the man of genius episode,

1237 Parallel of Ernest's and French conversation as opposed to Gerald and me and U.S.A. emotional bankruptcy.

1246 Do you know what your affair was founded on? On sorrow.

You got sorry for each other. (Did Ernest borrow this one?)*

1437 Ernest taking me to that bum restaurant. Change of station implied.

1819 Ernest would always give a helping hand to a man on a ledge a little higher up.

1825 Ernest Hemingway and Ernest Lubitsch—Dotty ''We're all shits.''†

1868 Bald Hemingway characters.

1918 People like Ernest and me were very sensitive once and saw so much that it agonized us to give pain. People like Ernest and me love to make people very happy, caring desperately about their happiness. And then people like Ernest and me had reactions and punished people for being stupid, etc., etc. People like Ernest and me ______

1924 Tom Fast's story of Ernest.

1979 Ideas on Fear as being removed as well as profit motive. We know the latter can—but the former. Some day when the psycho-an are forgotten E.H. will be read for his great studies into fear.

1995 Ernest and ''Farewell to Arms''—producer story.

1996 An inferiority complex comes simply from not feeling you're doing the best you can—Ernest's ''drink'' was simply a form of this.

2066 It is so to speak Ernest's 'Tale of Two Cities' though the comparison isn't apt. I mean it is a thoroughly superficial book** which has all the profundity of Rebecca.

*Printed in *The Crack-Up,* with parenthetical comment omitted.
†Hollywood director Ernst Lubitsch and Dorothy Parker.
***For Whom the Bell Tolls.*

2068 I want to write scenes that are frightening and inimitable. I don't want to be as intelligible to my contemporaries as Ernest who as Gertrude Stein said, is bound for the Museums. I am sure I am far enough ahead to have some small immortality if I can keep well.

Index